CRIME AND THE FAMILY

CRIME AND THE FAMILY

By

ALAN JAY LINCOLN

Professor of Criminal Justice
University of Lowell
Lowell, Massachusetts

and

MURRAY A. STRAUS

Professor of Sociology
University of New Hampshire
Durham, New Hampshire

CHARLES C THOMAS • PUBLISHER
Springfield • Illinois • U.S.A.

Published and Distributed Throughout the World by

CHARLES C THOMAS • PUBLISHER
2600 South First Street
Springfield, Illinois 62717

This book is protected by copyright. No part of it
may be reproduced in any manner without written
permission from the publisher.

© *1985 by* CHARLES C THOMAS • PUBLISHER

ISBN 0-398-05144-5
Library of Congress Catalog Card Number: 85-2862

With THOMAS BOOKS *careful attention is given to all details of manufacturing and
design. It is the Publisher's desire to present books that are satisfactory as to their physical
qualities and artistic possibilities and appropriate for their particular use.* THOMAS
BOOKS *will be true to those laws of quality that assure a good name and good will.*

Printed in the United States of America
SC-R-3

Library of Congress Cataloging in Publication Data

Lincoln, Alan Jay.
  Crime and the family.

  Bibliography: p.
  Includes index.
  1. Family violence—United States—Addresses, essays, lectures.
  2. Victims of crimes—United States—Addresses, essays, lectures.
  I. Straus, Murray Arnold, 1926–   .   II. Title.
  HQ809.3.U5L56   1985   362.8'2   85-2862
  ISBN 0-398-05144-5

For my parents and all the good
things they mean to me.
AJL

In memory of my father,
whose example made me human.
MAS

ABOUT THE CONTRIBUTORS

Michael Agopian is Professor of Public Administration, University of LaVerne, LaVerne, CA.

Federico Allodi is a Psychiatrist at Toronto Western Hospital.

Gretchen Anderson is with the University of Southern California.

Carl C. Buzawa is an Attorney for Congoleum Corporation.

Eva S. Buzawa is Associate Professor of Criminal Justice, University of Lowell.

Paul Cressey was Professor of Sociology, Wheaton College, Norton, Massachusetts.

D. P. Farrington, Gwen Gundry, and **D. J. West** are affiliated with the Institute of Criminology, Cambridge University.

David Finkelhor is Associate Chair of Family Research Laboratory, University of New Hampshire.

Richard Gelles is Dean of Liberal Arts and Professor of Sociology at the University of Rhode Island.

John T. Kirkpatrick is Assistant to the Dean, College of Liberal Arts, University of New Hampshire.

Irvin Waller and **Norman Okihiro** are affiliated with the Centre of Criminology, University of Toronto.

Kersti Yllo is Assistant Professor of Sociology at Wheaton College, Norton, Massachusetts.

ACKNOWLEDGMENTS

This book is one of a series of articles and books based on research done under the sponsorship of the Family Violence Research Program at the University of New Hampshire.* We are indebted to the National Institute of Mental Health and the Graduate School of the University of New Hampshire for the continuing support which made the program possible; and specifically to NIMH grant T32 MH15161 which funded the post doctoral research fellowship that enabled Alan Lincoln to pursue this research.

Our intellectual debts to colleagues in the Family Violence Research Program are numerous. Over forty persons have been active participants in that program, first in the sense of having been the author or coauthor of a paper or book chapter done under the sponsorship of the Family Violence Research Program; and second and equally important, in the sense of being insightful, severe, but supportive critics. In one way or another, all have contributed to this book, some directly, and others indirectly through their contributions to the theoretical and empirical development of the program of which this book is a part. It is a pleasure to acknowledge their contribution.

Chapter 5 is reprinted with permission from Richard J. Gelles and Murray A. Straus, "Violence in the American Family." Journal of Social Issues, Vol. 35, No. 2, 1979, pp. 15–39.

Chapter 6 is reprinted with permission from Michael W. Agopian and Gretchen L. Anderson, "Characteristics of Parental Child Stealing." Journal of Family Issues, Vol. 2, No. 4 (December, 1981), pp. 471–483. (c)1981 Sage Publications, Inc.

Chapter 11 is reprinted with permission from Paul F. Cressey, "The Criminal Tribes of India." Sociology and Social Research, Vol. 20, 1936, pp. 503–511.

Chapter 14 is reprinted from Federico Allodi, "Psychiatric Effects of Political Persecution and Torture in Children and Families of Victims."

---

*A brochure describing the program and a list of books and papers (some of which are available for distribution) will be sent on request to the Program Assistant, Family Violence Research Program, University of New Hampshire, Durham, New Hampshire 03824.

Canada's Mental Health, Vol. 28, No. 3, 1980, pp. 8–10.

Chapter 15 is reprinted from Ervin Waller and Norman Okihiro, Burglary: The Victim and the Public, by permission of the authors and University of Toronto Press. (c)University of Toronto Press, 1978.

CONTENTS

CRIME AND THE FAMILY

PART I
OVERVIEW

CHAPTER 1

A CONCEPTUAL FRAMEWORK
FOR UNDERSTANDING CRIME AND THE FAMILY

Murray A. Straus and Alan Jay Lincoln

This book is about two aspects of American society that have aroused wide interest and concern: the high crime rate and the changes that are occurring in the family. Typically, the two issues are studied independently by social scientists. One group of researchers studies crime and another group studies families. But there are some exceptions. A few social scientists have looked at limited aspects of how crime and the family are related to each other. One example is research on how family patterns affect juvenile delinquency. These studies have shown that family patterns are related to the chances of a child being delinquent: the closer the bond between children and their parents, the lower the chances that the child will be delinquent (Hirshi, 1969; Empey and Lubeck, 1971).

The research on how family patterns are related to delinquency is very important, but it is only one of many ways that the family and crime are linked. Despite studies on some aspects of this linkage, there does not seem to be a recognition of the general principle that crime and the family are interrelated, nor is there a group of researchers who take "crime and the family" as the focus of their work.

There are probably a number of reasons why crime and the family has not so far emerged as a clear field of study. One reason may be that it is something that most people do not want to think about because it forces one to come to grips with the fact that the family is less than the perfect institution which most people want it to be. But that is a shortsighted view. If one is truly "pro-family," then the wisest course is to face up to the problems so that they can be corrected and thereby enable the family to come closer to what most people hope and expect from the family. To paraphrase Schmookler (1984), a work preoccupied with the dark side of the family can be dedicated to overcoming the power of darkness.

Although the "perceptual blindness" towards the dark side of the family applies almost as much to social scientists as to the general public, another factor may be more important in accounting for the neglect of

5

this issue by social scientists. This is that absence of a conceptual framework to use in thinking about the issue and to use as a guide to research.
Without such a framework, it is difficult to know what to look for and
difficult to make sense of what is found by research or what is already
known. We intend this book to be a step toward filling that void. This
introductory chapter presents a conceptual framework which we have
found helpful in grasping the central issues, and perhaps others will also
find it useful. The framework evolved by bringing together ideas from
both traditional criminology, from the new field of victimology, and
from the field of family studies.

The remainder of the book is, in effect, the first use of this conceptual
framework because it was the basis for selecting what went into the three
main sections of the book. It led us to look at three main issues: crime
within the family, crime by the family, and crime against the family. We
hope that this method of organizing the scattered literature on crime and
the family will also help make sense out of a complex and controversial
issue. We also hope that it will encourage social scientists to do the
research needed to fill the gaps in knowledge revealed by looking at
crime and the family through the lenses of this framework.

IMPORTANCE OF UNDERSTANDING THE
INTERRELATION OF CRIME AND THE FAMILY

There are a number of reasons why studies of the interrelation of
crime and the family are important.

New Insights and New Facts

Preliminary evidence (see Chaps. 4 and 9) suggests that one of the
features of American family life is a surprisingly high level of involvement
in crime. As a starting point we need to know if this is true, because it can
tell us something important about the family and about crime.

Interdisciplinary studies are likely to reveal knowledge that would
not otherwise come to light. Criminology and family studies are both
well developed fields of knowledge. Many articles are published in
journals such as *Criminology, Crime and Delinquency, Journal of Marriage
and the Family, International Journal of Family Studies,* etc. These articles, and the many books which are published each year, indicate that
there is a continuing stream of important new knowledge about crime
and about the family. But as pointed out earlier, family researchers
have tended to ignore the possibility that crime may be as much a part
of the family as it is a part of other spheres of life, and criminologists
have tended to ignore the possibility that families may be involved in

crime as much as any other group or type of person.

This book tries to correct the oversight by putting what is already known about the interrelations of crime and the family into a systematic perspective. It makes use of the theories which have been developed in both fields. Family specialists might be able to achieve a better understanding of families if they can use the theories that have developed to explain criminal behavior, and criminologists might achieve a better understanding of crime if they can use some of the theories that have been developed to explain family behavior. That is one of the reasons why we are hopeful that the study of crime and the family will contribute to a better understanding of both families and crime than can be achieved by studying each in artificial isolation from each other. It may even help achieve a better understanding of all types of harmful behavior.

Practical Contributions

In addition to the theoretical contributions that could occur as a result of the dual focus on crime and the family, there are also important practical reasons for such an approach.

One reason the study of crime and the family has such practical importance is because so much crime takes place in or against families. Studies of physical violence within the family, for example, show that an average citizen is much more likely to be assaulted in his or her own home than on the streets of the most dangerous city in the United States (Straus, Gelles, and Steinmetz, 1980). So far, no one has done a study of a representative sample of families to find out how often nonviolent crimes are committed within the family. The preliminary study described in Chapter 4 is a first step in that direction. It reveals a high rate of nonviolent crimes within the family. When these nonviolent episodes are added to the violent criminal acts within the family, it suggests that *crime in the family may be more common than crime in any other setting.*

However, in many cases, these acts are not defined as crimes by either the perpetrators or the victims. Even when they are defined as criminal acts, victims rarely ask for protection by the police and the courts. The reasons for not doing so include shame, fear that it will cause more harm than good, a belief that they can "handle" the situation themselves, fear of retaliation from the perpetrator if reported, etc. These circumstances make crime in the family largely "hidden crime." One of our objectives is to bring it into the open because that is an essential first step in dealing with the problem. Or to put it more directly, anyone who is concerned about crime, should be concerned with crime and the family, simply because so much of it takes place in a family context.

Once the problem is recognized, the next step in doing something practical about it is to correct the myths and other barriers that stand in the way of working effectively with families. For example, many people believe that assaults and other crimes within the family happen only or mostly in lower class families. That and other similar issues need to be settled in order to design crime prevention and victim assistance programs that reflect the crime problems actually faced by families. If the police, prosecutors, and social service agencies are to act effectively, they need information on the causes, incidence rates, and consequences of crime affecting the family.

VICTIMOLOGY AND CRIMINOLOGY

Our approach to the study of crime in the family partly reflects the new and growing body of work on "victimology." This is in contrast to the main body of criminology which focuses on criminals and the causes of crime. Victimology gives primary focus to the victim of crime. It seeks to answer such questions as whether certain types of people or groups are more likely to be victims, and why this may be true. Victimology also gives greater attention to the consequences of crime for the victim and his or her career, as compared to the focus of classic forms of criminology on the criminal and his or her career.

The perspective of victimology is consistent with our objective of tracing out the links between crime and the family. A victimology perspective, for example, leads to asking if certain family members are more likely to be victimized than others, and if so, why that is the case. It also suggests looking at both the short term and long term effects of this victimization.

Of course, victimology does not completely ignore the classic concerns of criminology with types of crimes and with the background and careers of criminals, nor does criminology completely ignore the victim and the consequences of crime for the victim. However, there are advantages to maintaining the distinction between criminology in the traditional sense and victimology. This dual focus let us create a typology of family crime by cross-classifying who is the victim by who is the perpetuator of the crime, as shown in Figure 1-1.

The various combinations shown in Figure 1-1 of who is the victim of the crime, and who is the perpetrator, identify the aspects of crime and the family on which this book is focused. They reveal three types of family crime: (1) crime within the family, (2) crime against the family, and (3) crime by the family. Let us look at each of these three types in more detail.

CRIME WITHIN THE FAMILY is represented in the upper left box. It

```
                                    VICTIM
                        Family                 Non-Family
            :-----------------------:-----------------------:
            :                       :                       :
Family      : 1. Crimes Within      : 2. Crimes By          :
            :    The Family         :    The Family         :
            :                       :                       :
PERPETRATOR :-----------------------:-----------------------:
            :                       :                       :
            : 3. Crimes Against     : 4. Crimes Among       :
Non-Family  :    The Family         :    Non-Related        :
            :                       :                       :
            :-----------------------:-----------------------:
```

Figure 1-1. A Taxonomy of Family Crime.

refers to those situations in which *both* the criminal and the victim are members of the same family. Physical assault is a type of within-family crime that has recently come to public attention under labels such as child abuse, spouse abuse, and abuse of the elderly. Many other types of crime can and do take place within the family, including crimes such as larceny and robbery among family members, extortion between relatives, childnapping in custody fights, some child pornography cases, the selling of one's own children, vandalism and arson of family property, and so on.

CRIME AGAINST THE FAMILY includes those situations in which some person or group outside the family commits a crime against two or more members of the same family. Notable examples here include household burglary, household larceny, and many motor vehicle thefts. Also included in the crime against family type are mass killings, swindling by confidence men preying on families, hostage taking, kidnapping for ransom, community harassment of minority families, and others.

CRIMES BY THE FAMILY is the third aspect of crime and the family to which Figure 1-1 alerts us. It refers to criminal acts committed by the family as a collectivity (i.e. by two or more members of the same family) against victims who are not members of that family. This cell of Figure 1-1 raises the question of the extent to which such common crimes as larceny, burglary, arson, fraud, etc. are committed by members of the same family *acting together.* In addition, certain other types of crime meet our criteria for crime by the family, including: violent feuds between families, some illegal immigration practices, some child pornography and child prostitution, some organized crime, some vigilante activity, and hereditary criminal castes (see Chap. 11).

NONFAMILY CRIME. Finally, the fourth cell in Figure 1-1 refers to crimes involving nonrelated groups or individuals. This situation best fits what typically has been the public conception of crime—the mugging, rape, robbery, or attack of a stranger or acquaintance.

The relationships identified in cells 1, 2, and 3 of Figure 1-1, by calling attention to the several possible ways that families can be involved in crime, provides a kind of road map for studying crime and the family. Since it also identifies aspects of crime which have not usually been seen before, it also suggests the possibility that there may be a much greater amount of crime involving the family than has been suspected.

DEFINING FAMILY CRIME

Since almost everyone is a member of a family, any crime against an individual has an impact on that person's family and might be considered by family members as a crime against them as well. But such a loose conception of family crime would not be helpful in advancing our understanding of the major issues involved. We therefore need to clarify the question of what is a family crime. In fact, as soon as one starts trying to do so, it becomes clear that it is often difficult to identify the point at which a crime involves the family *per se*, and whether it really is a crime.

Crime Within the Family

Crimes within the family at first seem to pose little difficulty since we can fall back on a fairly clear criterion: whether both the victim and the perpetrator are members of the same family. However, there are at least two sources of ambiguity which need to be dealt with.

WHO IS A FAMILY MEMBER? First, there is the question of who is a family member. Shall it be restricted to members of the immediate family, i.e. husband wife and children? Or should it include grandparents, cousins, uncles, aunts, etc. If the latter, how distant a relative should be included? If the decision is made to restrict the definition to members of the immediate family, should an exception be made for a relative such as an uncle or cousin who is living in the same household as the immediate family? Conversely, if there are members of the immediate family who are living elsewhere, such as adult children, should they be included? There is no one best solution to these issues. Each alternative has both advantages and disadvantages. However, one must be clear about what is and is not included. Our decision was to include members of both the immediate and the extended family, and to include them irrespective of whether they lived in separate households. That decision, however, does not preclude considering differences between various categories of family members, and we will do this where the data permits.

WHAT ACTS ARE CRIMES? Another difficulty in identifying crimes within the family arises because different standards may be used to evaluate the same act inside and outside the family. Sex between unmarried consenting adults is no longer illegal. But what if they are brother and sister? Taking money from another person without their knowledge or consent is theft, and striking another person is an assault. But many people would be reluctant to consider money taken from a brother, sister, or parent as "Larceny," or punching a brother as "Assault." There may, in fact, be implicit rules in the family which permit this up to a certain point. These examples illustrate the tendency to apply different rules to behavior which occurs within the family than are applied to behavior between nonfamily members. This issue has so many subtle and perplexing aspects that it is discussed separately later in the chapter.

Crimes Involving the Family as a Unit

There are also important difficulties in identifying crimes committed *by* families, and even more difficulties in identifying crimes committed *against* families. The difficulty occurs because it involves a continuum rather than a clear presence or absence decision. When the Hatfields fought the McCoys, there is no doubt that this crime was committed by a family against a family. Such family feuds can continue for several generations, as was true in societies such as rural Albania.

But how do we categorize the crime when a burglar breaks into a home and steals? Is that a crime against the family or the individual members? There is no clear answer to this question. Rather we suggest evaluating each crime with three criteria in mind. If *one or more* of these are met, then we will consider the episode a family crime.

(1) *The family as a group is involved.* This criterion requires that two or more members of the same family be either the perpetrators of the crime (for it to be a crime *by* a family), or that two or more members of the same family are the victims (for it to be a crime *against* a family). These are extremely arbitrary distinctions, but we think they are necessary in order to distinguish family crime from other crime.

Some indication of just how arbitrary it is can be gained from considering the following examples. If a man carries out a rape or a robbery, that is not a family crime (for purposes of this book) even though his family may benefit financially from the robbery, or be injured both financially and socially if he is convicted of rape. However, if a father-son team does it, we consider it a crime by a family. It would be more of a family crime if the mother or a brother also participated. Turning to crimes against the family, if a woman is raped, that is not a crime against the family (for purposes of this book), however serious the impact may be on the woman's family. But if two sisters are raped, we define it as a family crime. Similarly, if a single individual is murdered (for purposes of this book), we do not consider it a crime against the family even though the person killed is almost always the member of some family.

(2) *The crime takes place in what might be called "family territory."* The distinction between crime in public places and private places is important for defining crimes against the family. When space, such as a home, used legitimately by the family is violated, then members of the family are more likely to feel collectively threatened or victimized.

We do not mean to say that if a member of your family is robbed in a parking lot, it does not affect the family. It does, and to that extent it is a crime against the family. But, as we pointed out before, since almost everyone is a member of a family, including such crimes means that all crime is family crime, i.e., it becomes a definition that does not differentiate anything. On the other hand, if that robbery occurs in one's own home, the crime takes on a unique additional characteristic. In effect, two crimes have been committed, one involves invasion of the person, and the other involves invasion of the home. Research on crime victims shows that violation of the family home often leaves deep emotional scars and fears that go well beyond the value of the property lost (Bard and Sangrey, 1979).

(3) *Whether the episode involves the collective property of a family* is the final criteria which influences whether a crime is to be considered a family crime. For example, when a home is robbed, items will often be taken which are in practice, even if not by law, the property of the family group rather than one individual: a TV set, stereo, silver tableware, etc. In these cases it is the family as a group that is victimized, not just one member.

In practice, there are many ambiguous events and anomolies which stand in the way of a straightforward application of these three criteria. Despite these problematic cases, we believe that there are enough situations which almost everyone would recognize as being family-related crime (using the three criteria suggested) to make this a useful device for advancing our understanding of both criminology and the family.

WHEN IS A CRIME A CRIME?

Defining "crime" is difficult and controversial, even without the complications involved when the parties are members of the same family. The essence of the definition given in Chapter 2 is that crime is anything the society declares to be illegal. So eating candy could be a crime if there was a law to that effect. In practice, the definition of and reaction to crime are not that straightforward. The criminal justice system takes into account a vast array of other considerations, such as the intent of the person, his age, sex, and demeanor, the relationship between perpetrator and victim, and a host of extenuating circumstances. These qualifications and circumstances are especially salient when the offending behavior occurs between members of the same family. They make it extremely difficult to know when to regard such behavior as a crime in the legal sense.

Should Within-Family Victimizations Be Defined as "Crime"?

Suppose sixteen-year-old "Junior" repeatedly takes money from his parents or from a brother or sister. In most cases, there is no way that the family members involved will treat either action as a crime in the legal sense. Even people outside the family will be reluctant to define it as a crime and, therefore, as an act which requires intervention by the criminal justice system (i.e., the police, the courts, juvenile authorities). It is regarded as "a family matter" and therefore something to be handled by the family. But if one of Junior's friends was to take money from Junior's parents or siblings, many if not most people would define that as stealing, i.e., as a crime. Similarly if a sixteen-year-old takes money from a teacher's desk, or merchandise from a store, the social perceptions and reactions are even more likely to be on the side of defining the child's actions as a crime. It seems that the closer the situation is to a family relationship, the more reluctant people are to consider the act a crime.

NORMATIVE AMBIGUITY. The problem, however, is that although this tendency exists, with a few rare exceptions, there are no societal norms or legal codes which unambiguously identify some of the acts mentioned above as crimes and others as not. In fact, there seem to be large differences between individuals and between families in respect to this idea. In one family almost anything will be tolerated as "a family matter"—even wife-beating—whereas in others, a single slap would lead the woman to end the marriage. There are also differences within the family, and between different outside observers. Mother may be more or less tolerant than father of Junior's taking the money; the victim may be more likely to define it as a crime than others in his or her family; a social worker may have still another view; and a police officer may simply not want to get involved without clear guidelines. We can only say that many acts which are tolerated within the family would be regarded as crimes if the victim and offender were not members of the same family.

LEGAL RECOGNITION OF FAMILY-STRANGER DIFFERENCES. To a certain extent distinctions based on whether the act involves members of the same family exist even in the law itself. Incest is one such example. It is also an example of the reverse side of the principle that many acts which are crimes between strangers may be tolerated if carried out between family members. In the case of incest, the fact that the sexual relation occurs within the family is part of what makes the act a crime.

One of the clearest examples of legal tolerance for behavior within the family that would be a crime outside the family is rape. In all but a few states which recently changed the law in this matter, there is what is known as the "marital exemption"—husbands cannot be charged with the rape of their wives (Finkelhor and Yllo, 1980). For purposes of this book, we will regard sex forced on a spouse as rape, even if it occurs in a state which has retained the "marital exemption."

More generally, *for purposes of this book, we will regard any act which occurs within the family as a crime if that same act is regarded as a crime when the parties are not related.* We made this decision in respect to intrafamily crime because we think it brings out issues which need to be considered and which might otherwise be overlooked. However, two things need to be kept in mind about this approach.

First, it is important to note that it is not a definition of intrafamily crime because it does not cover all cases. For example, it does not include acts which are a crime within the family, but are not criminal when the persons involved are unrelated, such as sex between brother and sister or parents and children. How then should intrafamily crime be defined? Our view is that the definition in Chapter 2 applies to the family as well as other crime—essentially that crime is what the law says it is.

Second, as explained below, applying the rules for nonfamily crime to the family may be appropriate as a tool for analysis, but that does not necessarily make it appropriate from the point of view of families, the criminal justice system, or society as a whole.

RESEARCH DEFINITIONS VERSUS SOCIAL POLICY. It is by no means clear whether families and society would be better off if the police, the courts, and the public, adopted the principle that the same standards should be used to judge crime within the family as outside the family. That rule might be helpful for the purpose of this book—to bring out issues which need to be addressed by theoretical analysis or empirical research—but it would not necessarily be helpful as a guide to conduct. A case can be made for not doing so.

For one thing, the state has conflicting interests. On the one hand there is the interest of the state in maintaining a "civil" society in which citizens can live without fear of victimization. This implies a commitment to vigorous action to prevent and punish crime. On the other hand, the state has an interest in encouraging and protecting the family as a social institution. Consequently, the family is subject to restrictions, protections, and exemptions which do not apply to other groups. The most obvious of these are the restrictions on terminating a family. Parents cannot just abandon children, and husbands and wives must also secure permission to terminate a marriage. For the same reasons, the state is reluctant to take actions which, however justified on other grounds, might break up a family.

A related reason for not applying the same rules about crime to families as to strangers is that families *are* different; not just in the law, but in what goes on in families compared to other groups, and this needs to be recognized. Crime is only one of many types of behavior for which there are different rules and expectations for the family as compared to other groups or situations. These differences are part of what makes the family such a unique and important institution. For example, the family is concerned with "the whole person," not just some specific aspect of the person. The head of the department where you work will be concerned about things that have to do with the quality of your work, whereas the family will be concerned, not only with your performance on the job, but also with your religion, your politics, and who you are going out with.

Finally, it can be argued that, even if the same norms about crime are applied within the family, there may be good reason for not involving the legal system in enforcing those norms. Even if they were willing to devote the time to the case, the police and the courts cannot be expected to understand the unique circumstances of each family, and they cannot be depended on to take actions which are in the best interest of either the person committing the crime or the family as a whole.

Family Status and Roles and the Definition of Crime

What is acceptable and unacceptable also varies *within* the family. As pointed out earlier, families, like the legal system, use a double standard — or really multiple standards. Age, sex, power, and family roles and obligations all are likely to influence the norms which define the boundary between "misbehavior" and "crime," i.e., how wrong an act is perceived to be. If a six-year-old takes money from his parents, that is usually treated as wrong, but not a crime with a capital C. But if a sixteen-year-old does the same thing, it is regarded as much more serious and the punishments may be more serious. Similarly, we suggest that most families will evaluate taking money as a less serious infraction if it is a sixteen-year-old who takes money from his or her parents, as contrasted with a parent who takes money that a sixteen-year-old earned from a part-time job.

Closeness Versus Kinship

There are still other complications and subtle distinctions. One of these is whether the crux of things is being a member of the same family, versus the closeness and intimacy of the relationship between perpetrator and victim, irrespective of whether they are related by blood or marriage? Just because a person is a family member may not lend any special character to the crime. Although there is wide agreement that intrafamily sexual abuse of a child is different from extrafamily sexual abuse, it can be argued that the important factor may be intensity or closeness of the relationship, and this is sometimes mistakenly presumed just because someone is "family." But abuse by a next door neighbor would be more like "family" abuse than abuse by uncle Charlie who lives a thousand miles away and is seeing the child for the first time. On the other hand, the counter argument is that what is at stake are social definitions of the situation. If society says that sexual contact by adult relatives makes such an act a particularly revolting crime, and if the victim accepts society's definition of the perpetrator as a member of his/her family, then he/she could well exhibit the negative reactions typical of serious moral transgressions, such as anxiety, shame, and guilt.

The Conceptual Framework as a Research Tool

Every reader of this book will probably think of additional complicating factors, exceptions, and contradictions. So it is important to keep in mind that the conceptual framework we have outlined is not intended to cover every possible situation. If it were to be judged by that criterion, it would no doubt fail the test. Rather, we offer it as a way of organizing one's thinking about these difficult issues in a way which helps to consider those issues systematically, and in a way which raises research questions and insights which would probably not otherwise have occurred. Only time will tell if the conceptual framework outlined in this chapter passes that test.

Historical Change and the Social Construction of Crime

The definition of crime, like every other aspect of society, has changed over the course of history and continues to change. What was once a religious injunction to "beat the devil out of him" is now either a phrase whose historical antecedents have been forgotten; or if acted on, is considered a crime—child abuse (see Clendinen, 1984 for some examples of such prosecutions). Similarly, in about ten states, the former immunity of husbands from being charged with rape of a wife has been removed.

These changes reflect the fact that crime is a "social construction" (Gelles, 1975; Gusfield, 1967), not an absolute. What is a crime in one society, or one historical era, can be a moral requirement in another. Some societies prohibit marriage between cousins, and in other societies a cousin is the preferred partner. Some societies permit or encourage polyandry or polygyny (more than one husband or more than one wife), whereas others jail people who have more than one spouse (Reiss, 1980). In a few societies—for example the Badaga of South India (Hockings, 1980)—an adult male relative is expected to initiate a girl into sexual activity, whereas in our society, it would be a crime.

In general, what is defined as a crime tends to reflect the economic imperatives and the power structure of the society. Societies with meager food supplies may require mothers to commit what we consider the crime of infanticide if a previous child is still nursing. Citizens in capitalist societies tend to view crimes by the poor (such as car theft), as more serious than crimes by the rich (such as a car manufacturer who conceals the fact that a certain model of car has unreliable brakes), even though the latter is more costly and produces more injuries. And in most societies, governments can engage in mass killing by declaring that it is morally right, i.e., by "declaring war."

In relation to crime in the family, an important trend has been to "criminalize" what once were legal acts. The English common law, which is the basis for the American legal system, gave husbands the right to "physically chastize an errent wife" (Calvert, 1974). It was not until the 19th century that the courts ceased to recognize this right, and it was not until the 1970s that any state enacted a statute which made clear that an assault on a wife is just as much a crime as an assault on a stranger.

WOMEN AND CHILDREN AS PROPERTY. In the 1980s some states of the USA, and a number of countries, recognized forced sex in marriage as rape. A still further development is occurring in countries such as Sweden, which enacted laws making physical punishment of children illegal. These changes raise the question of why there has been a "moral transformation" in respect to violence in the family, but not in respect to property crimes? Why do many people now want to end the "marital exemption" for rape, but in effect, retain it for larceny and other property crimes? That is an important question which only an insightfully designed study can answer.

A hypothesis worth exploring is that the difference reflects the ownership of material goods, as contrasted with the ownership of children, women, and sexual rights. In the western historical tradition, children are, in effect, the property of the parents. In ancient Rome, a father could even kill a child. In the case of girls, ownership has traditionally been transferred to the husband when a girl is "given in marriage," at which point the husband also acquired the exclusive right to her sexual services. (Of course, these rights have never been absolute since society also has an interest in furthering the family as a social institution and in making sure that there is a next generation.)

We suggest that one of the factors which led to the "moral transformation" (Gusfield, 1967) which criminalized previously tolerated behavior under the new concepts of "child abuse," "spouse abuse," and "marital rape," is the gradual replacement of the status of women and children as property by the idea of equality. In the case of women, the final *legal* step in this transition still awaits the passage of the equal rights amendment to the constitution; the final steps in the *de facto* transition to equality with men is much further off. In the case of children, there are inherent limits on equality due to their physical and mental immaturity, but the children's rights movement has made considerable headway and the idea of children as the property of the parents has been importantly diminished (Adams et al., 1971; Feshbach and Feshbach, 1978).

To the extent that women and children are given the same rights as adult men, they become the sole owners of their own bodies. Hence, any infringement on their body without consent cannot be tolerated. However, in the case of money and property, the situation is different because there is something of a presumption that wealth will be shared, at least within the immediate family. Perhaps the individualization of society will continue to the point where the underlying notion of shared wealth will cease to exist. To the extent that this occurs, we are likely to see a similar moral passage in respect to property crimes within the family as is occurring in respect to violent crimes.

CONFLICTING PRINCIPLES AND RESEARCH ON INTRAFAMILY CRIME. We regard these as welcome and long overdue changes in the legal system (Straus, 1983). But, as with most things in life, they are not an unmixed blessing. They raise questions about the extent to which the state should directly intervene in family life, questions about how far the trend should go, and questions about the effectiveness of criminal sanctions in dealing with family matters. These are large questions, but questions which can be addressed by empirical research, as illustrated by a Sherman and Berk's study (1984) in Minneapolis. The results of that study indicate that a policy of automatic arrest of wife-beaters makes a difference: the men who were arrested had a lower rate of repeating the offense than was the case when the police used mediation and referral to family therapists and other social services.

Similar research needs to be done on the effects of using the criminal justice system in respect to within-family property crimes. But even before that, we need information on such issues as to what extent do people allow a "family exemption" in respect to property crimes within the family? Conversely, are there crimes in addition to incest in which the criminality or seriousness of the act follows from the very fact that it occurs within the family? How do the circumstances and the characteristics of the victims and the aggressors (such as age, sex, and family role) affect evaluation of the seriousness of the offenses and whether it should be regarded as a crime?

If the act is defined as a crime, what are the consequences for the individuals involved, and for family cohesion? If parents and other family members do not treat an act which would be a crime outside the family as a criminal act, does that affect the probability of future acts of that type? Is parental disinterest in petty crime in the home related to delinquency outside of the home? One can argue that failure to react negatively to violations of the rights and property of others within the family sets the stage for the same behavior outside the family (Hirschi, 1969). Alternatively, one can argue that "criminalizing" such childish behavior by responding with outrage and punishment will only alienate the child. This list is only a small sample of the many issues on which research knowledge is needed.

THE KEY ISSUES

The three aspects of crime and the family identified by our conceptual framework (crime within, crime by, and crime against the family) are the first half of the conceptual framework used to organize this book. The other half consists of the five key analytic issues described below.

Incidence

The three types of family crime identified in Figure 1-1 are important because they alert us to the existence of aspects of crime and aspects of the family that have tended to be overlooked. The very existence of the taxonomy (i.e., the classification system in Fig. 1-1) leads us to ask about the "incidence" (the frequency of occurrence) of each of the types. Many of the articles in this book attempt to answer that question, but as you will see, the answer is often in the form of an informed opinion rather than truly reliable statistics.

Cause and Consequence

Knowing how much there is of a phenomenon is an important first step in science. Also, it is often of great practical value. But it may not be very crucial for scientific understanding of the issue. This is because the main concern of scientific analysis is in understanding *why* things are the way they are. That is, the core of science is concerned with issues of cause and consequence. In our case, this means trying to understand why the phenomena identified by the typology exist and what consequences they have for other aspects of life in the family and in the wider community.

Socialization

Since human behavior is overwhelmingly a function of what people have learned to do, a critical part of the explanation for crime is to be found in what sociologists call "socialization." Socialization is a specific type of learning. It refers to what is learned as a member of and as a part of functioning in a social system. It is part of the socialization of American children to learn to eat with a knife, fork, and spoon. Learning to use chopsticks, which is part of the socialization of a Chinese child, would not help an American child to get along in American society.

The family teaches a vast range of things to its members (both adult members and children). We think that among them is criminal behavior, including norms and values justifying crime and techniques for carrying out crimes. Even the most law abiding families may socialize children to commit such criminal acts as minor tax evasions, violation of liquor or traffic laws, etc. Socialization for crime, i.e., learning how to justify and carry out criminal acts, is such an important part of the links between crime and the family that we have singled it out for special attention throughout the book.

Crime Prevention and Treatment

There is some doubt if a society without crime is even possible (Erickson, 1966). There is, however, little doubt that some societies have a lot more crime than others, and that the United States is in that high crime group. Therefore, the issue of what can be done to prevent or control crime is even more important here than in some other countries.

Programs aimed at crime prevention are more likely to be effective if they are based on an understanding of the interrelations of crime and the family. We have already mentioned the possibility that families socialize their members (both adults and children) for criminal activities. The other side of the coin may be even more important. Families can help insulate members against pressures toward crime. Social scientists and criminal justice professionals are familiar with numerous cases in which children growing up in an environment where crime is common, nevertheless were able to avoid becoming involved and go on to successful legitimate careers (Dinitz et al., 1962; McCord and McCord, 1959).

Families are also important for other aspects of crime prevention.

They can teach members to take steps which will help protect them from crime, such as instructing children about how to deal with adults who make sexual advances; they can install burglary protection equipment; and the very existence of cohesive family units in a neighborhood is probably a deterrent to crime.

The Matrix

So far we have identified three aspects of crime and the family (crime within families, crime against families, and crime by families) and five key issues that need to be understood (incidence, causes, consequences, socialization, and prevention). The combination of the three aspects of crime and the family and the five analytic issues provides the conceptual framework for the book. Cross-tabulating these two classifications (see Fig. 1-2) shows that there are 15 separate but related issues.

	ASPECT OF FAMILY AND CRIME		
KEY ISSUES	Within Families	By Families	Against Families
INCIDENCE	4 5 6 7	9 10 12	13 15
CAUSES	5 6 7	9 10 11 12	13
CONSEQUENCES	6 7 8	11	14 15
SOCIALIZATION	5	10 11 12	
PREVENTION TREATMENT	6 7 8		14

Figure 1-2. Conceptual Framework of the Book.

The numbers in each cell of Figure 1-2 are the chapters of this book. That is useful as a guide to finding information on specific topics. It also gives an overview of what is already known about the interrelationships of crime and the family. Specifically, in view of the fact that these 15 issues have not been widely recognized, it is remarkable that we were able to find useful material on all but one or two.

On the other hand, Figure 1-2 also tends to overstate what is known about crime and the family. First, there are not as many different articles as it seems. Some chapters are listed in two or three of the cells because they cover more than one of the 15 issues. Second, Figure 1-2 says nothing about the quality of the information. As will be clear when you read the introductions to each of the main parts of the book, several of these articles, although useful, have limitations. Third, certain types of crime—such as child abuse—are well represented because the existence of child abuse has been recognized as a crime for a number of years. But other types of crime involving families that may be equally or more common than child abuse—for example, theft from other family members—have not been recognized by the public or researchers. Consequently, not much has been published yet. To help fill this void we began a series of studies designed to measure the range and frequency of crime involving the family. Using a sample of college freshman from two different state universities, we inquired about their experiences with crime by or against other family members and crimes that they committed along with other family members. The results of these studies are presented later in Chapters 4 and 9. They confirm that crime within the family is indeed a relatively common occurrence.

The five issues described in this section are clearly important for understanding crime and the family. However, there are alternative ways, or additional ways, of looking at this topic which are also valuable. For example, instead of organizing the book according to these five issues, a more abstract framework could have been used by focusing on causal theories such as functionalist or Marxist theories. Or we could have taken a more concrete approach by focusing on the nature of the crime, such as violent crime versus property crime. We organized the book on the basis of Figure 1-2 because we felt that it represents the best match to the scientific information now available.

REFERENCES

Adams, P. et al. (1971). *Children's rights.* New York: Praeger Publishers.

Bard, M., & Sangrey, D. (1979). *The crime victim's book.* New York: Basic Books.

Calvert, R. (1974). Criminal and civil liability in husband-wife assaults. In S. K. Steinmetz, & M. A. Straus (Eds.), *Violence in the family* (pp. 85–87). New York: Harper and Row (originally published by Dodd, Mead).

Clendinen, D. (1984, July 1). Cult and child beating: Defense and accusation. *The New York Times, 14.*

Dinitz, S., et al. (1962, August). Delinquency vulnerability: A cross group and longitudinal analysis. *American Sociological Review, 27,* 515–517.

Empey, L. T., & Lubeck, S. G. (1971). *Explaining delinquency.* Lexington: D. C. Health.

Erickson, K. T. (1966). *The wayward puritans.* New York: Wiley.

Feshbach, N. D. & Feshbach, S. (1978). The changing status of children: Rights, roles & responsibilities. *Journal of Social Issues, 34*(2).

Finkelhor, D., & Yllo, K. (1982). Forced sex in marriage: A preliminary research report. *Crime & Delinquency, 28*(3), 459–478.

Gelles, R. (1975, April). The social construction of child abuse. *American Journal of Orthopsychiatry, 45*(3), 363–371.

Gusfield, J. (1967, Fall). Moral passage: The symbolic process in public designations of deviance. *Social Problems, 15,* 175–188.

Hirschi, T. (1969). *Causes of delinquency.* Berkeley: University of California Press.

Hockings, P. (1980). *Sex and disease in a mountain community.* New Delhi: Vikas Publishing House PVT LTD.

McCord, W., & McCord, J. (1959). *The origins of crime.* New York: Columbia University Press.

Reiss, I. L. (1980). *Family systems in America* (3rd ed.). New York: Holt, Rinehart and Winston.

Sherman, L. W., & Berk, R. A. (1984, April). The specific deterrent effects of arrest for domestic violence. *American Sociological Review, 49*(2), 261–272.

Straus, M. A. (1983). Violence in the family: Wife beating. In S. H. Kadish (Ed.), *The encyclopedia of crime and justice.* New York: Free Press.

Straus, M. A., Gelles, R. J., & Steinmetz, S. K. (1980). *Behind closed doors: Violence in the American family.* New York: Doubleday/Anchor.

CHAPTER 2

CRIME AND VICTIMS

ALAN JAY LINCOLN

It is important to have knowledge of some of the key ideas, facts, and methods of criminology and victimology as a basis for understanding the interrelationships of crime and the family. This chapter is intended to provide that information for those who are not yet familiar with these fields.

DEFINING CRIME

In Chapter 1 we introduced the terms victimology and criminology. But just what are the differences between the two fields of study? They are considerable, even though there is also a great deal of overlap. For example, the traditional way of thinking about crime is to assume that if a crime has been committed, then there must have been a victim. But it turns out that this is not always true. In fact, in recent years a whole class of crime has been reexamined and given the name "victimless crime" (Schur, 1965).

Schur defines these victimless crimes as ". . . . the willing exchange, among adults, of strongly demanded but legally proscribed goods or services" (Schur:169). Included would be such crimes as gambling, sexual relations between consenting adults (or even many kinds of sexual acts between husband and wife), prostitution, some drug offenses, and perhaps some pornography violations. Common features of these crimes include the questionable amount of harm to any person and the relatively private nature of the acts.

What then makes something a crime? Tappan suggests the following definition:

> "Crime is an intentional act or omission in violation of criminal law (statutory and case), committed without defense or justification, and sanctioned by the state as a felony or misdemeanor" (1960:10).

Several aspects of this definition need to be clarified. A crime can only occur when there is some intent to commit an act that is prohibited. The specific consequences of the action may be unanticipated—such as shooting at one person and missing but hitting a second bystander. Most legal scholars agree that if a reasonable person could have expected that the act could have produced these effects, then "general intent" is present. General intent is sufficient for criminal activity if the other criteria of this definition are met. Note that legally determining an actor's intent is not a simple task. Yet the determination of intent may be the difference between legal and illegal activity or the severity of the charge as in "degrees of homicide."

Second, there must be actual behavior or a failure to act when required to do so. The latter is illustrated by the offense of failing to file an income tax return or failing to provide care and food to your children. Refusing to act when not required to do so—such as not trying to rescue a drowning man—would not be a *criminal* offense.

A third issue in this definition of crime involves "defense or justification." A crime has not been committed if the law recognizes a legal defense or justification for the behavior. This category includes the legitimate use of force to protect one's self or property. Several states currently are debating the passage of laws increasing the rights of homeowners and others to use "deadly force" under clearly specified, threatening circumstances. These circumstances typically involve intrusion into one's home by a stranger who is perceived to be a threat to an individual or his/her family. There are other legally-recognized defenses including insanity, mistake of fact, duress, entrapment, and so on.

It also is possible to be a victim (for example, of being struck by lightning) when no crime was committed. But not all accidents are as free from liability as the term "accident" suggests. Consider the following problem. While crossing a campus street on the way to your next class you are struck by a car while in the cross walk. The car is free from mechanical defects and properly registered, but the driver is intoxicated. This common "accident" is not an accident at all, but rather a violation of laws. Liability is recognized easily here. But the issues are not always this clear. For example, a machine operator has his hand crushed while operating a large and complex metal stamping machine. The factory owners have complied with every existing law which applies. But many people might still think that the factory was run in an unsafe way and as the expression goes, "*it's a crime* that they did not have better safety protections," even though no law required it. If the factory owner should or could have done things differently, even though no law required it, then in a strict legal sense there was no crime, even though there was a victim. The victim's family also will experience hardship as a result of the "accident."

We should point out that legal definitions and statutes may change over time. At some subsequent point in history, the same legal act indeed may become a crime. In fact, in other states or societies this act may already be a crime. This is well illustrated in the history of legislation involving children. It used to be common practice to employ children as young as nine for a ten- or twelve-hour workday. Now, of course, these practices are illegal in our society. Until recently, children within the privacy of their own home might be physically punished with a large rod until severely bruised and not have legal recourse. Recent changes in laws regarding the punishment and treatment of children have altered this. In fact, children's rights are undergoing change in three areas: (1) The state versus the child as in delinquency proceedings; (2) The state on behalf of the child as in abuse and neglect proceedings; (3) The child making claims against the parent or the state as in seeking confidential medical treatment. These rights currently are in a state of flux showing us that the legal process is one of change and redefinition.

VICTIMOLOGY AND CRIMINOLOGY

The fact that all crimes do not have easily identifiable victims, and all victims are not necessarily in that situation because of criminal acts, is only one reason for the distinction between criminology and victimology. The most important reason for making the distinction between the two is that, despite the fact that both deal with crime, the two fields of study call attention to different aspects of crime. Knowing what causes some people to engage in crime does not necessarily tell us what causes some people to be victims of crime, sometimes repeatedly. Family crime, like other crime, needs to be viewed from both perspectives. Figure 2-1 summarizes some of the main differences between criminology and victimology.

Each of the differences identified in Figure 2-1 is discussed in one or more places in this book. The first row of Figure 2-1, which identified the importance of considering the characteristics of *both* the criminal and the victim, is the basis for the conceptual framework presented in Chapter 1 and is discussed further in the section which follows. The second row of Figure 2-1, the type of crime and the type of victimization, is covered in this chapter and in Chapter 13. The third row of Figure 2-1, the causes of crime and of family-related crime, is discussed in Chapter 3. The last row of Figure 2-1, the effect of the criminal justice system on the criminal and the victim, is addressed in this chapter and in Chapter 3.

Criminology focuses on:	Victimology focuses on:
The perpetrator or criminal	The victim
The type of crime (murder, burglary, etc.)	The type of victimization: direct and indirect costs, material and psychological costs
The causes of crime, i.e., why crime rates vary, why some people commit crimes and others do not, etc.	The causes of being victimized, i.e., how and why victimization rates vary, why some people become victims and others do not
Criminal careers and the effect of the criminal justice system upon offenders	Effects of victimization on careers of the victim

Figure 2-1. Aspects of Crime Given Primary Attention by Criminology and Victimology.

Criminals vs Victims

Criminologists tend to focus on the perpetrator or criminal. This focus might be manifest in attention to a person's position, as indicated by characteristics such as age, sex, race, social class, or place of residence. Psychological factors including personality traits, needs and motives, or physical states including genetic makeup, nutritional conditions, and appearance might be emphasized. This does not exhaust the possible interest in the criminal. Some researchers tend to place more importance upon some combination of social, biological, and psychological factors. For example, the effects of family relationships, status among peers, and educational or occupational opportunities for the potential offender could be examined.

In contrast, the victimologist emphasizes the physical, social, or psychological characteristics of the victim or group of victims. Typical studies in this developing field would include determining whether the sex, age, or physical condition of a person effects the chances of being a victim. Place of residence, income level, and life-style have been shown to affect victimization. The status of the victim within the family, birth order, or relationships with friends might provide some clues to the victimization process. Likewise, racial or ethnic identity often is linked to victimization patterns, but the patterns may differ depending upon regional and community conditions. Psychological characteristics of victims, such as "learned helplessness" and "dependency," have been examined as possible links to victimization. Thus it is true that the focus of the criminologist and the victimologist are in different directions. However, the specific factors that each considers useful in helping to gain an understanding of the respective problems may be quite similar.

Type of Crime or Type of Injury

A second major difference between criminology and victimology involves the interest in the type and characteristics of crime as opposed to the impact of the crime. Certainly the two are not unrelated. Yet many researchers tend to emphasize one or the other. Criminology places importance upon the patterns of crime. This is illustrated by the Uniform Crime Reports published annually by the FBI. Nationwide statistics are tabulated for 29 different offenses. The relationship between the type of crime and factors such as population size, geographic location of crime, seasonal and monthly variations, and crime rate increases and decreases are examined.

DIRECT AND INDIRECT COSTS OF CRIME

Victimologists, however, would be interested in the impact of these different types of crime. One useful way to examine the impact of crime is to consider both the *direct* and *indirect* costs. Whenever an individual or several people are victimized, costs are incurred. The direct costs include those resulting from a particular crime and include the value of property lost or damaged, the amount of money taken, medical costs for injuries received, and wages lost due to injury. All of these could be the direct results of a particular victimization. Although not as easy to measure, the indirect costs might be even more devastating for a victim or a victim's family in the long term. Here we could consider all changes that are the result of the fear of or anticipation of crime. For example, if a homeowner installs a $3,000 security system to prevent anticipated burglaries, then we are dealing with indirect costs. Personal security costs are not the only indirect costs. In fact, according to Conklin:

> There is the cost of maintaining the vast but undermanned criminal justice system that processes suspects. There are expenditures for the police, the courts, and the correctional institutions. Aside from these easily measured expenses, there are losses to inmates and to society from time spent in jails and prisons. Inmates working at prison jobs earn only a fraction of the money they could make in the outside world. Not only do they suffer the loss of earning power and dignity, but their families are not provided for and often require welfare assistance, an additional cost to society. Society also suffers in the incarceration of inmates because of the expense of maintaining prisons and their staffs, and because of the loss to the economy of the full productive effort of the inmates" (1975:4).

These costs are staggering. Expenditures for criminal justice activities in the United States for Fiscal Year 1978 were over $24 billion. Over half of this total was for police protection ($13 billion) and $5.5 billion was used for corrections. In 1983 there were nearly 60,000 public agencies involved with criminal justice. More than 1.1 million persons were employed on a full-time basis just in police-related jobs in the public sector. This does not include the massive force of private security personnel. Except for the few states with legislated budget cutbacks, these costs are continuing to rise. According to the Department of Justice (1979), criminal justice-related expenditures increased 129 percent between 1971 and 1978. These costs are shared by all taxpayers, not merely those people who have become victims or members of victims' families. The indirect costs of crime affect us all.

From the viewpoint of an individual victim or a person who fears victimization there are other indirect costs.

> "The indirect costs of crime also include the changes in attitude and behavior by people who fear their own victimization. They stay off the streets at night and lock their doors. If they go out, they walk only in groups and avoid certain areas of the city. They use taxis or cars to protect themselves from street crime. If they have to drive through high crime-rate areas of the city, they roll up their car windows and lock the doors. To avoid possible victimization, people do not use library and educational facilities at night, they stay away from meetings of social groups and organizations, and they keep out of parks and recreational areas. Some forfeit additional income by refusing overtime work which would force them to go home after dark. Some even carry firearms or knives. Many take security measures to protect their homes—additional locks on doors and bars on windows, brighter lights on porches and in the yards, burglar-alarm systems, and watchdogs. Judging by the types of precautions that people take, they seem to fear personal attack more than the loss of property through theft. One extreme but fairly common reaction to both personal and property crimes is a desire to move, to escape from the community where crime poses such a great threat" (Conklin, 1975:6).

Costs to Families

We have seen that crime can affect both the society and the individual. The family as a unit can be affected as well. Direct and indirect costs for the family include those referred to above but also some additional problems that affect the members as a group. Here we might consider the strain on family relationships brought about by crime or the fear of crime. For example, parents may choose not to go out in the evening, because they are afraid to leave their young children with babysitters or their older children alone. Under these conditions parenting might become perceived by adults as an added burden restricting their own

freedom. The gruesome toll of crime on the family unit could be seen in
the recent wave of child-killings in Atlanta that occurred in the late
1970s. Activity patterns of black families in particular were altered
dramatically. Children in many families were not allowed out without an
adult even before the imposed curfew. The fear instilled in many children placed added strain on their relationships with siblings and parents.
This fear is likely to occur whenever children are threatened and may
lead to changes at the community as well as the family level.

> Pain relievers, nasal spray, candy, orange juice. Poisons, acids, pins and
> needles. There seems to be no limit to the numbers, targets or methods of copy-
> cats seeking to emulate their demonic hero, the still unknown poisoner who
> murdered seven people (and, it was disclosed last week, might have come hair-
> raisingly close to killing an eighth) by placing cyanide in Tylenol® capsules.
>
> Provoked by such incidents, and the prominent display they got almost
> nightly on TV news last week, more than 40 communities in the U.S. banned
> Halloween trick-or-treating. "I feel like the Grinch—you know, the one who
> stole Christmas." said Councilman Paul Sharp of Hammond, La., which
> enacted a ban. Rhode Island Governor J. Joseph Garrahy urged parents to
> substitute Halloween house parties for trick-or-treating, and New Jersey Gov-
> ernor Thomas Kean signed a law mandating six months in jail for anyone
> convicted of contaminating Halloween candy, even if no one was harmed
> (Time, 11/8/82:27).

Families also can experience the costs of crime from episodes that
affect only its own members. Although the impact may not be as widespread as in Atlanta, or in the cities banning trick-or-treating, it can be as
intense. The following account of an attack against family members
sleeping in their home points this out.

> A 50-year-old Hingham man was stabbed repeatedly early yesterday by a
> would-be rapist who had assaulted his daughter in the family home.... O.
> _____, his wife D. _____ and his daughter had gone to bed about 8:45 P.M.
> Thursday in their rented duplex house. They left their front door unlocked
> because they have always felt secure in their suburban neighborhood of small
> houses where they have lived for four years. Five hours later, D._____ was
> awakened by her daughter's screams and found her husband sitting on a chair
> bleeding and the kitchen swimming with blood."

There are obvious direct costs from this episode—some immediate
and some long-term.

> "The arm wound almost cost him his life. The muscles were cut to the bone.
> The wound to the arm severed a main artery, cut one of the major nerves to
> the hand.... He (surgeon) described O.'s _____ prognosis as excellent, but
> with some residual nerve damage." The indirect costs are not as apparent, but
> certainly are as real.

Relationships, feelings about one another, and life-style all are subject to change.

> "D._____, who works as a waitress and is the mother of three other children who are married said she will 'never again feel at home in my house. There's been dirt in my house.' Now (the daughter) is worried because she feels if she didn't scream, her father wouldn't have been injured" (Boston Globe, 4/25/81).

The family also can be affected by crime against the elderly. Persons over 65 typically have victimization rates substantially *lower* than persons between 12 and 35. Even though the victimization rate against the elderly is relatively low, the consequences of each episode may be considerably higher for the victim. Direct costs may be higher in that a robbery may result in the loss of "only" sixty dollars, but this loss may mean a choice between heat and food. Similarly, a purse snatching all too frequently results in a fall and subsequent serious injury to the victim. Indirect costs or reactions to crime and the fear of crime also can be devastating for the elderly.

> "As a result, old people—black and white alike—live like prisoners in the decaying sections of the city. One woman was even afraid to put out her trash; she stuffed it in plastic bags, which she stored in a spare room. When one room would fill up, she would seal it off and start filling up another. At times she lived on candy bars, tossing coins out of a window to children who would go to the store for her. Visiting The Bronx, a reporter from the *New York Times* talked to _____ 64, who had moved her bed into the foyer of her apartment and slept fully dressed so she could dash out the door the next time someone tried to break into her bedroom—which had happened three times before. 'They're not human,' she cried, 'They're not human'." (TIME, 11/29/76:21).

During the summer of 1983 a severe heatwave struck portions of the country. Fear of crime escalated the effects of the weather.

> (St. Louis) The heat wave blamed for 15 deaths in the St. Louis area has been particularly hard on elderly people, who often are afraid to open their windows or go outside because of robberies, officials said Thursday. . . .
> "St. Louis has a high crime rate and a dense population, and people might hesitate to open their windows," said Dr. Arthur Meyers, a police department statistician. He said fear of being mugged prevents many people from cooling off at night (A.P., Aug. 15, 1983).

In any case, elderly victims often have to seek assistance from their grown children or grandchildren. At times the adult children feel so badly (guilty?) about the plight of their elderly parents that they insist on "getting the parents out of that neighborhood." This support may take the form of financial aid, intensive health care, emotional and psychological support, or simply a place to live. These added burdens on the host family may not be entirely positive experiences.

Costs to Families of Criminals

So far we have talked about the family or a family member being the victim of a crime. Crime impacts upon the family in another way. When a family member is the *perpetrator* of a crime then there are potential serious costs to that person's family. These would include the immediate impact when another family member is the victim of the crime or the indirect impact of the perpetrator being caught up in the criminal justice system. In 1982, over 10 million arrests were made for various offenses. Even though many persons were arrested more than once, millions of families experienced the hardships of one of their members being arrested and charged with a crime. These effects range from financial (as in meeting bail, providing support when a wage earner is detained) to psychological (dealing with shame, stress, fear, etc.).

MEASURING CRIME

Programs to deter, control crime, or to modify the effects of crime, need to be based on information about the incidence and patterns of crime. However, assessing criminal behavior is not an easy task. Like other social problems that tend to be hidden by the participants, criminal behavior is not always apparent to the naive observer. The social scientist and the criminal justice professional utilize a variety of measurement techniques designed to assess patterns of crime and its effects. Each of these techniques have strengths and weaknesses. The choice of one or another depends on the immediate goals of the researcher or practitioner, the type of data desired, and the resources available. We will examine four of the diverse measurement techniques including: (a) Uniform Crime Reports, (b) victimization surveys, (c) offender surveys, and (d) agency records.

Uniform Crime Reports.

The oldest continuous crime measurement program is the Uniform Crime Reports (UCR) of the Federal Bureau of Investigation. The data they provide to the FBI are "crimes known to the police."

Since the publication of the first report in 1930, the number of reporting police departments has grown from about 750 to over 15,000 today.

'*Reporting procedures*' On a monthly basis, law enforcement agencies report the number of Crime Index offenses (murder and nonnegligent manslaughter, forcible rape, robbery, aggravated assault, burglary, larceny-theft, and motor vehicle theft) that become known to them. A count of these crimes, which are also known as Part I offenses, is taken from records of all complaints of crime received by law enforcement agencies from victims, officers who discovered the infractions, or other sources.

Whenever complaints of crime are determined through investigation to be unfounded or false, they are eliminated from the actual count. The number of 'actual offenses known' in Part I is reported to the FBI whether anyone is arrested for the crime, the stolen property is recovered, or prosecution is undertaken. Additionally, each month law enforcement agencies report the total number of these crimes cleared. Crimes are 'cleared' in one of two ways: (1) at least one person is arrested, charged, and turned over to the court for prosecution; or (2) by exceptional means when some element beyond police control precludes the physical arrest of an offender. The number of clearances which involved only the arrest of offenders under the age of 18; the value of property stolen and recovered in connection with Part I offenses; and detailed information pertaining to criminal homicide are also reported (United States Department of Justice) (1978).

Despite the fact that the program is costly and that only certain crimes are included in the reports, the UCR is a valuable tool for law enforcement personnel, other criminal justice professionals, social scientists, legislators, and others. The UCR is one of the most complete and readily available sources of data on reported crime. There are strong controls on the reporting of incidents and the use of standardized definitions which cut across the 50 different state legal codes. Furthermore, current rates and trends over time can be examined, and comparisons between different regions and states can be made. Overall, the UCR is a rich source of data on crimes that come to the attention of law enforcement agencies. A sampling of the information available in the UCR is shown in Table 2-1.

Recent (1982) statistics on known crime are presented in Table 2-3. The rates in that table are the actual number of a particular crime for every 100,000 residents. Notice that the rate of Part I crimes varies from 9.1 (per 100,000) for murder to 3,069 for larceny theft. The rate of violent crime (for murder, forcible rape, robbery, and aggravated assault) is 555 per 100,000 persons. This is only about one-ninth of the rate for property crime (4,998 per 100,000). Despite this difference, most Americans are more concerned about the threat of violent crime than that of property crime.

Also of interest in Table 2-2 are the varying crime rates for different population areas. The "Standard Metropolitan Statistical Area" refers to a core city or cities with a combined population of 50,000 or more, the county in which it is located, and the surrounding counties if they meet certain criteria such as a certain proportion of the population who

Table 2-1. Partial Contents of Uniform Crime Reports

commute to the central city. "Other cities" are those outside the SMSAs. As you might expect, crime rates in rural areas tend to be lower than those in other cities, which in turn are lower than the rates in the SMSAs. The only exceptions are the rates for murder which tend to be highest in metropolitan areas and lowest in "other cities."

The seriousness of murder has prompted the FBI to present data on the relationship between the assailant and the victim. These findings appearing in Table 2-4 are of interest for our study of crime and the family. Notice that approximately 15 to 20 percent of all murders occur among family members, with half of these involving the husband and the wife. What does this mean in real terms? In 1979, approximately 3,500 victims were murdered by members of their own family. The alleged reasons for these murders vary tremendously, but "arguments" between family members are prime factors.

Table 2-2.—Index of Crime, United States, 1982

Area	Population[1]	Crime Index total	Modified Crime Index total[2]	Violent crime[3]	Property crime[3]	Murder and non-negligent man-slaughter	Forcible rape	Robbery	Aggra-vated assault	Burglary	Larceny-theft	Motor vehicle theft	Arson[1]
United States Total	**231,534,000**	**12,857,218**		**1,285,705**	**11,571,513**	**21,012**	**77,763**	**536,888**	**650,042**	**3,415,540**	**7,107,663**	**1,048,310**	
Rate per 100,000 inhabitants		5,553.1		555.3	4,997.8	9.1	33.6	231.9	280.8	1,475.2	3,069.8	452.8	
Standard Metropolitan Statistical Area	173,143,110												
Area actually reporting[4]	98.5%	10,842,834		1,139,844	9,702,990	17,226	67,321	515,306	539,991	2,863,742	5,888,469	950,779	
Estimated total	100.0%	10,947,153		1,147,049	9,800,104	17,327	67,833	517,075	544,814	2,890,551	5,949,751	959,802	
Rate per 100,000 inhabitants		6,322.6		662.5	5,660.1	10.0	39.2	298.6	314.7	1,669.5	3,436.3	554.3	
Other Cities	24,155,265												
Area actually reporting[4]	94.5%	1,133,571		75,764	1,057,807	1,329	4,555	12,690	57,190	261,103	748,903	47,801	
Estimated total	100.0%	1,203,568		80,091	1,123,477	1,418	4,878	13,447	60,348	276,425	796,372	50,680	
Rate per 100,000 inhabitants		4,982.6		331.6	4,651.1	5.9	20.2	55.7	249.8	1,144.4	3,296.9	209.8	
Rural	34,236,625												
Area actually reporting[4]	90.2%	646,598		52,684	593,914	1,978	4,528	5,729	40,449	226,878	332,843	34,193	
Estimated totals	100.0%	706,497		58,565	647,932	2,267	5,052	6,366	44,880	248,564	361,540	37,828	
Rate per 100,000 inhabitants		2,063.6		171.1	1,892.5	6.6	14.8	18.6	131.1	726.0	1,056.0	110.5	

[1]Populations are Bureau of the Census provisional estimates as of July 1, 1982, and are subject to change.
[2]Although arson data are included in the trend and clearance tables, sufficient data are not available to estimate totals for this offense.
[3]Violent crimes are offenses of murder, forcible rape, robbery, and aggravated assault. Property crimes are offenses of burglary, larceny-theft, and motor vehicle theft. Data are not included for the property crime of arson.
[4]The percentage representing area actually reporting will not coincide with the ratio between reported and estimated crime totals, since these data represent the sum of the calculations for individual states which have varying populations, portions reporting, and crime rates.

Table 2–3. Circumstance by Relationship, 1982

[Percent distribution]

Victim	Total	Felony type	Suspected felony type	Romantic triangle	Argument over money or property	Other arguments	Miscellaneous non-felony type	Unable to determine
Total¹	100.0	100.0	100.0	100.0	100.0	100.0	100.0	100.0
Husband	3.4	.2	.1	3.2	2.9	8.0	2.8	.8
Wife	4.8	.2	.2	7.1	1.1	8.5	7.3	1.8
Mother	.6	.2	.1			.9	1.1	1.1
Father	.7	.1	.1		.6	1.4	.9	.3
Daughter	1.0	.4	.3	.4		.4	3.6	.4
Son	1.7	.6	.1	.2	1.1	1.2	5.0	.9
Brother	1.1	.1		.2	1.1	2.5	1.1	.4
Sister	.2				.2	.3	.3	.2
Other family	3.3	1.0	.2	.4	3.7	6.2	4.5	.9
Acquaintances	29.7	20.7	5.8	60.3	61.4	42.1	35.3	9.7
Friend	3.4	1.2	.8	6.1	11.2	4.4	4.9	1.3
Boyfriend	1.4	.2		3.6	1.1	2.9	1.2	.3
Girlfriend	1.9	.1	.2	7.8	1.1	3.3	2.1	.7
Neighbor	1.6	1.9	.5	1.3	4.0	2.4	1.2	.4
Stranger	16.9	41.6	7.1	6.3	6.1	8.4	15.2	15.8
Unknown relationship	28.1	31.5	84.4	3.2	4.3	7.2	13.3	66.0

¹Because of rounding, percentages may not add to total.

VICTIMIZATION SURVEYS

As an alternative to using data on known or reported crimes, researchers may choose to collect crime data directly from those involved with criminal behavior. There are several levels of "involvement" including perpetrator, victim, and observer of crime. When we seek information related to being the victim of a crime, then we are conducting a "victimization survey." The victims of crime can be rich sources of information about their own victimization and its direct and indirect costs. Examining the responses of nonvictims in the same sample provides comparative information on the relevant characteristics of the victims and the nonvictims.

The earliest systematic, large-scale victimization survey was conducted in 1965 by the National Opinion Research Center. In this study of 10,000 scientifically selected households, the crime rates were found to be approximately twice as high as the comparable UCR statistics. This was explained in part by the fact that while 21 percent of respondents reported being the victim of a crime, only half of those victims reported the episode to the police.

Following the "success" of the NORC survey, the Law Enforcement Assistance Administration designed and implemented a series of national victimization surveys. Beginning in the early 1970s, the United States Bureau of the Census conducted systematic surveys in selected cities and across the nation. These surveys included as many as 200,000 respondents, including a sample of commercial establishments. The focus of these National Crime Surveys was on:

> "...certain criminal offenses, whether completed or attempted, that are of major concern to the general public and law enforcement authorities. For individuals, these offenses are rape, robbery, assault, and personal larceny; for households, burglary, household larceny, and motor vehicle theft; and for commercial establishments, burglary and robbery. In addition to measuring the extent to which such crimes occur, the surveys permit examination of the characteristics of victims and the circumstances surrounding the criminal acts, exploring, as appropriate, such matters as the relationship between victim and offender, characteristics of offenders, victim self-protection, extent of victim injuries, economic consequences to the victims, time and place of occurrence, use of weapons, whether the police were notified, and, if not, reasons advanced for not informing them" (United States Department of Justice, 1979:iii).

Victimization Rates

What do the crime patterns uncovered by victimization surveys look like? Remember that we are describing incidents reported by the victims

Crime and the Family

themselves, whether or not the police were notified. Table 2.4 contains victimization rates for males and females over the age of 12. These victimization rates are for the number of crimes per 1,000 persons while UCR rates were for the number of crimes per 100,000 persons. This means, for example, that an aggravated assault rate of 9.2 must be multiplied by 100 (920) to equate it with the corresponding UCR rate for 1980 of (291). This disparity is typical of the victimization, the rates being higher than rates for most reported crimes.

Table 2-4

Victimization rates for persons age 12 and over, by type of crime and sex of victims, 1981.
(Rate per 1,000 population age 12 and over)

Type of crime	Both sexes (186,336,000)	Male (89,109,000)	Female (97,227,000)
Crimes of violence	35.3	46.2	25.4
Rape	1.0	a0.1	1.8
Completed rape	0.3	a0.0	0.5
Attempted rape	0.7	a0.1	1.2
Robbery	7.4	9.8	5.2
Robbery with injury	2.4	2.9	1.8
From serious assault	1.2	1.7	0.7
From minor assault	1.2	1.3	1.1
Robbery without injury	5.1	6.9	3.4
Assault	27.0	36.2	18.5
Aggravated assault	9.6	14.4	5.3
With injury	3.2	4.7	1.7
Attempted assault with weapon	6.5	9.6	3.6
Simple assault	17.3	21.9	13.1
With injury	4.5	5.3	3.8
Attempted assault without weapon	12.8	16.6	9.3
Crimes of theft	85.1	90.7	80.0
Personal larceny with contact	3.3	2.7	3a7
Purse snatching	1.0	(aZ)	2.0
Pocket picking	2.2	2.7	1.7
Personal larceny without contact	81.9	88.0	76.3

NOTE: Detail may not add to total shown because of rounding. Numbers in parentheses refer to population in the group.

(Z) Represents less than 0.05.
aEstimate, based on zero or on about 10 or fewer sample cases, is statistically unreliable.

Victim characteristics thought to be associated with crime patterns can be examined easily. Table 2.5 provides information on the age and sex of victims and their reported victimization rates. Two strong effects are apparent. First note that males at every age were more likely than females to be victims of both violent crimes and crimes of theft (sexual assaults being the exception). Secondly, the overall and specific victimization rates peak at relatively low ages (usually 16–19) and then decline continuously with age. In fact, the lowest reported rate is for respondents over 65. However, also keep in mind that as mentioned earlier, the impact of a particular episode may be more devastating for the aged. The personal impact, as we discussed earlier, tends to be masked by the aggregate data common to both the UCR and victim surveys.

Also of interest are data examining the relationship between the victim and the offender. Crime survey data show that both crimes of violence and crimes of theft are more likely to be committed by a stranger than by a nonstranger. However, the pattern of reporting the crime to police is not as clear. While rape victims are somewhat more likely to report rapes by a stranger, robbery victims are more likely to report robberies by a nonstranger. There also is the possibility that respondents were reluctant to report some crimes to the survey interviewers. We suspect that this is true particularly for those involved with crimes in their immediate family. In fact, the behavior (such as the unauthorized taking of money from a parent's wallet or punching a sibling) may not even be defined by the "victim" as a crime in the legal sense.

Advantages/Disadvantages of Victimization Surveys

Among the major limitations of victimization surveys is an inability to use the technique to study all types of crime. Many victimless crimes and murder are not easily studied with victim surveys. In addition, the victims must be aware of their own victimization in order to describe it. Even if this is the case, victim surveys typically ask the respondent to recall experiences that occurred months or years earlier, resulting in some distortion and selective retention. Finally, when using trained interviewers, large scale victim surveys may be prohibitive in cost. Recent advances in the use of telephone surveys, although subject to some methodological problems, have reduced the costs dramatically.

On the other hand, victim-focused research has several advantages over other techniques. It has been shown that many respondents will identify episodes that were not reported to the police. Thus, we can obtain a more accurate portrayal of the incidence of crime as opposed to crime reporting. Secondly, the victim often can provide detailed information about both the circumstances surrounding the crime and the characteristics of the offender even when the offender is never apprehended. Almost any potentially related variable could be examined as part of a victimization study. One of the important issues suitable for victimization surveys is the examination of the short-term and long-term impact of crime upon the victim and the victim's family. Finally, a well

Table 2-5

Victimization rates for persons age 12 and over,
by sex and age of victims and type of crime, 1981.

(Rate per 1,000 population in each age group)

Sex and age	Crimes of Violence	Rape	Robbery			Assault			Crimes of theft	Personal larceny	
			Total	With injury	Without injury	Total	Aggra-vated	simple		With contact	Without contact
Male											
12-15 (7,394,000)	72.5	a0.0	17.1	4.4	12.7	55.4	20.1	35.3	131.7	3.8	127.9
16-19 (8,072,000)	96.9	a0.4	18.7	6.5	12.2	77.9	31.8	46.2	139.4	4.0	135.4
20-24 (10,348,000)	90.8	a0.2	17.2	4.2	13.0	73.4	31.9	41.5	147.9	5.1	142.9
25-34 (18,918,000)	52.5	a0.1	9.2	3.3	5.9	43.2	16.1	27.1	105.7	2.9	102.7
35-49 (18,479,000)	28.7	a0.1	6.8	1.8	5.0	21.9	9.6	12.3	76.5	1.6	75.0
50-64 (15,660,000)	14.8	a0.0	4.7	2.0	2.7	10.1	3.4	6.7	49.1	1.4	47.8
65 and over (10,240,000)	9.9	a0.0	4.8	a0.7	4.1	5.1	a0.8	4.3	26.8	2.3	24.5
Female											
12-15 (7,112,000)	44.7	2.9	6.2	a2.1	4.1	35.6	7.5	28.1	124.3	a1.2	123.1
16-19 (8,068,000)	38.6	4.5	5.9	a1.5	4.4	28.2	9.0	19.1	124.5	3.3	121.1
20-24 (10,765,000)	46.6	3.7	7.5	1.9	5.7	35.4	9.3	26.0	118.3	3.8	114.5
25-34 (19,521,000)	35.1	2.6	6.2	2.7	3.5	26.4	8.0	18.4	96.1	4.7	91.4
35-49 (19,383,000)	18.1	a0.7	4.2	1.3	2.8	13.3	4.8	8.5	79.0	3.7	75.3
50-64 (17,582,000)	11.8	a0.4	4.6	1.5	3.0	6.8	1.8	5.1	52.6	4.2	48.4
65 and over (14,796,000)	6.4	a0.2	3.4	1.8	1.6	2.8	a0.8	2.0	19.1	3.3	15.8

NOTE: Detail may not add to total shown because of rounding.
      Numbers in parentheses refer to population in the group.

aEstimate, based on zero or on about 10 or fewer sample
cases, is statistically unreliable.

designed victim study can obtain over 90 percent response rate thereby facilitating generalization of the findings.

The study of crime within the family described in Chapter 4 is based partly on a victim survey. But not all the data in that study is from victims. A third technique for measuring crime—the offender survey was used.

OFFENDER SURVEYS: SELF-REPORTED CRIME

Suppose you are interested in why juveniles commit crimes or how many they commit. You might simply ask an appropriate sample of juveniles. The offender survey in one sense represents this direct approach. Naturally, there are strengths and weaknesses of this approach. Victimless crimes, which are missed by victimization surveys, can be examined by questioning those engaging in such acts. Gambling, drug offenses, illegal sexual practices, and other offenses are amenable to self-report data. The motivations and precipitating factors surrounding crime can be clarified by offenders themselves as can their perceptions of the criminal justice system. On the other hand, the shortcomings of this approach include a failure to give full disclosure of criminal activities, and perhaps sometimes the opposite—a tendency to exaggerate one's criminality. There are also ethical and legal issues involved with obtaining information about previously unreported crime. As is true with all survey research, the generalizability of crime data obtained by self-report depends upon the sample used. The majority of juvenile offender research has used high school or college students, or institutionalized groups, and these groups may not represent a wide spectrum of the population. Finally, offender surveys are not very effective in uncovering the most serious crimes, either because the offenders are not in the sample or if they are, they are "not talking."

Examples of Offender Surveys

One of the major conclusions from various offender surveys is that "ordinary" people do extraordinary things. In a groundbreaking study, Wallerstein and Wyle (1947) had nearly 1700 men and women of varying ages and backgrounds complete anonymous questionnaires about their behavior. Ninety-nine percent indicated that they had committed, as an adult, at least one of the 49 offenses included on the survey instrument. Both the men and the women reported an average of over ten offenses each. More recent studies by Short and Nye (1958), Clark and Tifft (1966), and Krohn et. al. (1974) also have shown that ordinary people do commit some criminal acts. In fact, had these actions been called to the attention of the police many of the respondents could have been labeled officially as delinquents or criminals depending upon their ages.

Offender surveys typically ask respondents to recall behavior from months and years past. However, it is possible to structure offender-focused research to examine more immediate behavioral episodes. Participation in looting, urban disorders, and other forms of illegal public behavior typically are examined after the events are over—either by the use of arrest data or a general survey. Sometimes scheduled public events such as rock concerts and championship contests (World Series, Super Bowl, etc.) are prone to disruption. The patterns, causes, and consequences of criminal behavior at these events can be clarified by studying potential and actual offenders at the scene.

Hillery and Lincoln (1978) in response to concerns of officials in New Orleans (Mardi Gras) and Ft. Lauderdale (College Spring-break) attempted to identify some of the correlates of participation in violent episodes at the two events. In this study student volunteers systematically asked other crowd participants to respond to a brief series of questions about their background, reasons for attending the event, perceptions about freedom and social control at the event, and their participation in conflict and violence while at the Mardi Gras or Spring Week. Several distinct patterns emerged. Thirteen percent of the respondents at the Mardi Gras had been involved in an assault while at the festivities compared with 4 percent of the Ft. Lauderdale sample. This difference was explained in part by the proposition that high levels of anticipated freedom coupled with deprivation of this anticipated freedom resulted in high levels of conflict and violence. The Mardi Gras sample had the highest level of anticipated freedom (believed that they could do whatever they wanted to do in New Orleans) and the highest level of deprivation of freedom (felt that their behavior was being overcontrolled by authorities in New Orleans).

The implications of the Hillery and Lincoln findings—that being deprived of anticipated freedom may lead to violence—relate to violence in the family. Perhaps family members who feel that they are not allowed the freedom that they deserve in the family setting are more likely to become assailants. This might be especially likely at certain critical times. The stage of adolescence in which growing children feel that they "deserve" or are ready for more freedom might plead to assaults on parents. The stage in marriage when a wife feels she should have more power in decision making within the family might produce wife beating. The birth of a child that is seen as restricting the freedom of one or both parents might increase the chances of child abuse. Each of these situations and others may be perceived as freedom restricting at a time when greater freedom is being expected.

Family Offender Surveys

Recent studies of the patterns of family violence have included data from offenders. Straus, Gelles, and Steinmetz (1980) found that the marital violence rate of husbands (12.1 per 100 families) was only slightly higher than that of wives (11.6 per 100). Interviews with the victims and the offenders yielded similar findings. There was no evidence that offenders were "covering up" their actions. In fact, offenders reported a slightly higher rate of violence than did their victimized spouses.

An offender survey sometimes is used when the victims are inaccessible as in the case of homicide, victimless crime, and unknown victims. Similarly, research on victimized children often is restricted for ethical reasons. In this case, studying their abusers provides needed information for social scientists and social service agencies. Gelles and Straus (Chapter 5) report data from a nationally representative sample of 1146 American families with a child between the ages of three and seventeen. In half of these families interviews were conducted with the father and in the other half the mother was interviewed. "Child abuse was defined as an attack by a parent involving punching, kicking, biting, hitting with an object, 'beating up,' or using a knife or gun." The study found that 10 percent of the men and 18 percent of the women abused a child in the family at least once during the year. Isolated incidents, moreover, were uncommon. Abusing parents averaged 10.5 assaults per year. Despite the risk of "cover up," data on serious and violent offenses can be obtained with a well designed offender survey.

EXISTING RECORDS: AGENCIES, COURTS, CORRECTIONS.

The Uniform Crime Reports of "crimes known to the police" are not the only source of official information about criminal behavior. Each step in the complex criminal justice system triggers some type of record keeping process (see Fig. 2-4). This process may begin at the early stage of reporting a crime, giving rise to the UCR, or continue to an arrest and to a middle stage such as arraignment or trial, or progress even further to sentencing or treatment. Even after completing one stage of a treatment program there may be followup information of probationers or parolees. At every stage, records (sometimes confidential) are generated. Many of these records provide valuable insights into some aspects of crime in the United States. Records of arrests, trials, convictions, sentencing, and prison populations often are the major sources of historical information about crime patterns.

Records related to activities of the police, the courts, and the prisons reflect the official responses of the criminal justice system to crime in America. Like the UCR, these records are subject to underreporting since not all actions are recorded. Biases present at specific times or places may affect the operation of the system. For example, at some time in our history, Irish immigrants in the Northeast, or Mexican immigrants in the Southeast, were viewed with suspicion or animosity, and there may have been a greater tendency to arrest, convict, or sentence members of these groups.

Some information about juvenile crime can be obtained by using existing records. The juvenile justice system involves not only the police, courts, and secure treatment facilities, but a host of prevention, treatment, and support agencies. Each of these may have information about juvenile crime patterns within their local areas. Typically, individual records would be unavailable to "outsiders," but summary data often can be obtained. Comparisons between different sets of agency or institutional data provide different perspectives on the problem of juvenile crime. To illustrate, Hackler and Lautt (1969) compared five measures of delinquency for a sample of delinquents: (1) self-report questionnaires, (2) juvenile court/police referral records, (3) head counselors' discipline ratings, (4) teachers' discipline ratings, and (5) number of friends with police contacts. In this study the official records tended to correspond with the self-reported episodes again pointing out the value of each of the varied measures of crime and delinquency.

CRIMINOLOGY, VICTIMOLOGY, AND FAMILY CRIME

Each of the issues and each of the problems discussed in this chapater concerning the definition and measurement of crime and victimization apply, to greater or lesser degree, to crimes involving the family. In fact, the conceptual framework presented in Chapter 1 is based on considering who is the victim and who is the criminal. Each of the other aspects of criminology and victimology listed in Figure 2-1 needs to be considered, including:

• The type of crime (e.g., violent crime versus property crime) and the type of victimization (e.g., material, physical, psychological).

• The factors which affect who commits a family related crime (e.g., mother, father, male child, female child) and the factors which affect who is the victim (e.g., other member of the family versus outsiders).

• The effect of intervention of the criminal justice system in respect to family crime, e.g., does it help either the offender or the victim, or does it serve to produce a new level of victimization.

Finally, although all the methods of gathering data on crime discussed in this chapter are applicable, some are better suited to certain aspects of family-related crime than others. "Victim surveys" are probably the best way of finding out about crimes against the family, and Chapter 13 presents the results of a nationwide survey of "households touched by crime." But victim surveys are not effective in getting information about crimes *within* the family because so many respondents do not consider these acts as crimes, or are reluctant to report criminal acts by their own husband, wife, or child. This calls for "offender surveys," and Chapters 4, 9, and 10 use this method.

REFERENCES

Clark, J. P., & Tifft, C. L. (1966). Polygraph and interview validation of self reported deviant behavior. *American Sociological Review, 31*, 516–523.

Conklin, J. E. (1975). *The impact of crime.* New York: MacMillan.

Hackler, J., & Lautt, M. (1969). Systematic bias in measuring self-reported delinquency. *Canadian Review of Sociology and Anthropology, 6:*92–106.

Hillery, G., & Lincoln, A. (1978). Crowds, leisure, and conflict. *Journal of Leisure Research, 10,* 219–225.

Krohn, J., Waldo, G. P., & Chiricos, T. G. (1974). Self-reported delinquency: A comparison of structured interviews and self administrated checklists. *Journal of Criminal Law, Criminology and Police Science, 65,* 545–553.

Schur, R. M. (1965). *Crimes without victims: Deviant behavior on public property.* Englewood Cliffs, NJ: Prentice Hall.

Short, J. F., & Nye, F. I. (1958). Extent of unrecorded delinquency: Tentative conclusions. *Journal of Criminal Law, Criminology and Police Science, 49,* 296–302.

Straus, M. A. (1980). Victims and aggressors in marital violence. *American Behavioral Scientist, 23,* 681–704.

Straus, M. A., Gelles, R. J., & Steinmetz, S. K. (1980). *Behind closed doors: Violence in the American family.* New York: Anchor Press/Doubleday.

Tappan, P. (1960). *Crime, justice, and correction.* New York: McGraw Hill.

United States Department of Justice (1978). *Uniform crime reports for the United States.* Washington, D.C.

United States Department of Justice (1979). *Expenditure and employment data for the criminal justice system.* Washington, D.C.

United States Department of Justice (1979). *Criminal victimization in the United States.* Washington, D.C.

United States Department of Justice (1982). *Criminal victimization in the United States.* Washington, D.C.

Wallerstein, J. S., & Wyle, C. J. (1947). Our law-abiding lawbreakers. *Probation* (38), 107–118.

CHAPTER 3

CRIMINOLOGICAL THEORY AND FAMILY CRIME

ALAN J. LINCOLN AND JOHN T. KIRKPATRICK

Criminologists seek to understand why crime occurs and how to control crime. The pursuit of these two goals requires knowledge from many disciplines, including anthropology, economics, history, medical science, political science, psychology, and sociology, among others. However, this diveresty in training and intellectual backgrounds makes for a rather fragmented body of knowledge. The purpose of this chapter is to help readers organize this knowledge, and specifically: (1) to familiarize the reader with some of the key theories about what causes crime and (2) to show possible connections between the family and crime.

The diversity of theories explaining why crime occurs is so great that some sort of framework is necessary to group them into categories so that we can see the similarities and the differences between the explanations which have been offered. We have elected to group the various theories of crime under three general headings. The first, *The Individual Focus*, includes theories that emphasize individual traits when explaining crime. Psychological and biological explanations, for example, fall in this category. *The Social Structural and Social Process Focus*, the second heading, actually represents two sociological bodies of theories tying the origin and proliferation of crime to the ways in which societies are constructed or to the social processes which facilitate becoming a criminal. The third category focuses on certain aspects of the interdependent relationships between individuals and societies. We have called this last category *The Societal Reaction Focus* and it includes, among others, labeling theory.

In the course of presenting this conceptual framework, we identified eight propositions that pertain to the family and crime. Each of these propositions appears in several studies of criminal behavior. At times the link between crime and the family is clear. Other times it is less so. There may be other propositions that are not here delineated. Yet, when taken together, these eight propositions indicate the close connection between the family and crime in American and other societies. We will develop these propositions as we proceed through the chapter.

THE INDIVIDUAL FOCUS

A long-standing controversy surrounds the idea that crime is caused by innate characteristics of individuals, i.e., the idea that the causes of crime lie within the biological and psychological constitutions of individuals. Criminal behavior, according to these scientists, results from some anatomical, physiological, genetic, or psychic dysfunction.

Biological Theories

BODY TYPE. Much of the early research on the link between biology and crime can be traced to the work of a single scientist, Cesare Lombroso. Lombroso, an Italian physician of the late nineteenth century, focused his work upon the anthropometric characteristics and physical irregularities of criminal offenders. He was convinced that the study of the unique physical composition of the criminal held the most promise for understanding why crime occurs. Heavily influenced by the evolutionary thought of Darwin and the phrenologists or "skull-feelers," Lombroso proposed that criminals were less advanced than noncriminals in the evolutionary scale, and that some unusual recombination of ancestral genes left criminals with a relatively high propensity for illicit behavior.

Lombroso often measured the degree of atavistic composition through the appearance of physical irregularities. In a study of female offenders (see Lombroso and Ferrero, 1898), Lombroso compared the physical attributes of a select group of female felons with those of a group of noncriminal women. Female criminals, according to Lombroso, are much like male criminals in that they show "atavistic" characteristics, such as low sensitivity to pain, and long lower jaws which Lombroso believed to be characteristics of a genetic order that programs them for criminal behavior.

Lombroso's research had several flaws. He drew his criminal samples only from prisons. Consequently, offenders who eluded arrest, conviction, and sentencing—probably the majority of offenders—were not studied. He tended to ignore alternative explanations for the differences he discovered. Cultural variation, for example, might explain why one group of people look different than another.

Other scientists who followed Lombroso's lead examined the link between physical constitution and crime. In England, Goring (1913) reported minimal differences between the physical attributes of criminals and noncriminals. In the United States, Hooten (1939) shared Lombroso's belief that behavior arises from organic bases though Hooten did acknowledge the role of environmental forces in criminal behavior. Sheldon (1949) constructed a typology of body types, consisting basically of fat, medium, and skinny body categories, and drew a relationship between body type and criminal propensity. According to Sheldon, because of the particular body temperature they maintained, people of medium build were more likely than the other two groups to engage in crime. Although the research designs of these scientists were often marred by the same errors that detracted from Lombroso's work, their collective works helped carry biological theories to the present.

GENES. The possible link between genetic factors and crime has been investigated in four different ways (Ellis, 1982). The various methods employed each share a similar focus. They attempt to determine whether some genetic factor helps explain the variation in criminal behavior observed among the population. Among the earliest studies were those examining family heritage or pedigree. In addition, studies of twins, adoptees, and chromosome irregularities have been used.

One function of the institution of the family is reproduction. It is therefore not surprising that several of Lombroso's peers chose the family as a context in which to test the genetic transmission theory. The family is a social unit where genes are passed from one generation to the next. Dugdale (1910) traced the intergenerational passing of criminal traits in the Jukes family. Nearly forty years later, Goddard (1915) attempted a similar study of the Kallikak family. Goddard had a natural control group, since there were two branches of the Kallikak family tree: a criminal and a noncriminal branch. Both Dugdale and Goddard identified genes as the transmitter of criminality, although an alternative explanation might be that the socialization process is the primary transmitter. In Goddard's study, the two family branches were likely to exhibit different genetic compositions over time but they also were likely to use different manners of childrearing. The problem is that from the research designs of the two studies, it is not possible to determine which of the two transmitters is operational.

STUDIES OF TWINS AND ADOPTED CHILDREN. The best research on the relative importance of genetic and social factors in influencing criminal behavior have studied twins and adopted children, particularly those adopted soon after birth. Since identical twins are genetically identical while paternal twins share only 50 percent of their genetic makeup, the identical twins should be more alike in their behavior patterns if the behavior is biologically influenced. After reviewing these studies, Ellis states that:

> Several criminologists have recently presented reviews of twin studies of criminality. Although their emphasis and depths of treatment vary, all have been left with the same general conclusions as that reached here: Even though

the studies' results are clearly consistent with the idea of some genetic involvement in criminal behavior they are not unequivocally so. Regarding adoption studies, while the number of studies is small, the evidence they provide of genetic involvement in criminality is now approaching the limits of certainty. The simplest way to reflect the persuasive nature of these adoption studies is to note that they show that an adopted person's chances of being convicted of serious criminal behavior can be more accurately assessed by knowing if that person's genetic parents (with whom no significant social contact has ever occurred) were similarly convicted than by knowing if the parents who reared that person had been similarly convicted (1982).

Ellis's optimism about the biological significance shown in adoption studies is based in part on work by Hutchings and Mednick (1977). Their studies of Danish adoption and crime records found that a higher percentage of the convicted adoptees genetic fathers (31%) had a conviction record than did the adopting fathers (13%).

CHROMOSOME VARIATION. The fourth technique used to study the possible link between genetics and crime is the study of chromosome variation. The most well known of these attempts is the suggestion that having an extra male chromosome leads to a greater likelihood of aggressive criminal behavior. Ellis indicates that the findings of these and other chromosomes are highly "suggestive of some genetic involvement in criminality."

Much of the current research on this topic is plagued by the imperfect designs and negative reactions to the earlier research. There is a general uneasiness at the mention of a connection between biology and crime. Jeffery (1980) argues that this uneasiness amounts to the intellectual censorship by the public and academic communities of an entire set of ideas.

To completely ignore biological explanations of crime would be to shortchange our larger understanding of the phenomenon. There are some intriguing research findings that suggest significant links between criminal behavior and electrodermal activity, chromosomal disorders (see Mednick and Christiansen, 1977), hormonal imbalances, certain biochemical reactions (see Jeffery, 1980), nutrition, and intense or prolonged exposure to physiological stress (Humphrey and Palmer, 1982).

This brief overview of the biological basis of criminal behavior suggests the first of the eight propositions concerning the family and crime which will be identified in this chapter:

1. Criminality is genetically transmitted through the family.

Readers should evaluate this proposition cautiously. The fact is that criminologists cannot now offer overwhelming evidence either in support of or against the proposition. However, there does appear to be some meeting ground for both camps of the "nature—nurture" controversy. More scientists are recognizing the interplay of biological and social influences of behavior. The question yet to be answered concerns the extent of the balance between these two possible criminogenic forces.

Psychological Theories

Psychological theories of crime causation, like biological theories, focus on internal characteristics influencing criminal behavior. The two sets of theories differ in that psychological theories trace criminal behavior to psychic, rather than biological, anomalies. Most psychological formulations of criminal behavior assume that the more intense the psychological impairment, the greater the chance that criminal actions will result.

A student of Lombroso's, Raffaele Garofalo, departed from his mentor's dependence upon anthropometry to explain crime. Instead he argued that a "psychic anomaly" separates the criminal from the crowd. The individual trait assigned to the criminal by Garofalo can be loosely translated as moral turpitude. A depravity such as this was thought to be deeply imbedded in the psyche of each criminal. Garofalo believed that this singular psychic trait might be genetically passed from one generation to the next, but he allowed that the "psychic anomaly" may arise from environmental sources. Garofalo's recognition that psychological impairment may accrue through the workings of the sociocultural environment led the way to an increasing role for psychological formulations in criminological theory.

Several psychological paradigms influenced much of the criminological research undertaken since Garofalo introduced "psychic anomaly" to the literature. Healy (1969) published a volume in 1917 reflecting Lombroso's influence as well as Freud's. Criminal misconduct, believed Healy, arises from some form of mental conflict, often the repression of an unresolved primal event, idea, or emotion. This would seem to borrow from psychoanalytic notions of behavior. At the same time, however, Healy was convinced of the criminal's "distinct inner urge" toward wrongdoing. He speculated that the urge may have some organic base. While Healy proposed a largely psychological theory of crime, his work also reflected the wide influence of biological theories of crime.

Other researchers in the early to mid 1900s included mental impairment in their studies of criminals. Fernald (1920) noted inferior mental capacities among the female offenders she studied. The Gluecks reported similar findings among both male and female offenders (1930, 1934). In a study of prostitution and sexual promiscuity among women, Thomas (1925) alluded to adjustment problems as sources of such behavior. These and other studies of the period each emphasized the inner psychic state of the individual. Several of these formulations reflected the trend toward IQ testing, psychoanalytic theory, and behaviorism in the discipline of psychology at the time.

Some of the more recent work on the psychological bases of criminal behavior still mirrors these trends. Palmer (1960) reported that his sample group of murderers experienced greater psychological and physical trauma early in life than did a control group of nearest-aged brothers. Palmer proposed that the intense psychological frustration experienced by murderers eventually drove them to their lethal behavior. Eysenck (1964), like Healy before him, asserted that criminals manifest some innate predisposition toward criminality. He added that the predisposition translates into actual criminal behavior through inadquate or improper socialization. Presumably, the criminal's moral and social conscience is not appropriately developed. Bromberg (1965) offered a psychiatric analysis of crime. He characterized embezzlement, larceny, and gambling, for example, as offenses most often committed by passive-aggressive personalities. In each of these studies, traces of psychonalytic thought, behaviorism, and developmental psychology can be identified.

A common goal in many psychological studies of crime appears to be the definition of the "criminal personality." In one way, this approach is similar to that of the biological studies that attempt to identify the "criminal gene." In the 1940s, Abrahamsen (1969) tried to identify the components of the criminal mind. More recently, Yochelson and Samenow (1976) attempted a similar venture: to probe the thought patterns of the criminal and to define the criminal personality.

Yochelson and Samenow present an exhaustive analysis of case studies largely taken from their work at a hospital for the criminally insane. They delineate a series of psychological traits that comprise the criminal personality as they understand it. Fear, anger, distrust, sentimentality, pride, poor decision-making ability, and a sense of victimization are only a few such traits. The researchers are careful to cast the criminal personality as a continuum, where the greater its operation, the greater the chance of criminal behavior.

Throughout most of these studies are references to the importance of the family. The psychoanalytically-inclined psychologists, for instance, emphasize that trouble-producing trauma usually surfaces early in life, within the folds of the family. An overbearing parent, a dispassionate one, sibling conflict, and abandonment are several examples of trauma occurring within the family that are tied to later criminality. The molding and shaping of the "criminal personality" within the family is another thread running throughout the psychological literature on crime. This aspect of the psychological theories of crime can be summarized as our second proposition:

> 2. *Criminal propensity is a function of psychological trauma and maladjustment early in the family experience.*

THE SOCIAL PROCESS AND SOCIAL STRUCTURAL FOCUS

Theories of crime that emphasize social structures and social processes are in the mainstream of contemporary criminology. Such formulations trace the origin crime to the nature of society itself, including the organizational structure, the cultural norms, and the processes by which those structures and norms are maintained. As we see it, there are six themes in this body of theory. Each of these themes and its relevence to the family is considered in this section.

Learning Theories

The first theme concerns the role of *learning* in criminal behavior. Even though learning has an important individual component, what one is given an opportunity to learn depends upon one's group identity and the way in which the society is organized. In addition, various social pressures affect the way individuals use what was learned. With this in mind we treat the learning theories of crime within the social and structural focus. Those who choose to emphasize the role of individual differences as they relate to what is learned would probably discuss learning theories in the previous section.

Edwin Sutherland, often identified as the father of modern criminology, was one of the first scientists to apply learning principles of behavior to understanding crime. All criminal behavior, Sutherland believed, is learned behavior (Sutherland and Cressey, 1974). He further suggested that the likelihood of criminal behavior is dependent upon the quality and quantity of contact an individual or group may have with criminal elements and definitions favoring crime. How young one is at initial criminal contact, the strength of that relationship between learner and teacher, the frequency of contact, and its duration through time are dimensions which Sutherland thought affected the learning of crime. Presumably the younger one is at first contact, the stronger the relationship between learner and teacher, the more frequent and long-lived the contact, the greater the prospect that an individual will learn to behave criminally. Small intimate groups were thought to be ideal settings for learning the skills and attitudes necessary for crime. The family, of course, is a small, intimate group.

Following a similar line of thought, Bandura (1973) suggested that criminal violence is a manifestation of social learning processes. Through the shaping and molding by either violent significant others or by primary groups, an individual may be socialized to accept and commit violent behavior. Since the family plays such a crucial role in socialization, the ideas set forth by both Sutherland and Bandura point to the family as a powerful transmittor of crime.

The role of the family in the learning process can be manifest in additional ways. For example, not only can children learn how to become criminals, but they can learn not to become one as well. If the child's prosocial and conforming behavior are praised and rewarded in other ways or if the child's deviance or delinquency are punished by the family, then the child should learn to avoid committing those actions. At least he or she should avoid committing them when around his or her family. Whether and how the family punishes early delinquency depends in part on the values and attitudes of the family members. These in turn may be influenced by the social position of the family within the framework of the society.

Subcultural Theories

Other theorists have also drawn from learning principles to explain crime. Wolfgang and Ferracuti (1967) identified pockets of customs within a larger culture that promote and condone the commission of violent acts. They termed these pockets "subcultures of violence." Individuals integrated with such subcultures have greater exposure to violent customs in daily life than those having little contact with a subculture of violence. Put another way, a person may commit a crime because he or she has learned the value of such actions. Entire families as well may be suject to these subcultural patterns.

The concept of the subculture can help to illuminate the role of the family in the proliferation of crime. For example, various ethnic groups have been tied to organized crime and often the organizational aspect of the illicit behavior is provided by the family. Much has been made, for instance, of the part played by a segment of the Sicilian-American community in organized crime. Popular books and films celebrate the history of the mafioso in the annals of American crime. If members of an extended family are engaged in organized crime the entire family may be likened to a subculture of violence since the promotion of crime and the enlistment of new criminal members may be persistent pressures on family members.

From the criminological theories involving learning principles, we may extrapolate two more propositions about the links between the family and crime:

> 3. *Criminality is transmitted through the socialization process operating within the family.*

> 4. *Criminality is encouraged by families entrenched in criminal subcultures.*

Social Disorganization Theory

Another structural theory of crime causation emphasizes forces at play within society which lead to a breakdown of social organization and social integration. In a classic study of suicide, Durkheim (1952) described a condition of "normlessness" that can pervade a society. This condition, which he termed "anomie" and defined as the increasing separation between individuals and the social rules that govern them, was believed to generate suicidal behavior. The importance of Durkheim's formulation rests in the suggestion that a breakdown of societal norms—the building blocks of social structure—may engender deviant behavior, including crime as well as suicide.

Merton (1957) proposed a model of cultural strain to explain crime. In American society, there is a schism between the goals of wealth and success so widely prescribed by the culture, and the low chance of obtaining wealth by the socially acceptable means such as hard work, education, and sustained effort. Illegitimate means, according to Merton, often supplant legitimate efforts to reach the ends. In one sense, American culture has enshrined the ethic which beautifies money and success. Wealth then becomes a state of grace. The achievement of that state may become primary, and the primacy of the work ethic can give way to the more expedient means of criminal behavior. In this case, the ends justify the means, and one might anticipate crime to be high in societies where the ends are emphasized beyond the means or the availability of acceptable means is structurally limited.

Value Conflicts

Cloward and Ohlin (1960) posited that, in competitive societies, not all individuals can "win." Some must necessarily "lose." That is to say that the channels to success in the legitimate world may not be open to all. There may be structures of opportunity in both the acceptable and criminal worlds. Just as one learns to be a successful lawyer through education, career entry, hard work, and partnership in a firm, one might also follow a similar path of education, entry, and apprenticeship to be a successful thief.

The role of cultural values has been pursued as a possible explanation for the relatively high crime rate in American society. Theories formulated by Baron (1974) as well as Taft and England (1964) cite several of these cultural features and values that may contribute to crime. They include a set of standards that are constantly in flux, an emphasis upon success, materialism, independence and individuality in thought and action, and the admiration of "toughness." Within our society these may be useful traits to have, but they also may contribute to the propensity for crime.

The importance of cultural values is treated in a different way by Cohen (1955) who found that the criminal involvement of juveniles usually involves some rejection of dominant values such as ambition, responsibility and respect for property. Delinquents may choose to follow their own interpretation of the cultural values. Finally, Sellin (1938) wrote of the role of clashing cultures in crime, either conflict of norms and values between two different cultures, or conflict because of social changes within a single culture. Using Sellin's formulation, we might expect violence in urban areas where separate ethnic or racial neighborhoods border one another. The reports of sporadic violence coming from communities in the United States that rapidly absorbed refugees from Southeast Asia during the seventies add credibility to Sellin's theory. This may occur in part because of the conflict between cultures and also in part because of changes occurring within the culture of the migrants.

What can these theories of cultural values contribute to our knowledge of the link between the family and crime? What can they tell us about crime within, against, and by families? We can infer a fifth proposition to add to those already stated:

> 5. *Families as well as individuals are affected by cultural pressures to commit crime.*

Families in conflict with the dominant or competing values of the community may stand at greater risk of criminal activity than those families who do not encounter such forces.

Conflict Theory

The fourth theme among the social and structural theories of crime causation centers upon the notion of social conflict. The conflict approach is mainly concerned with the relationship between socioeconomic forces and illicit behavior. Vold (1958) outlined the rudiments of the conflict perspective for many criminologists who would follow him. Put simply, this perspective attributes crime to inequality in society. Since conflict theory highlights socioeconomic disparities in the explanations of crime, it owes much to the writings of Marx. This perspective became popular among certain groups of criminologists in the 1970s, under the name of "New" or "Radical" criminologists.

Chambliss (1976) succinctly characterizes the essence of the conflict hypothesis. Criminal and noncriminal behavior, he writes, arise from people acting compatibly with their social class position in society. Crime is primarily viewed as a reaction to the oppressive life conditions of an individual's lower-class standing. Moreover, the upper classes control the mechanisms of law making and law enforcement and exercise that control over subordinate classes. In societies where great class struggle can be found, continues Chambliss, high crime rates are also to be found.

Some of the pioneer work showing that what constitutes a crime reflects the political system of a society was done by Quinney (1970). According to Quinney, crime is a definition of human behavior created and maintained by those in power. Behavior defined as criminal is most often conduct which threatens the class interests of the ruling authorities. Criminal justice systems, then, are viewed as tools of the "haves" in society to confirm the status quo and retain control over the "have-nots." Quinney argues that this is the reason why our prisons are populated by the poor while so much white collar crime escapes detection or prosecution. In a society marked by an inequitable distribution of economic resources, "crime in the streets" and not "crime in the suites" becomes the target of most enforcement and corrective public policy. In Quinney's view, the ruling classes would not want it any other way.

Although conflict between economic classes has been the main focus of conflict theory explanations of crime, the applicability of conflict theory is much broader (Thio, 1978). Many crimes, such as rape and most assaults, have little to do with economics, but a lot to do with power. Feminist scholars, for example, have shown that the more inequality between the sexes in a society, the higher the rape rate (Sanday, 1981). Following the lead of Brownmiller (1975), they interpret this correlation as showing that rape is one of many ways in which men keep women in a fearful and subordinate role. Moreover, the criminal justice system itself, as a male-dominant institution, makes it extremely difficult to secure a conviction for rape. Finally, when women commit crimes, although they may escape criminal detection more easily than do men, once detected, women often receive stiffer penalties than men for the same offenses (Smart, 1976). The criminal justice system, which is an important part of determining how much crime and what type of crime characterizes a society, tends to reflect the conventions of a male-dominated society.

Proposition 5, which was based on cultural theories of crime, suggested that families are exposed to and reflect *cultural* pressures to commit crime. The conflict theory of crime just reviewed suggests a parallel proposition about crime and the family:

> 6. *Families as well as individuals are affected by social inequality and resulting structural pressures to commit crime.*

By structural forces, we mean political, economic, and social exigencies that impinge on the lives of various groups in society. This can be illustrated by comparing the pressures encountered by a low-income family with a single female as the sole adult member of the household to the economic pressures and opportunities typical of a well-to-do family with both husband and wife present.

Social Stress

The fifth theme among theories emphasizing social structure and social process is comparatively new but rapidly developing. Several recent studies have discovered some relationship between social stress and crime. Stress is defined as the process in which individuals or groups are required to adjust or adapt to new conditions and situations. Stress that flows from the sociocultural environment is termed sociogenic stress. Stress that springs from the psychological adjustment to life change is called psychogenic stress (Dodge and Martin, 1970). The effects of mass immigration on a community would be an example of sociogenic stress and the adjustment required of a recent divorcee would exemplify psychogenic stress. In many studies, high levels of stress have been shown to have deleterious effects on mental and physical health.

Both sociogenic and psychogenic stress have been found to be related to stress. Linsky and Straus (1982), for example, find an association between sociogenic stress and certain types of crime. Using the fifty states as units of analysis, they constructed an index to measure the stressfulness of life in each of the states, using indicators such as rates of business failures and infant deaths. They found that the higher the score of a state on the stress index, the higher the rate of violent and nonviolent crime. In a study of the relationship between psychogenic stress and criminal homicide, Humphrey and Palmer (1982) find that criminal homicide offenders exhibit higher levels of life-stress, such as divorce, death of a close one, and loss of a job, than do nonviolent felons. Straus (1980) found that the more stress a family was under during the year of his study, the greater the probability of an incident of wife-beating during that year.

The findings of these studies hold sufficient promise to warrant a proposition on stress:

7. Families under stress generate crime.

THE SOCIETAL REACTION FOCUS

The third major theme among criminological theories can be termed the societal reaction focus. The term implies that crime, in part, is a product of the very mechanisms in society created to control crime. This perspective brings to light the paradox that crime control begets crime.

The societal reaction theory of crime rests on the sociological formulations of George Herbert Mead, Charles Horton Cooley, W. I. Thomas, and Herbert Blumer and others at the University of Chicago earlier in this century. They pointed out that people construct their behavior by interpreting and defining the actions of others relative to themselves, and that this is largely done through "labels" and other symbols.

Human actors typically use labels to capture the essence of other actors' social statuses and positions. Black, white, young, aged, husband, wife, child, rich, and poor are frequently referenced words in conversations.

> Man is a language using animal. In the nature of language, he divides
> things into groups, categories, or classes, including some objects with others,
> because they have a characteristic in common, although they are dissimilar in
> an infinite variety of ways. In order to speak and write about these groups of
> things that are alike in some respect, he places a label (tag, name, or counter)
> on them (Sagarin 1975:127).

The societal reaction theory of crime combines this tendency to label behavior with the fact that people base their self-image and behavior in part on the image of themselves which they receive from interaction with others. If people label a person as creative, he or she is more likely to act creatively. If the person is labeled as bad or criminal, there will be a tendency to behave in a way which is consistent with the label. In short, the way society reacts to people influences their behavior, including deviant behavior such as crime.

Thus, Lemert (1967), one of the pioneers of the societal reaction theory, regards deviance, such as crime or mental illness, as a process of becoming. An individual may initially behave in a manner that evokes negative responses from others. Lemert calls this "primary deviance." Over time, a person labeled as "insane," "bad," or "criminal," may come to view him or herself as such and to incorporate the label into a self-image, and then may begin to behave according to the expectations of that image of self. Lemert calls this final stage of a self-fulfilling prophecy "secondary deviance." Some thirty years before Lemert, Tannenbaum wrote of a tendency in human interaction for "a gradual shift from the definition of the specific acts as evil to a definition of the individual as evil, so that all his acts come to be looked upon with suspicion (1938:20)." The labeled individual is caught in a psychological web spun by social forces.

Suppose that a spirited adolescent finds herself in the classroom of a particularly sour and spiteful teacher. For any number of reasons, the teacher displays a singular disdain for the hapless girl. Perhaps she wore her hair in a certain way, or, in the eyes of the teacher, she dressed in an inappropriate fashion. The teacher begins to belittle the girl before her peers. Soon, some other students begin to mimic the teacher's approach to her. Eventually, she acquires a reputation as a troublemaker in the classroom though she has done little to deserve it. This view is reinforced as the teacher relays an impression of her to colleagues, students, and friends. Consequently, her reputation spills outside the school and circulates in the community. Parents refuse to let their teenaged sons and daughters associate with the girl. In their view, she is "bad news" and they fear her condition is a socially contagious one. The labeled girl finds it increasingly difficult to maintain a positive self-image against such odds. She questions her every action and thought. Perhaps she is, she believes, as bad as "they" say she is, so she might as well do the bad things attributed to and expected of her. This in turn strengthens her entrenchment in the role of a wayward youth.

Many researchers have shown similar "processes of becoming" in studies of crime and deviance (see, for example, Eisner, 1969 and Kaplan, 1975). Moreover, the social reactions that may contribute to crime are not confined to informal social relationships. The criminal justice system, the formal network designed to control and contain crime, may inadvertently contribute to the perpetuation of crime. Rubington and Weinberg (1968) view the justice system as a series of "criminal corridors." The official criminal processing of an alleged offender—from arrest through prosecution to punishment—serves to reinforce the criminal label. The further one moves through criminal processing, the more difficult it is to escape the power of the criminal label. In a sense, the criminal justice system, with all its invested authority and official trappings, may encourage as many criminal careers as it interrupts. Once one is publicly identified as a criminal, it is difficult to dispel the perception. If an appropriate allegorical slogan of some individual focus theories is "Birds of a feather flock together," the complementary slogan for societal reaction theories is "If you can't beat them, join them."

For our purposes, we can refer to labeling as typescripting since it involves not only the labeling of a person as criminal but also the prescription of a criminal role. Labelers view the criminal as a "type" of individual who acts according to a criminal "script."

The labeling process, and the criminal behavior which it tends to evoke, also apply to families. Consequently, the eighth proposition about crime and the family derived from this analysis of theories of crime is:

> *8. Crime is a product of criminal typescripting within, by, and against families.*

The tagging of a family member as a "bad egg" exemplifies typescripting within families. Long-standing feuds between families where the familial parties characterize each other as ne'er-do-wells is an example of typescripting by families and the government's investigation of particular families as "child abusers" or because of their political views provides further illustration of typescripting against families.

PRACTICAL IMPLICATIONS OF CRIME THEORIES

In the context of a brief chapter such as this, which is focused on summarizing the major theories of crime and drawing out their applicability to the family, it was not possible to also present a careful evaluation of the validity of each of these theories, nor of the propositions about the family and crime derived from these theories. Each of the theories is supported by at least some empirical research. However, regardless of their level of validity, theories of crime have implications for the treatment and prevention of crime. Even theories thought by most social scientists to be weak may impact upon the way we deal with crime. This is particularly likely to occur if those with decision-making powers believe that a theory is useful. One question to keep in mind is: if the theory is correct, then what are the implications for the treatment and prevention of crime? Policies and legislation often are made in response to popular theories of crime. For example, the belief that crime was passed down through families had an influence upon the passing of laws in several states in the 1920s that dealt with the castration or sterilization of habitual offenders. The belief that hyperactivity, nutrition, and delinquency are linked led to recent attempts to alter the behavior of both delinquency prone children and aggressive prisoners by changes in their diet.

Theories emphasizing the importance of social conditions in the neighborhood have been used in part to justify the expenditure of large sums of money to rebuild and restructure portions of our major cities. Theories focusing on either the role of social learning or the labeling process have had impact on the treatment of both juvenile and adult offenders. The fact that juvenile offenders typically are kept separate from adult offenders within the criminal justice system and are categorized in many states as Children in Need of Services ("CHINS") rather than delinquents reflects the importance placed on the implication of theories, in this case labeling theory. In sum, if a theory is believed to be true, then there may be attempts to implement programs based on the theory.

LINKING CRIME AND THE FAMILY

Criminological theory and research have not often directly addressed the relationship between crime and the family. Yet while this is true, our review of these theories and research provided clues to possible linkages between the two and led to the formulation of the following eight propositions about the interrelationships of crime and the family:

1. Criminality is genetically transmitted through the family.
2. Criminal propensity is a function of psychological trauma and maladjustment rooted in early family experience.
3. Criminality is transmitted through the socialization processes operating within the family.
4. Criminality is encouraged by families entrenched in criminal subcultures.
5. Families as well as individuals are affected by cultural pressures to commit crime.
6. Families as well as individuals are affected by social inequality and resulting structural pressures to commit crime.
7. Families under stress generate crime.
8. Criminality is a product of criminal typescripting within, by, and against families.

These propositions are not intended to be exhaustive of the ways crime and the family are interrelated, nor are they intended to be mutually exclusive. There are also likely to be additional propositions that have escaped us. Most important of all, they should not be regarded as established facts, but as guides to thinking about the issues, as hypotheses, or as a provocative introduction to an important aspect of criminology and victimology.

REFERENCES

Abrahamsen, D. (1969). *Crime and the human mind.* Montclair, NJ: Patterson Smith.

Bandura, A. (1973). *Aggression: A social learning analysis.* Englewood Cliffs, NJ: Prentice-Hall.

Baron, M. L. (1974). The criminogenic society: Social values and deviance. In A. S. Blumberg (Ed.), *Current perspectives on criminal behavior.* New York: Alfred A. Knopf.

Bromberg, W. (1965). *Crime and the mind.* New York: Macmillan.

Brownmiller, S. (1975). *Against our will: Men, women, and rape.* New York: Simon and Schuster.

Chambliss, W. J. (1976). Functional and conflict theories of crime: The heritage of Emile Durkheim and Karl Marx. In W. J. Chambliss, & M. Mankoff (Eds.), *Whose law? What order? A conflict approach to criminology.* New York: John Wiley and Sons.

Cloward, R. A., & Ohlin, L. E. (1960). *Delinquency and opportunity: A theory of delinquent gangs.* New York: Free Press.

Cohen, A. K. (1955). *Delinquent boys: The culture of the gang.* New York: Free Press.

Dodge, D. L., & Martin, W. T. (1970). *Social stress and chronic illness.* Notre Dame, IN: University of Notre Dame Press.

Dugdale, R. L. (1910). *The Jukes.* New York: G. P. Putnam.

Durkheim, E. (1952). *Suicide.* New York: Free Press.

Eisner, V. (1969). *The delinquency label: The epidemiology of juvenile delinquency.* New York: Random House.

Ellis, L. (1982). Genetics and criminal behavior. *Criminology, 20,* 43–65.

Eysenck, H. J. (1964). *Crime and personality.* Boston: Houghton, Mifflin.

Fernald, M. R., Holmes, M., Hayes, S., Dawley, A., & Ruml, B. (1920). *A study of women delinquents in New York state.* New York: The Century Co.

Fernald, M. R., Holmes, M., Hayes, S., Dawley, A., & Ruml, B. (1914). *Criminology.* Boston: Little, Brown.

Glueck, S., & Glueck, E. (1930). *Five hundred criminal careers.* New York: Alfred A. Knopf.

Glueck, S., & Glueck, E. (1934). *Five hundred delinquent women.* New York: Alfred A. Knopf.

Goddard, H. H. (1915). *The criminal imbecile.* New York: Macmillan.

Goring, C. (1913). *The English convict: A statistical study.* London: T. Fisher Unwin.

Healy, W. (1969). *Mental conflicts and misconduct.* Montclair, NJ: Patterson Smith.

Humphrey, J. A., & Palmer, S. (1982). Stressful life events and criminal homicide. Paper presented at the National Conference on Social Stress Research, Durham, NH.

Hooten, E. (1939). *The American criminal.* Cambridge, MA: Harvard University Press.

Hutchings, B., & Mednich, S. A. (1977). Criminality in adoptees and their adoptive and biological parents: A pilot study. In S. Mednick and K. O. Christiansen (Eds.), *Biosocial bases of criminal behavior* (pp. 127–141). New York: Gartner Press.

Jeffery, C. R. (Ed.). (1977). *Biology and crime.* Beverly Hills, CA: Sage.

Jeffery, C. R. (1980). Sociobiology and criminology: The long lean years of the unthinkable and the unmentionable. In E. Sagarin (Ed.), *Taboos in criminology.* Beverly Hills, CA: Sage.

Kaplan, H. B. (1975). *Self-attitudes and deviant behavior.* Pacific Palisades, CA: Goodyear.

Kitsuse, J. (1962). Societal reaction to deviant behavior: Problems of theory and method. *Social Problems, 9,* 247–256.

Lemert, E. M. (1967). *Human deviance, social problems, and social control.* Englewood Cliffs, NJ: Prentice-Hall.

Linsky, A. S., & Straus, M. A. (1982). *Crime and other maladaptive responses to stress.* Paper presented at the National Conference on Social Stress Research, Durham, NH.

Lombroso, C., & Ferrero, W. (1898). *The female offender.* New York: D. Appleton and Company.

Mednick, S. A., & Christiansen, K. O. (Eds.). (1977). *Biosocial bases of criminal behavior.* New York: Gartner Press.

Merton, R. K. (1957). *Social theory and social structure.* Glencoe, IL: Free Press.

Palmer, S. (1960). *The psychology of murder.* New York: Thomas Crowell.

Palmer, S. (1980). Sex differences in criminal homicide and suicide in England and Wales and the United States. *Omega, 11,* 255–270.

Quinney, R. (1970). *The social reality of crime.* Boston: Little, Brown.

Rubington, E., & Weinberg, M. S. (Eds.). (1968). *Deviance, the interactionist perspective: Text and readings in the sociology of deviance.* New York: Macmillan.

Sagarin, E. (1975). *Deviants and deviance: An introduction to the study of disvalued people and behavior.* New York: Praeger.

Sanday, P. R. (1981, Fall). The socio-cultural context of rape: A cross-cultural study. *Journal of Social Issues, 37,* 5–27.

Schur, E. M. (1971). *Labeling deviant behavior: Its sociological implications.* New York: Harper and Row.

Sellin, T. (1938). *Culture, conflict, and crime.* New York: Social Science Research Council.

Sheldon, W. H. (1949). *The varieties of delinquent youth.* New York: Harper and Row.

Simon, R. J. (1975). *Women and crime.* Lexington, MA: D. C. Heath.

Smart, C. (1976). *Women, crime and criminology.* Boston: Routlege and Kegan Paul.

Straus, M. A. (1980). Social stress and marital violence in a national sample of American families. In F. Wright, C. Bahn, & R. W. Reiber (Eds.), *Forensic Psychology and Psychiatry, Annals of the New York Academy of Sciences, 347,* 229–250.

Sutherland, E. H., & Cressey, D. R. (1974). *Principles of criminology.* New York: J. B. Lippincott.

Tannenbaum, F. (1938). *Crime and the community.* Boston: Ginn.

Taft, D. R., & England, R. W., Jr. (1964). *Criminology.* New York: Macmillan.

Thio, A. (1978). *Deviant behavior.* Boston: Houghton Mifflin.

Thomas, W. I. (1925). *The unadjusted girl.* Boston: Little, Brown.

Vold, G. B. (1958). *Theoretical criminology.* New York: Oxford University Press.

Wolfgang, M. E., & Ferracuti, F. (1967). *The subculture of violence.* London: Tavistock.

Yochelson, S., & Samenow, S. E. (1976). *The criminal personality.* New York: Jason Arnson.

Part II
CRIME WITHIN THE FAMILY

The definition of crime given in Chapter 2, although complex, provides a way of differentiating criminal acts from noncriminal acts. However, it offers less guidance concerning the question of whether the behaviors in question are crimes when committed within the family. Several additional criteria often are necessary. When strangers, acquaintances, or friends take money or property from each other without permission, there usually is clear agreement by the victim, the perpetrator and courts, that the act in question is a crime. On the other hand, if a husband or a wife steals from their marriage partner, the principle of immunity may apply. Immunity of spouses occurs because of the nature of the marriage relationship and the presumption of at least a joint ownership or interest in property. Consequently what might otherwise be "larceny," may not be defined as a crime if it occurs between husband and wife.

Larceny between other members of the immediate family, although not covered by a statutory or common law exemption, is often dealt with leniently. Part of the reason for such leniency is the difficulty in determining whether the person taking the property had either explicit or implied consent to use or take the item in question. If for example a boy had in the past been allowed to borrow his brother's stereo for the weekend, then there may have been grounds for him to believe that subsequent use might be appropriate as well. It certainly would be difficult to clearly establish all of the facts of this type of case in a court of law.

The chapters that follow recognize these legal difficulties, but at times consider actions that, even if not clearly recognized as a crime within the family by current legal standards, would be a crime if committed in another setting. Regardless, of whether these are legal or customary exemptions, criminal actions within the family can have negative consequences for the family, and can affect the larger community and society as well.

Crime Within The Family As Criminal Socialization

A number of studies have looked into the relationship between family characteristics and crime and delinquency outside the family. Typically these studies were designed to try to determine which, if any, characteristics of the family influence the amount or type of crime and delinquency committed by family members in settings other than the family. These studies have examined a bewildering array of family characteristics. But ironically they have rarely investigated the relationship between the commission of crime within the family and outside the family.

Perhaps this omission is because it seemed so obvious that patterns of crime observed or experienced within the family become generalized to other settings. But the history of science is replete with "obvious" facts that research later proved to be false. Anyone can "see" that the sun revolves around the earth, and as recently as 1600 the Italian philosopher Giordano Bruno was burned at the stake for insisting that it is the earth which revolves around the sun. The social sciences have even more instances of "obvious" truths that turned out to be false. To take just one of many examples, it was widely believed that, on the average, the rural people are healthier (both physically and mentally) than are city people. But countless studies show just the opposite. So the relationship between crime within the family and crime outside the family cannot be taken for granted. It needs to be carefully investigated. Such studies are, as just indicated, scarce. Still, there is indirect evidence, and logical or theoretical reasons for expecting such a relationship.

Families exert a variety of influences upon their children including biological, psychological, and social factors. Thus, the family is a significant factor in the behavior patterns of youth, including delinquency. Haskell and Yablonsky (1983) review many of the family characteristics which could affect delinquency; for example, in their choice of residential neighborhood, their influence or lack of influence in the child's selection of friends, and by the type of preparation given for school. The pattern of interaction between parents and children may contribute to or deter crime and delinquency, especially the "quality" of interaction (McCord and McCord, 1959; Alexander, 1973) as well as patterns of discipline within the family (Glueck and Glueck, 1950; Hirschi, 1969).

A   eal of research has centered on the question of the role of
                    ies" in producing delinquency. It has been shown that the
                    is associated with higher levels of delinquency than the
                    but the relationship is not a simple one. The absence of a
                    e less important than the kind of interaction with the

remaining parent in influencing delinquency (Shaw and McKay, 1942; Monahan, 1957; McCord, McCord, and Thurber, 1962; Chilton and Markle, 1972; Datesman and Scarpitti, 1975).

Haskell and Yablonsky put these various studies in perspective as follows:

> The family is therefore an important determinant of whether or not a child will become delinquent. The family, as the basic agent of socialization, determines a child's socioeconomic class, and its structure and process is vital in the personality formation of the individual. All these factors— socialization, class, and dynamics—impinge on the development of either a law-abiding or a delinquent child. These factors are inextricably bound together. (1982:80)

The various chapters in Part II reveal that an extraordinarily wide range of crimes take place within the family. The episodes cover the full range of severity from petty theft or vandalism to assault, rape, and murder. A second point to consider is that there is variation in terms of who the participants are. "Within the family" includes actions between siblings, between parents, between parents and child, and multigenerational incidents such as grandchild-grandparent. Here is one of many examples:

> After buying a new Thunderbird, a Jaguar and a $25,000 Lincoln Continental to make herself popular and change her humdrum life, a high school student has been charged with second-degree forgery in the theft of about $32,000 from her parents' savings accounts.
>
> Police detectives said last Wednesday that Sandra Lee Smart, 19 years old of Boulder, also bought four horses and two horse trailers paid off a friend's $1,400 bank loan, spent about $1,500 on gasoline over the summer and bought $500 worth of clothes and a $56 belt buckle.
>
> The money disappeared from her parents' two savings accounts between March and June, while Miss Smart was a senior at Boulder High School.
>
> She told the tellers that her parents were ill and wanted to withdraw some money, Mr. Dillman said. She asked if she could take withdrawal slips home for them to sign. The tellers let her do it more than once.
>
> He said she even persuaded a small-town notary public to notarize a signature of her father "who had a broken leg" on a form to get a new passbook for withdrawals from a savings account.
>
> Mr. Dillman said that both parents were in good health and did not know that their savings accounts were depleted until "one bright sunshiny day when they went to visit their money and were told that they had withdrawn it" (Associated Press, 6/12/83).

The Chapters In Part II

CHAPTER 4. The first chapter in this section describes a study designed specifically for this volume. To our knowledge, this is the first and only study of the incidence of nonviolent crimes within the family. It shows that the rate of property crimes within the family far *surpasses* the rate of similar crimes known to occur outside the family. This appears to be true for both blue collar and white collar families.

CHAPTER 5. Gelles and Straus present the findings on physical violence between family members in a nationally representative sample survey of American families. Similar to the patterns of property crime, crimes of violence were found to be more common than suggested by "official" statistics. The importance of this chapter, however, goes beyond revealing the high incidence of violence within the family. Perhaps the most important part of the findings reported by Gelles and Straus is the information on *why* violent incidents occur in the family. They discuss a variety of factors related to the patterns of family violence, including income, occupation, stress, prior experience with violence and norms and attitudes approving of violence.

CHAPTER 6. Public attention in recent years has been drawn to the problem of parental kidnapping. Agopian and Anderson explore the nature of this serious problem within families and help to explain some of the underlying factors likely to lead to attempts to steal a child.

CHAPTER 7. Finkelhor and Yllo present an exploratory study of marital rape and develop a typology of forced sex experiences including battering rapes, nonbattering rapes, and obsessive rapes. The importance of the consequences of marital rape, legal issues, and public attitudes also are discussed.

CHAPTER 8. Whereas the first four selections dealt with the incidence rates, the causes, and the consequences of various types of crime within the family, the final selection by Buzawa and Buzawa focuses on the official treatment of and legislative responses to domestic violence. This chapter also considers the ways in which legislative changes affect the criminal justice system's response to domestic violence, the impact on police response, reasons for the relative ineffectiveness of the police in dealing with domestic violence, and prosecutorial and judicial responses to family violence.

REFERENCES

Alexander, J. F. (1973, April). Defensive and supportive communication in normal and deviant families. *Journal of Consulting and Clinical Psychology, 14,* 223–231.

Andry, R. G. (1950). Faulty paternal and maternal-child relationships, affection and delinquency. *British Journal of Delinquency, 1,* 34–48.

Chilton, Roland, & Markle (1972). Family disruption, delinquent conduct and the effect of subclassification. *American Sociological Review, 27,* 93–99.

Datesman, S. K., & Scarpitti, F. R. (1975, May). Female delinquency and broken homes. *Criminology, 13,* 33–56.

Glueck, S., & Glueck, E. T. (1950). *Unravelling juvenile delinquency.* New York: Commonwealth Fund.

Haskell, M., & Yablonski, L. (1983). *Criminology: Crime and criminality.* Boston: Houghton-Mifflin.

Hirshi, T. (1969). *Causes of delinquency.* Berkeley: University of California Press.

McCord, J., McCord, W., & Thurber, E. (1962, May). Some effects of paternal absence on male children. *Journal of Abnormal and Social Psychology, 64,* 361–369.

McCord, W., & McCord, J. (1959). *The origins of crime.* New York: Columbia University Press.

Monahan, T. P. (1957, March). Family status and the delinquent child: A reappraisal and some new findings. *Social Forces, 35,* 250–258.

Shaw, C. R., & McKay, H. D. (1942). *Juvenile delinquency and urban areas.* Chicago: University of Chicago Press.

CHAPTER 4

NON-VIOLENT CRIME WITHIN THE FAMILY

Murray A. Straus and Alan Jay Lincoln

There is a growing national awareness of the fact that more violence takes place in the family than in any other setting in civilian life (see Chapter 5). The recognition of family violence as a widespread problem began in the early 1960s with the "discovery" of child abuse (Pfohl, 1977). In reality, child abuse is an age old problem that had been ignored. But by the mid 1970s every state had passed legislation to require those who know about a child abuse case to report it, and had set up special services to protect such children and to help parents deal with the child non-abusively. These efforts have often been inadequately supported, but at least the effort has been made.

Spouse abuse came into national consciousness about a decade later than child abuse—largely as a result of efforts by the women's movement. By 1983 there were about 700 "shelters" where battered women could find safety and help. Another important contribution of the women's movement is that it has kept the issue before the public. As a result, a number of states changed their laws to give better protection to battered women, and some states have helped to fund shelters (Lerman, 1981; Buzawa and Buzawa, Chapter 8).

In the 1980s still another recurring problem, abuse of the elderly, began to come to national attention (Kosberg, 1983). Even at this early stage, some states and communities have passed protective legislation and appropriated money to provide services.

All in all, there is a growing awareness of *violent* crime within the family, and a growing number of remedial steps. None of these steps are adequate—not even close. But at least there is an effort.

In respect to nonviolent crimes (so-called "property crimes") the situation in respect to public awareness is quite different. The current situation in respect to such crimes is similar to the lack of public awareness of physical violence in the family before the early 1960s: Few people even think of the possibility of one family member committing a property crime against another member of his or her own family. But, "thinking the unthinkable" is part of what social scientists are trained to do. It is one of the ways that new and important information can come to light. It was in the spirit of that tradition of social inquiry that we decided to try to find out if, as is the case with violent crimes, property crimes occur in the family more often than outside the family. If that is true, it has profound implications for what we think of as "the crime problem" in the United States. Crime, like charity, may begin at home, and if so it is something to be considered in formulating prevention and control measures.

HOW THE STUDY WAS DONE

No accurate and representative information has ever been collected about property crimes within the family. Part of the reason, as noted above, is that no one thought it was worth investigating. Another reason may be the conceptual difficulties which were discussed in Chapter 1, and the measurement difficulties which will be discussed below. In addition, the cost of doing a study of a sample that is large enough and representative enough to come to definitive conclusions might have seemed out of line with what might be learned in view of the conceptual and methodological problems. Given these problems, the research described in this chapter was undertaken as a preliminary or "pilot study," designed to explore the type of questions it is possible to ask on this topic, and the type of questions to avoid; and to get a preliminary idea about how frequently property crimes occur within the family. We felt that even if nothing else is achieved, the study would at least provide concrete data on the problems and pitfalls of research on crime in the family.

The Families Studied

SAMPLE. We did the study by giving questionnaires to 450 students in two New England colleges. The questionnaires were distributed in randomly selected sections of required classes. When the questionnaires were handed out we told the students that if they did not want to answer them, they could just hand in a blank questionnaire. Since no names or other identifying information was included, no one would know if they chose to complete the questionnaire or not. Actually, almost everyone completed the questionnaires. Of the 450 questionnaires distributed, 437 were completed. This means that 97 percent completed the questionnaire. So we know that the results are at least representative of students in the classes where the questionnaires were distributed. In one of the two universities the sampled classes were also representative of all "lower division" required courses.

FAMILIES ARE THE UNIT OF STUDY. An important thing to remember is that although students completed the questionnaires, most of the data is about the families of these students, and what went on in those families. We achieved this by asking each student to complete the questionnaire by providing information about what the situation was during the year they were seniors in high school if they were living at home that year, as almost all were. In most cases (74%) our respondents were freshmen who were being asked to recall events that had occurred the previous year.

ADEQUACY OF STUDENT SAMPLES. A sample of the families of college students is by no means representative of all American families, but it will do for purposes of a pilot study. In fact, college students have been very helpful in providing information on a great many issues. Straus' research on wife-beating and child abuse began with a pilot study almost identical to this study, and the rates produced by that study are remarkably close to the rates from his later study of a nationally representative sample of families (see appendix in Straus, Gelles, and Steinmetz, 1980).

In addition to the convenience and economy of a pilot study using data provided by college students, they are obviously above average in intelligence and education, so questions which might be too difficult for the general public can be asked. Of course, these characteristics also show that college students are not representative of the population as a whole. The same thing applies to their families. On the average, college students come from families that are better educated and have a higher income than families generally. They are also more stable families than is generally the case—only 5.5 percent of our sample came from "broken homes." Since income, family stability, and education tend to be associated with less crime (at least less of the usual types of crime), the crime rates that we are about to report are probably lower than would be the case if we were able to study a truly representative sample of families. So the "incidence rates" for the crimes described in this chapter could be *under*estimates of how much of this type of crime goes on within the family.

There are three other reasons why the actual rates of crimes within the family may be higher than reported to us. First, some of the crime experiences were undoubtedly forgotten. Second, it is very likely that others were covered up and not reported to us. Third, there could well have been crimes which fit our definition that the respondent did not know about; for example, a crime committed by the respondent's parents.

The Questionnaire

The objective of the questionnaire was to ask questions which would provide a rough indication of the extent to which crime occurs within

American families. The crime rates which can be computed from such a questionnaire cannot be directly compared with the Uniform Crime Reports (UCR) published each year by the FBI. It might seem as though such a comparison could be made by using the same words to describe crimes in a questionnaire as are used in the UCR. Unfortunately, that is not possible because the UCR uses technical terms that most people do not really understand. How many people for example, know the difference between robbery and burglary?

We are not the first researchers to run into the problem of how to ask people about crimes. When interview surveys of crime began in the United States in the early 1970s, they encountered the same problem (Garofalo and Hindelang, 1977). Both the National Crime Survey and the study we are describing found that it is impossible to word questions that the public will understand and also have them exactly match the UCR categories. So, although interview and questionnaire studies of crime are intended to measure "crime," they do not always reflect exactly the same things as are reported in the UCR.

Another reason why legal terms for crimes were not used is the possibility that some respondents would not recognize what had happened if we had used legal terms such as robbery, assault, and larceny. People do not think of what goes on in the family in those terms. If "robbery" is used to refer to an incident in which a student forcefully took the property of a brother or sister, or had property forcefully taken from him or her, some students might deny, even to themselves, that this is "robbery." Consequently, we felt that describing *acts* rather than using legal terms, would come closer to obtaining a full accounting of what happened, i.e. a more complete tally of acts which are crimes in the eye of the law, even if not in the thinking of some respondents.

On the other hand, a danger with this method is that punching a brother might be friendly "rough housing" rather than an assault. Or signing a parent's name to a credit card charge might be done with their consent rather than as a means of defrauding the parents. Consequently, steps had to be taken to make sure that our "crime" measures included only events that the respondent regarded as wrong or noxious. To achieve this, the list of criminal acts, although not labeled as "crime" for the reasons given above," was headed "PROBLEMS WITH...." The instructions which followed that heading used the negative phrase "done to each other." In addition, the list of possible criminal acts within the family came right after a list of crimes which uses such terms as "violated," "laws," and "stole" (see Chapter 9 for the list), thus further helping to establish the idea that only noxious events should be reported.

Nevertheless, it is likely that many of the acts reported in response to our questionnaire were *not* regarded as "crimes" in the legal sense by the people involved—just as wrong or bad things done by someone in their family. This raises the question of whether something is a crime if the persons involved (both the victims and the perpetrators) do not define it that way. That is an extremely difficult question because there are arguments on both sides. However, as explained in Chapter 1, we think that for purposes of carrying out research of this type (as contrasted with crime prevention and control), it is best to count as a crime any act which the legal system defines in that way.

Briefly, the part of the questionnaire dealing with property crimes within the family asked the respondents about the following eight acts. The phrases in parenthesis, which were not in the questionnaire, are the approximate legal equivalents. *1:

1. "Signed other's name to something" (forgery)
2. "Took money without using force" (larceny)
3. "Took money using force" (robbery)
4. "Took property without using force" (larceny)
5. "Took property using force" (robbery)*2
6. "Intentionally damaged property" (vandalism)
7. "Borrowed money and never returned it" (larceny—fraud)
8. "Demanded some kind of payment for not 'telling on' or not beating up another person in the family" (extortion)

These questions were repeated a number of times to get information about whether the student who answered the questionnaire had done any of these things to another member of his or her family, and then which crimes (if any) each person in the family had committed against the respondent during the last year the student lived at home before going to college.

HOW FREQUENT ARE CRIMES WITHIN THE FAMILY?

The Overall Rate of Property Crime

The first of the questions about property crimes that we will try to answer is the extent to which family members commit "property crimes" against each other. How often does this occur? How does the rate compare to property crimes known to the police—which are almost always crimes against nonfamily members? The answer—at least for this sample—is given in the first row of Table 4-1. It shows that, during the year of this survey, a property crime occurred within 73 percent of the families in our sample.

The difference in definitions and populations covered by our survey,

Table 4-1. Overall Rates For Specific Within-Family Property Crimes.

===

Crime	Perecent Of Families*
PROPERTY CRIME INDEX (one or more of the first six crimes listed below)**	73
LARCENY-FRAUD (Did not return borrowed money)	59
FORGERY (Signed another's name to something)	42
LARCENY-MONEY (Took money without using force)	36
LARCENY-PROPERTY (Took property without using force)	33
VANDALISM (Intentionally damaged property)	20
EXTORTION (Demanded payment for not "telling" or not beating up)	12
ROBBERY-MONEY (Took money using force)**	5
ROBBERY-PROPERTY (Took property using force)**	5

* The percentage of families in which the crime or crimes occured once or more, i.e., for purpose of these statistics, a family was included only once, even if there were repeated instances of a crime.
** Robbery was excluded from the overall property crime index to conform to the UCR classification of crimes.

and the Uniform Crime Reports (UCR), and the National Crime Survey (NCS) are so great that there is no point attempting specific numerical comparisons with the overall property crime rates from these three sources, except to say that the within-family rate from this is much greater. Actually, with a figure of 73 out of every hundred families, there is no need for a comparison to grasp the magnitude of these events.

Readers with an irresistible urge to compare these data with the UCR or the NCS rates need to keep in mind that multiplying by 100,000 will not produce a rate comparable to the UCR rate, nor will multiplying by 1,000 produce a rate comparable to the NCS rate. This is because many other things also differ. For example, our rates are per FAMILY, whereas the NCS rates are per person age 12 and over, and the UCR rates are per person of all ages. Moreover, the list of crimes is different in all three sources of data.

Another major difference is that the UCR and NCS count the number of "crimes," not the number of "criminals." Thus, the 73 percent figure is not comparable to the UCR or NCS data on crimes since our figures are more like the number of criminals than the number of crimes. The difference between the two types of statistics occurs because there are far more crimes than criminals. One criminal often commits many crimes. So the number of crimes per 100,000 population is much greater than the number of criminals per 100,000 population.

The same principle applies to crimes within the family. Although "only" 73 percent of the families in this sample were "criminal" in the sense of having had a property crime occur within the family, the rate of "crimes" committed was much larger. This is because, where there was one offense, it was rarely an isolated instance. In fact, our respondents reported an astounding total of over 15,000 property crimes. If we translated that into a rate per 100,000 persons it is more than 100,000 per 100,000. It is difficult to grasp or believe figures of this magnitude, but we have no reason to think that our respondents exaggerated the number of property crimes which took place in their families during the year of the study. No doubt some "telescoping" occurred (reporting crimes that actually took place earlier) and this would serve to inflate the rate. On the other hand, it is equally likely that some events were forgotten or deliberately not reported, and the two types of error may balance each other out.

One factor which at least partly explains why these rates are so high is that the data includes many petty crimes, such as the theft or extortion of small sums of money. Although this is also true of the larceny category in the UCR (since it includes such crimes as purse snatching, pocket picking, shoplifting, and bicycle theft), crimes involving loss of only a small sum are almost certainly a much larger proportion of the events reported in this survey than they are of crimes reported to the police.

Another factor inflating the rate of crime in this survey of families can be traced to limitations of the questionnaire (see next section). For example, we could not distinguish failure to repay money borrowed from a brother resulting from inability to do so, from deliberate non-payment, i.e., fraud. Thus, the data includes some acts which are not crimes at all.

Despite these problems, some general answers can be given to the question of how often property crimes occur within the family:

1. Property crimes occur in most families—an astounding 73 percent in any one year, if one takes the figures literally.

2. When there is one property crime in a family, there are likely to be many. In fact, in those families where one such crime was reported, only 1 percent were instances of a single crime during the year of the study.

3. The within-family rate of property crimes is many times greater than the rate of property crimes against nonfamily members. But because the data are not directly comparable, we cannot say precisely how many times greater. Nevertheless, our data do suggest that the risk of being a victim of property crime is much greater within the family than it is outside the family.

Specific Crimes Against Other Family Members

Not all property crimes are equally serious. Most people regard robbery as more serious than burglary since robbery is also a violent crime. Forgery, as it occurs within the family, may be something that most people regard as serious (if a check for money is forged) or fairly trivial. A forgery that most people are likely to regard as fairly trivial is illustrated by a child who skipped school, and then wrote an excuse and signed the parent's name. So it is important to look separately at each of the eight crimes in Table 4-1.

Table 4-1 was arranged to put the most frequently occurring crimes first. This shows that, roughly speaking, the more serious the crime, the less frequently it occurred. Heading the list in frequency is not returning borrowed money. This occurred in 58 percent of the families. There is some question as to whether this is a crime. For it to be a crime (as compared to a bad debt), there would have to be evidence that the loan was sought with the intent to defraud by not paying it back. Probably most of these instances were not crimes in that sense. However, to keep the questionnaire to a reasonable length, we could not ask for details about each of the 15,000 crimes reported to us. So we do not have information on this issue.

The next most frequent property crime which occurred within this sample of families was forgery (42 percent of the families). Probably most of these forgeries were relatively trivial in their seriousness. Yet some may have involved signing another's name without permission to checks, credit card slips, and other documents.

Next in frequency was someone taking another family member's money or property. This occurred in 36 and 33 percent of the families we studied. Again, we do not know the specifics of these crimes (but there are some hints in the data to be presented in the next section). Probably most of the money thefts were instances of a child taking small sums from a brother or sister or their parents.

Vandalism occurred in what at first seemed like a surprisingly large percent of the families (20% or one out of five families). But on second thought, that does not seem very high, given the frequency of conflict in families (Gelles and Straus, 1979), and the fact that in the course of these conflicts, people may not only yell and scream and hit each other, but also smash things.

Extortion occurred in 12 percent of the families in this study. In the next section we will look at data on who was the extortionist and who was the victim.

Finally, robbery (taking money or objects using force) was the least frequent property crime within this sample of families. It occurred in "only" five percent of the families. That, of course, is a very high rate. Translating into the equivalent of a UCR rate by multiplying by 1,000 (to make it a rate per 100,000 families), and dividing by four (to make it closer to a rate per person rather than per family) produces a robbery rate of 1,250, which is several times greater than the 1980 UCR robbery rate.

The Relationship Between Family Role and Property Crime

The public tends to think that crimes occur because there are "criminals." That is the truth, but not the whole truth. The whole truth is much more complex. There are many other factors besides the fact that some people are more inclined to crime than others. The first block of data in Table 4-2 illustrates one of the most obvious of these other factors—the characteristics of the victim.

CRIMES COMMITTED BY THE RESPONDENT. All the rates in the first block of data refer to crimes committed by the students who completed the questionnaire. The percentage of these students who took money or property from another member of the family varies widely, depending on who the other person is. Forty-one percent committed a property crime in which the victim was the mother of the student, but only 1.6 percent committed such a crime against a relative outside their immediate family. So the occurrence of crime depends on the characteristics of the victim as well as the criminal. That in turn raises the question of what causes such large differences. We can only speculate about that because the need to keep the questionnaire short prevented us from asking detailed questions about each of the crimes.

We think that the reason for such a low rate of victimizing "other relatives" is that the questionnaire asked about crimes against other persons who lived in the respondents' house, and very few had relatives living with them. This is what criminologists call the "opportunity"

Crime and the Family

Table 4-2. Relationship of Perpetrator to Victim in Within-Family Property Crime.

```
================================================
                                     Percent of
    Perpetrator          Victim      Families*
------------------------------------------------

Respondent          Brother            38.0
     "              Sister             29.3
     "              Father             33.9
     "              Mother             41.4
     "              Other Relative      1.6

Brother             Respondent         43.0
Sister                 "               29.7
Father                 "               14.9
Mother                 "               16.5
Other Relative         "                1.9

Father              Mother             21.5
Mother              Father             25.2

------------------------------------------------
```

* See footnotes to Table 4-1.

factor in crime. Members of the immediate family are available to be victimized, whereas other relatives are much less available.

It is more difficult to suggest why more of our respondents stole from mothers than fathers, and why more stole from brothers than sisters. Perhaps more stole from brothers because boys tend to have more money than girls. If so, it is another aspect of "opportunity." The same principle can apply to mothers because, in many households, mothers keep "grocery money" in a known place. It also is possible that mothers were seen as better victims in the sense that they might respond less severely than would fathers.

THE RESPONDENT AS VICTIM OF PROPERTY CRIMES. The second block of data in Table 4-2 gives the percentage of respondents who reported that they had been a victim of a property crime carried out by another member of their own family. The first two rows in this block of data show that the students in our sample were more likely to have had things stolen by a brother than a sister. We interpret this as showing that girls are less inclined to crime than boys. This suggests another of the many factors influencing crime—social roles, in this case "gender roles" (Adler, 1975; Datesman and Scarpiti, 1980; Jensen and Eve, 1978; Simon, 1975).

The third and fourth rows of the second block of data in Table 4-2 show that parents stole from our respondents even less often than sisters. That can also be regarded as a function of a social role, in this case, the explicit and implicit norms involved in the "parental role." However, there is another aspect of this data which should not be overlooked. Except for "other relatives" (who we will not consider here because the low rate stems from the fact that there were so few living with the respondents of this study), the rate for property crimes committed by parents against children is the lowest for any family role-relationship. But this should not blind us to the fact that about one out of seven of the students in this sample were aware of some things being stolen from them by their parents.

The last two lines of Table 4-2 are interesting by themselves and also by contrast with the figures on thefts from children. The rate for stealing from a spouse is about 1.5 times greater than the rate for stealing from a child. Actually, the difference may be much greater than that because of a "methodological artifact:" Our respondents probably did not know all the instances in which one parent misappropriated the property of the other parent, whereas there would be relatively few instances in which they did not know when they themselves were the victims.

Assuming that the parents victimize each other much more often than they victimize a child, the next question is why. Our speculations follow the same line of reasoning as was used to interpret the other statistics in this table. First, there may be an opportunity structure factor which exists because one's spouse usually has more money and property to steal than do one's children. Second, is the possibility of a social role factor because stealing from one's child may be more inconsistent with the parental role than stealing from one's spouse.

CRIME, CLASS, AND FAMILY

The Class Difference Controversy

There has been a long and heated debate about social class and juvenile delinquency, and only a somewhat less heated debate about the existence of class differences in adult crime (Hindelang, 1983). On one side are those who cite official crime statistics from many countries, including the United States. These statistics consistently show higher crime rates in low socioeconomic status neighborhoods, and higher arrest rates of low socioeconomic status persons.

On the other side are those who believe that these differences do not reflect differences in the true incidence of crime. They argue that the differences in official crime statistics reflect less skill or less interest in concealing their crimes on the part of low status children, and a greater willingness by the police to arrest low socioeconomic status persons. In support of this belief, the opponents of class differences in juvenile delinquency cite numerous "self-report" studies of juvenile crime. A "self-report" study is one based on interviews or question-naires, such as the one used for this research. Such instruments are thought to be a way around the limitations of the official statistics since self-report data provides information about crimes which are not re-ported to the police, and the rates are not affected by bias in arresting procedures.

Recent research has thrown a further complication into the picture. This shows that middle-class persons have a greater tendency to reveal their failings than do working-class persons (Klech, 1982). Consequently, the lack of social class differences in self-report measures of crime might reflect a greater tendency for working class persons to cover up their crimes when interviewed or when completing a questionnaire.

We have no way of resolving this conflict. We presented the pros and cons only to provide information on some of the things which can affect the self-report data on within-family crime that we are about to present.

Socioeconomic Status of the Sample

Before presenting the findings on the relationship between socioeco-nomic status (SES) and intrafamily property crime, we need to identify the type of families which were included in the study. This will tell us how different the families in this sample are from a representative sample of families. It is also important because we need to know if there is enough variation in the SES of these families to make it worth using this sample to study class differences. As noted earlier in this chapter, families that send a child to college tend to be higher status than the national average. If they were all high in SES, we obviously could not use such a sample to compare SES groups. So we need to determine if the sample includes a broad enough range of SES to make it worth compar-ing families of different socioeconomic levels.

The *education* of the parents in these families shows a broad distribution, ranging from those who did not complete high school to those with advanced degrees. The *income* level is, as expected, higher than the US average. But when the fathers in this sample are compared to similar-aged men the differences are not that great. It turns out that although the sample includes a larger percentage with incomes of $30,000 or more, and a smaller percentage with incomes under $10,000, the median income is slightly *less* than the US median income for men age 45 to 54. Finally,

Table 4-3. Socioeconomic Status of the Sample Families.
==

SES Indicator	Percent*
Father's Income:	
Less than $10,000	7.8%
$10 - $14,999	9.7%
$15 - $19,999	14.2%
$20 - $29,999	31.7%
$30,000 and over	36.6%
Mother's Income:	
Less than $10,000	65.2%
$10 - $14,999	21.0%
$15 - $19,999	8.3%
$20 - $29,999	4.0%
$30,000 and over	1.5%
Father's Education	
Less than High School diploma	10.6
Completed High School	24.0
Some College	26.6
Completed College	20.3
Post-Graduate Education	18.5
Mother's Education	
Less than High School diploma	9.2
Completed High School	48.7
Some College	18.4
Completed College	15.9
Post-Graduate Education	7.8
Father's Occupation	
Blue Collar	37.7
White Collar	62.3
Mother's Occupation	
Blue Collar	34.0
White Collar	32.8
Housewife	33.1

* Although 437 families are in the sample, the N's in this table average about 400 because of missing information, such as when a student did not know the father's income.

in respect to *occupation,* over a third of the parents in this sample were blue collar (i.e. manual) workers. This is important because many studies show that the line between manual and nonmanual workers is the most powerful indicator of social position in American society (Kahl, and Davis, 1955).

Socioeconomic Status and Property Crime

We correlated each of the SES indicators in Table 4-3 (and also a composite family SES index) with the measures of intrafamily property crime. Altogether over two hundred correlations were computed. We also did cross tabulations to check for relationships which might be covered up by a correlation coefficient.

Almost none of the correlations were large enough to be either important or statistically significant. In addition, when so many correlations are computed, there is a possibility that at least some statistically significant coefficients will occur just by chance. It seems therefore that the evidence of this study is on the side of those who hold that the social class difference in crime shown by official statistics are a function of the biases of the criminal justice system. When one can peek behind the closed doors of the family, the level of property crime is remarkably similar within both low and high socioeconomic status families.

SUMMARY

Our survey of the families of over 400 college students revealed important new information about the extent to which "property crimes" such as larceny occur within the family:

• Acts which fall within the legal definitions of property crime occurred during the year of this survey within almost three-quarters of the families in our sample.

• When a crime of a certain type occurred, such as larceny, it was rarely an isolated instance. Rather, there tended to be multiple offenses. Consequently, an astounding total of over 15,000 crimes were reported within these 437 families within the year of the study. In some respects this is an overestimate of the true incidence because the questionnaire included some acts which are not always prosecutable crimes. In other respects, however, this figure is an underestimate because there are bound to be acts which were forgotten or covered up, and there were probably also criminal acts between other family members which our respondents did not know about.

• These rates are many times greater than property crimes against nonfamily members.

• As in crimes known to the police, the more serious the crime, the less often it occurs within families.

• The most frequent perpetrator-victim relationship within the family was that of brother-to-brother, but mothers were the second most frequent victims, probably because they frequently keep "grocery money" in a known place, but perhaps also because there is less fear of severe negative response.

• Parents had a high rate of property crime against each other (about 1 out of 4), but a low rate of victimizing their children. Even so, about one out of seven mothers and one out of seven fathers victimized our respondents.

• The families in this study varied considerably in respect to socioeconomic status. Despite this, there were no important differences in the extent to which property crimes were reported in the families of low and high socioeconomic status.

REFERENCES

Adler, F. (1975). *Sisters in crime.* New York: McGraw Hill.

Datesman, S. K., & Scarpitti, F. R. (Eds.). (1980). *Women, crime, and justice.* New York: Oxford University Press.

Federal Bureau of Investigation. (1983). *Crime in the United States.* Washington D.C.: United States Department of Justice, Uniform Crime Reports.

Garofalo, J., & Hindelang, M. J. (1977). *An introduction to the National Crime Survey. Applications of the National Crime Survey, victimization and attitude data, analytic report SD-VAD-4.* Washington, D.C.: U.S. Government Printing Office.

Gelles, R. J., & Straus, M. A. (1979). Determinants of violence in the family: Toward a theoretical integration. In W. R. Burr, R. Hill, F. I. Nye, & I. L. Reiss, *Contemporary theories about the family.* New York: Free Press.

Hindelang, M. (1983). Class and crime. *Encyclopedia of Crime and Justice.* New York: The Free Press.

Jensen, G. F., & Eve, R. (1976). Sex differences in delinquency: An examination of popular sociological explanations. *Criminology, 13*(4), 427–428.

Kahl, J. A., & Davis, J. A. (1955, June). A comparison of indexes of socio-economic status. *American Sociological Review, 20,* 317–325.

Klech, G. (1982, June). On the use of self-report data to determine the class distribution of criminal and delinquent behavior. *American Sociological Review, 47*(3), 427–433. Comment on Hindelang et al., *American Sociological Review, 44*(6), 995–1014, 1979, December, and on Tittle et al., *American Sociological Review, 43*(5), 643–656, 1978, October.

Kosberg, J. I. (Ed.). (1983). *Abuse and maltreatment of the elderly: Causes and interventions.* London: John Wright PSG Inc.

Lerman, L. (1981). *Prosecution of spouse abuse: Innovations in criminal justice response.* Washington, D.C.: Center for Women Policy Studies.

Loftin, C., & McDowall, D. (1982, June). The police, crime, and economic theory: An assessment. *American Sociological Review, 47,* 393–401.

Pfohl, S. J. (1977). The "discovery" of child abuse. *Social Problems, 24*(3), 310–323.

Simon, R. J. (1975). *Women and crime.* Lexington, MA: Lexington Books.

FOOTNOTES

1. Readers can gain some idea of the extent to which there is correspondence and discrepency between these questions and the definitions used in the Uniform Crime Reports from considering the following definitions taken from the annual summary of UCR data (FBI, 1983)

MURDER AND NONNEGLIGENT MANSLAUGHTER. Murder and nonnegligent manslaughter, as defined in the Uniform Crime Reporting Program, is the willful (nonnegligent) killing of one human being by another.

The classification of this offense, as for all other Crime Index offenses, is based solely on police investigation as opposed to the determination of a court, medical examiner, coroner, jury, or other judicial body. Not included in the count for this offense classification are deaths caused by negligence, suicide, or accident; justifiable homicides; and attempts to murder or assaults to murder, which are scored as aggravated assaults.

FORCIBLE RAPE. Forcible rape, as defined in the Program, is the carnal knowledge of a female forcibly and against her will. Assaults or attempts to commit rape by force or threat of force are also included; however, statutory rape (without force) and other sex offenses are not included in this category.

ROBBERY. Robbery is the taking or attempting to take anything of value from the care, custody, or control of a person or persons by force or threat of force or violence and/or by putting the victim in fear.

AGGRAVATED ASSAULT. Aggravated assault is an unlawful attack by one person upon another for the purpose of inflicting severe or aggravated bodily injury. This type of assault is usually accompanied by the use of a weapon or by means likely to produce death or great bodily harm. Attempts are included since it is not necessary that an injury result when a gun, knife, or other deadly weapon is used which could and probably would result in serious personal injury if the crime were successfully completed.

BURGLARY. The Uniform Crime Reporting Program defines burglary as the unlawful entry of a structure to commit a felony or theft. The use of force to gain entry is not required to classify an offense as burglary. Burglary in this Program is categorized into three subclassifications: forcible entry where no force is used, and attempted forcible entry.

LARCENY-THEFT. Larceny-theft is the unlawful taking, carrying, leading, or riding away of property from the possession or constructive possession of another. It includes crimes such as shoplifting, pocket-picking, purse-snatching, thefts from motor vehicles, thefts of motor vehicles, thefts of motor vehicle parts and accessories, bicycle thefts, etc., in which no use of force, violence, or fraud occurs. In the Uniform Crime Reporting Program, this crime category does not include embezzlement, "con" games, forgery, and worthless checks. Motor vehicle theft is also excluded from this category inasmuch as it is a separate Crime Index offense.

MOTOR VEHICLE THEFT. In Uniform Crime Reporting, motor vehicle theft is defined as the theft or attempted theft of a motor vehicle. This definition excludes the taking of a motor vehicle for temporary use by those persons having lawful access.

ARSON. Arson is defined by the Uniform Crime Reporting Program as any willful or malicious burning or attempt to burn, with or without intent to defraud, a dwelling house, public building, motor vehicle or aircraft, personal property of another, etc.

Only fires determined through investigation to have been willfully or maliciously set are classified as arsons. Fires of suspicious or unknown origins are excluded.

2. The UCR classifies robbery as a "violent crime." We included it in this list of property

crimes because it also involves taking property. However, to be consistent with the UCR property crime index, robbery was excluded for purposes of computing our summary index of all property crimes which occurred within the family.

CHAPTER 5

VIOLENCE IN THE AMERICAN FAMILY

RICHARD J. GELLES AND MURRAY A. STRAUS

With the exception of the police and the military, the family is perhaps the most violent social group, and the home the most violent social setting, in our society. A person is more likely to be hit or killed in his or her home by another family member than anywhere else or by anyone else. Nearly one out of every four murder victims in the United States is a family member. Similarly, in Africa, Great Britain, and Denmark the greatest proportion of murders are intrafamilial (Bohannan, 1960; Curtis, 1974).

Although increased public attention to the problem of family violence would suggest that there has been a rapid increase in the level of family violence, most historical evidence suggests that the family has always been one of society's more violent institutions (see, for example, Bakan, 1971; DeMause, 1974, 1975; Newberger, Reed, Daniel, Hyde & Kotelchuch, 1977; Radbill, 1974). But despite the family's long history as a violent social setting, for many years the issue of violence in the home was subjected to "selective inattention" (Dexter, 1958). Battered children, women, husbands, and parents were the missing persons of the social problems literature until the late 1960s and early 1970s. While there were occasional articles on the "pathology" of child battering are rare articles on wife-beating, there was no systematic socialscientific study of the issue of family violence.

By contrast, the decade of the 1970s has produced a proliferation of books, articles, and monographs on the subjects of child abuse, wife abuse, and family violence. However, the available research evidence is clouded by problems of conceptualization and operationalization of key terms, (for example, the term "child abuse"). Moreover, the state of knowledge about child abuse is limited by a number of methodological problems involved in most past studies. This paper reviews some of these problems. It also draws heavily on data collected from a major national survey of violence in the American family (e.g., Gelles, 1978; Straus, Gelles & Steinmetz, 1979). That study, the first to employ a nationally representative sample of families, explored the extent of family violence and attempted to identify which families were more likely to be violent.

FAMILY VIOLENCE AS A SOCIAL ISSUE

Decades of overlooking family violence as a social problem were followed by one decade of intense public and professional interest. What accounted for the change in public and scientific attitudes toward family violence, and what accounted for family violence being discovered as a social issue? Straus (1974a) proposes that numerous streams of thought and action converged in the United States in the late 1960s and early 1970s to help uncover this hidden side of family life. First, the 1960s was a decade of public or visible violence. Race riots, political assassinations, rising rates of interpersonal violence, and an unpopular war that produced tens of thousands of casualties, all drew public attention to the problem of violence. The National Commission on the Causes and Prevention of Violence was formed as a response to the assassinations of Martin Luther King and Robert Kennedy. The Commission produced the first comprehensive national study of attitudes and experiences with violent behavior. The questions which dealt with family violence opened the eyes of many people, who previously had thought that family violence was uncommon as well as deviant. The evidence indicated otherwise. For example, Stark and McEvoy's (1970) analysis of the Commission data showed that one in four men and one in six women approved of a husband slapping a wife under certain conditions.

A second force which brought family violence into public attention was the women's movement. The struggle to gain liberation and equality for women brought women of all ages and backgrounds together for "consciousness-raising sessions." One latent function of these sessions was to help many participants discover that they shared similar dark secrets: they had been battered by their husbands. These collective sessions served to inform battered wives that being beaten and battered by their husbands was neither their own fault nor their own unique experience. There has been a children's rights movement somewhat paralled to the women's movement. Much of that effort has focussed on maltreatment or abuse of children. This, too, has heightened public awareness of violence in the family.

Finally, while such social movements gathered steam, some American social scientists began to use a "conflict model" of human behavior, rather than the long dominant "consensus-equilibrium model." Sprey (1969) argues that a conflict model of family relations is much better suited for the study of family violence than the previously dominant model, which had been designed for studies of mate selection and similar issues.

Other social scientists have postulated that family violence and child abuse were "created" as social problems as a result of the entrepreneurial efforts of certain professional groups. Pfoul (1977), for example, argues that the "discovery" of child abuse as a social problem was due to the efforts of diagnostic radiologists, who at that time constituted a marginal speciality within the field of medicine, but who used the issue of battered children to create a mandate for this professional speciality.

Major Questions in the Study of Family Violence

The social issue of family violence and violence toward children has typically focused on three major questions. First, there has been considerable concern over exactly how widespread the phenomenon actually is. Concern with measuring the incidence of family violence is perhaps best viewed as a reaction to the general belief that family violence is really quite rare and is confined to a few mentally disturbed people (Steinmetz & Straus, 1974).

The second question deals with the demographic distribution of family violence. Work on this particular problem has ranged all the way from some early studies arguing that, since child abuse was found in all social groups, social factors (such as socioeconomic status) could not be used to account for such violence (e.g., Steele & Pollock, 1974), to later studies arguing that violence is either confined to or more prevalent in certain social groups (e.g., poor; certain racial or ethnic minorities, etc.) (see Pelton, 1978; Steinmetz & Straus, 1974).

The third major question concerns what causes people to be violent. Early investigators of child abuse and wife beating employed a psychodynamic model of abuse and violence. Consequently, they directed their efforts toward "discovering" the personality traits and disorders that were associated with, and that "therefore" caused people to abuse family members. Other investigators have developed models emphasizing sociological, social psychological, or ecological factors, or various combinations of these. (For a review of 17 theories of violence, see Gelles & Straus, 1979.)

Conceptual and Methodological Problems in the Study of Family Violence

The development of a knowledge base in the area of family violence, and especially in the study of violence toward children, has been hampered by two major difficulties, one conceptual and the other methodological. The conceptual problem is that the study of violence toward children is almost always subsumed within investigations of child "abuse." There are some studies of physical punishment of children (see, for example, Sears, Maccoby & Levin, 1957; Eron, Walder, & Lefkowitz, 1971). One notable exception is the analysis of the data collected by the National Commission on the Causes and Prevention of Violence (Owens & Straus, 1975; Stark & McEvoy, 1970). But by and large, there have been few studies of violence toward children which were conducted outside of the rubric of child abuse research.

This poses a major problem for investigators who want to determine how widespread violence is and what causes parents and caretakers to use violence toward their children. Usually, "child abuse" is defined to include behaviors beyond the use of physical force: malnourishment, failure to care for and protect a child, sexual assault, failure to clothe a child, and psychological abuse. The wide and varied definitions of the concept "child abuse" makes it nearly impossible to compare the findings of various investigators or even separate out of the data the part that pertains to the use of physical violence. It is therefore difficult to develop cumulative knowledge about violence toward children.

At the heart of the problem is the fact that the term "child abuse" is intended to draw attention to acts which are believed to deviate from appropriate standards of behavior for caretakers. Such standards vary over time (e.g., stubborn child laws in the seventeenth and eighteenth centuries allowed parents to put unruly children to death, although there is no evidence that such deaths occurred), across cultures (e.g., some cultures allow infanticide), and between social or cultural strata (e.g., physicians who physically injure their children are much less likely to be labeled "child abusers" than unemployed fathers who injure their children).

A second important problem in the study of violence in the family is that the issue is, at the very least, sensitive. There are taboos against talking about the subject with either friends or strangers. The private and intimate nature of the family makes it very difficult to use traditional research strategies to measure the extent and patterns of physical violence (Gelles, 1978).

Because violence in the family is a sensitive topic, it is difficult to study in terms of securing access to subjects, establishing rapport with them, and getting reliable and valid self report data from them. Researchers often try to design their studies to aid these problems. In doing so, they create other problems. One way to try to deal with these problems is to operationally define "child abuse" as those cases or families that have been officially labeled as "child abuse." This often insures that cases will be available for study. But it confounds the measurement of abuse with factors which lead a family to be publicly labeled a "child abuser" (for example, is poverty a correlate of high rates of child abuse, or are poor people simply more likely to be labeled child abusers?).

Other critics of past child abuse studies (and by inference, of research on violence toward children) have noted that these studies typically employ at-hand clinical cases, that they do not test hypotheses or build theory, and that they fail to employ adequate control or comparison groups (Spinetta & Rigler, 1972; Gelles, 1973).

The result of these conceptual and methodological limitations is that we have little valid and generalizable information about how extensive violence toward children actually is, and about how it is distributed in the population. In order to overcome some of these problems, Straus et al. (1979) designed and carried out a national survey of a representative sample of American couples. That study investigated the extent of violence in the American home and tried to learn more about which families are the most likely to engage in violent behavior within the family settings. Most of this paper will present results of that study and discuss the implications of those results. (The study is presented in more detail in Gelles, 1978; Straus, 1979a; and Straus et al., 1979.)

A NATIONAL SURVEY OF FAMILY VIOLENCE

The national survey of family violence defined violence as "an act carried out with the intention or perceived intention of physically hurting another person" (Gelles & Straus, 1979). The "physical hurt" can range from slight pain, as in a slap, to murder.

There were a number of important issues which had to be dealt with when we developed this definition. First, the definition includes acts which are not normally considered violent (and certainly not abusive), such as spanking a child. Our definition viewed spankings as violent for two reasons. First, a spanking is an act intended to cause physical pain. Second, a spanking, if administered to someone who is not a family member, would be viewed as assault in the eyes of the law.

A second problem was that our definition of violence did not take into account whether an injury is produced by the violent act. Many definitions of child abuse view an act as abuse only if it produces some harm or injury. However, harm or injury often depends on events or contingencies which are external to the behavior (e.g., aim, size and strength of actor and intended victim, luck, availability of weapons, etc.). We chose to focus only on acts rather than on outcomes.

Study Methods

The data are based on interviews with a nationally representative sample of 2,143 American couples, of whom 1,146 had one or more children aged 3 to 17 years old living at home at the time of the interview. Interviews were conducted with the husband in a randomly selected half of the families and with the wife in the other half. A more complete discussion of the methodology is given in Straus et al. (1979).

We measured violence and incidence of violence in American families using a series of questions called the "Conflict Tactics Scales" (CTS). The CTS were first developed at the University of New Hampshire in 1971. They have been used and modified in numerous studies of family violence in various countries (United States, Canada, Israel, Japan, Finland, Great Britain, and British Honduras). Data on validity and reliability of the scales are given in Straus (1979b).

Each person was asked to consider two time frames: (1) conflicts that took place in the preceding 12 months; and (2) conflicts during the duration of the marriage or the lifetime of his or her children. The first time frame is used to compute annual incidence rates; since we interviewed our subjects from January to April, 1976, these can be thought of as rates for 1975. The second provides more limited information about violence that had occurred during the duration of the relationship.

In our national survey, we interviewed each respondent with respect to *one* of his or her children (randomly chosen). To interview each parent with respect to all their children would have been too time consuming. Furthermore, it would have introduced some additional methodological problems involving order effects. The interviews covered a wide range of acts, from the "normal violence" of physical punishment such as spanking to more extreme forms of violence (hitting, biting, beating, threatening with a knife or gun, etc.).

Proportion of Families in which Violence Toward Children Occurs

Estimates of the extent of child abuse and violence toward children vary widely. In any case, most of them are estimates of overall incidence with no breakdown by age, sex, or demographic characteristics of the children or parents. Since much of the research on child abuse relies on officially compiled statistics, they are probably underestimates of the true level of abuse. David Gil's 1968 survey of officially reported and validated cases of child abuse yielded 6,000 cases (Gil, 1970), but this data was collected before all fifty states had enacted mandatory child abuse reporting laws. The American Humane Association documented 26,438 reports of child abuse in 1976, but this number represents only reported child abuse and for only the 31 states that participated in the American Humane Association's national child abuse clearinghouse (American Humane Association, Note 1).

A national household survey in 1965 produced an estimate of between 2.53 and 4.07 million individuals who knew of a case of child abuse (Gil, 1970). Richard Light (1973) corrected for instances where the same case could be known to a number of people and estimated that there are 500,000 children abused each year.

Nagi's (1977) survey of community agencies produced an estimate that there are 167,000 annual reports of child abuse plus 91,000 unreported cases. Other investigators have projected an annual rate of child abuse as low as 30,000 abused children (DeFrancis, 1973) to as high as 1.5 million cases (Fontana, 1973). The estimates of how many children are killed each year as a result of abuse are also varied, from a low estimate of 365 (One child dies daily, 1975) to a high estimate of 5,000 deaths per year (United States Senate, 1973).

The limitations of the data on incidence of child abuse are compounded when it comes to determining if violence toward children is actually increasing. Certainly, if one goes by officially reported cases of child abuse, the evidence supports the claim that violence is increasing. However, official statistics cannot be relied upon to answer this question. They reflect public media campaigns aimed at increasing public knowledge about and concern with child abuse and child abuse reporting. Furthermore, they are based on varying definitions of child abuse. Since 1968, by which time all 50 states had enacted child abuse and neglect laws, there has been a tendency to *broaden* legal definitions of "child abuse." Thus, more behaviors are now defined as under the legal definition of child abuse.

The matter is further complicated when we attempt to study physical violence toward children as different from, though overlapping with, "child abuse." Past research indicates that the use of physical punishment in childrearing is nearly universal in the United States. Between 84 and 97 percent of all parents use some form(s) of physical punishment of their children at some time(s) during the childrearing relationship (Erlanger, 1974; Newson & Newson, 1963; Stark & McEvoy, 1970). Drawing the line between "normal" physical violence used as a routine part of child training, and physical violence which results in a "recognized" case of "child abuse" involves social, political, legal, and moral, as well as scientific, issues.

In our national survey, the milder forms of violence were, of course, the most common. Of our respondents, 58 percent had used some form of violence toward their child during the current year; 71 percent had done so at some time. Since other studies have shown that 90 percent or more of all American children have been hit at least once by their parents, these figures must be regarded as underestimates of actual violence in families.

Of greater interest are age differences. Among 3 and 4 year olds, and also among 5 to 9 year olds, 82 percent had been hit during the year of the survey. Two-thirds (66%) of the preteens and early teenage children (10 to 14 year olds) had been hit that year. "Only" one-third (34%) of the 15 to 17 year olds had been hit by their parents during the year. These are likely to be substantial underestimates; but the differences may be accurate.

The more dangerous types of violence occurred less often. But even for these extreme forms of violence, and even for these underestimates, there are an astoundingly high number of American children who were kicked, punched, bit, threatened with a gun or knife, or had guns or knives used on them. Approximately three children in 100 were kicked, bitten or punched by their parents in that year; many more (8 in 100) had it happen at one time or another in their lives. Slightly more than one of 100 children were beaten by a parent in that year; 4 in 100 were beaten at least once while growing up.

One child in 1,000 faced a parent who threatened to use a gun or knife during the survey year. Nearly 3 children in 100 have been threatened with a gun or knife by a parent at least once in their lifetimes. The same proportions hold for children whose parents actually *used* a gun or a knife. These data are truly astonishing when we remember that these numbers are based on parents' *own* testimony.

Frequency of Violence in Families Where It Does Occur

We were surprised, although perhaps we should not have been, to find that the extreme forms of parental violence are not likely to be one shot events. These extreme forms of parental violence occur periodically and even regularly, in the families where they occur at all. For example, if a beating is considered an element of "child abuse," then our findings show that child abuse is a chronic condition for many children, not a once in a lifetime experience for them.

With the exception of being threatened with a knife or gun, or having a knife or gun used on them, children whose parents were violent to them generally experienced such violence more than once. Children who had something thrown at them had that happen an average of 4.5 times during the reported year. Children who were pushed, grabbed or shoved experienced that an average of 6.6 times over the prior 12-month period. As expected, spankings and slappings were the most frequent.

They occurred an average of 9.6 times the previous year. The average for kicks, bites, and punches was 8.9 times that year, while children who were hit with objects had it happen an average of 8.6 times. For those who were beaten, it was repeated almost once every two months, on the average 5.9 times over the year. Where a gun or knife was used, though, it happened "only" once in the survey year.

Child Abuse Index

To estimate how many American children were "at risk" of being physically injured, we developed a Child Abuse Index that combines the items which imply a high probability of injury or damage to the child (kicks, bites, punches; beatings; threats with a gun or knife; use of a gun or knife). More than three out of every hundred children (3.6%) are at risk of serious injury each year from their parents using at least one of these dangerous forms of violence. Assuming that each of these acts has a high probability of causing harm to a child victim, then *between 1.4 and 1.9 million children in the United States were vulnerable to physical injury from their parents during the year of our study.* Moreover, as shown by the frequency data on individual violent acts, when such assaults occur, they tend to reoccur. In fact, "single incident" cases make up only 6 percent of all child abuse cases. The average number of serious assaults per year experienced by those children whose parents committed at least one abusive act was 10.5. The median, probably a better estimate for such data, was 4.5.

Being at risk of injury from parental violence is not the same thing as being a victim of child abuse. Many a child has been slammed against a wall or punched and kicked by his or her parents, who did not end up with a concussion or broken bones. Nevertheless, these figures probably are the best available ones for estimating how many children might be abused each year in the United States, because they are the only estimates ever generated from a nationally representative sample using consistent measurement procedures. If they represent a reasonable estimate of *potential* child abuse, then they offer some new and surprising information:

First, the estimates are *at least 1.2 million children higher than previous estimates of the incidence of physical abuse* (which are 150,000 to 250,000).

Second, even these figures probably *underestimate* the true level of abuse for five important reasons. First, they are based on self-reports of the parents. Underreporting is quite likely when sensitive questions about socially disapproved behavior are asked. Second, the survey deals with only seven specific forms of violence. There are others (e.g., burning). Third, the data on violence toward a given child refers to violent acts by only one of his or her parents. Fourth, the children we studied were between the ages of 3 and 17. Previous research suggests that much violence and abuse is directed toward children between three months and three years of age, who are not covered in our survey. Had they been included, our figures would necessarily have been higher. Fifth, we studied only "intact" families (husbands and wives who were living together). The literature on child abuse suggests that violence may be even more common in families where only one parent lives with the child. Had we studied single parent families, we might have found a higher rate of violence toward children. All of these suggest that the actual violence that children experience is probably much more frequent than even the astonishing figures we report here.

Factors Related to Variations in Rate of Child Abuse

Most studies of child abuse show the rate to be greatest among infants and very young children. Our Child Abuse Index revealed a slightly different pattern with regard to age of the child. The rates peaked at two ages: the youngest in our sample (3 and 4 year olds) and the oldest (15 to 17 year olds). One reason for the difference in results may be that previous studies measured abuse on the basis of injuries sustained by a child, whereas this study measured abuse by the severity of the violent act. The predominance of infants and young children among the abused in previous research is probably in part because such children are more likely to require medical attention when subjected to violence, compared to an older child subjected to the same degree of force. However, that does not explain why our data show a peak at these two ages (3 to 4 and 15 to 17). Part of the explanation might be that infancy and adolescency are both ages at which many parents find verbal controls, such as reasoning, explaining, or ordering ineffective. But these unexpected findings deserve further exploration.

We found a small, but significant, difference between mothers and fathers in the use of physical violence on their children. Mothers were slightly more likely to use violence on their children than were fathers. Mothers were also more likely to use abusive violence, as defined by our Child Abuse Index.

Boys were slightly more likely than girls to be the targets of parental violence, and, for all age groups, were also more likely to be abused.

Other Forms of Violence in the Family

We can perhaps get a better understanding about violence toward children by examining, briefly, the violence in other aspects of intra-family relationships which form part of the context of violence toward children.

One out of every six couples in our study (16% of the 2,143 surveyed) reported that they had engaged in at least one of the eight violent acts, toward the *spouse*, at least once during the survey year. These data are presented and analyzed in detail in Straus (1977) and in Straus et al. (1979).

As with violence toward children, the least dangerous acts of marital violence were the most common, but dangerous violence was also very common. We compiled an index of abusive violence toward spouse, paralleling our Child Abuse Index. It contained the five violence items which are the most likely to cause physical injury (the same four items used in the Child Abuse Index—kicking, biting, punching; beating up; threatening with knife or gun; using knife or gun; plus one additional item—hit with something). By this criterion, almost 1.8 million wives are physically abused by their husbands each year (3.8 percent), while nearly two million husbands are physically abused by their wives (4.6 percent).

We were particularly intrigued by the latter finding, especially in light of the traditional view that men are more violent than women. When we compared husbands and wives in terms of each of the eight violence items, we found that husbands and wives had similar rates of violence. Although most research suggests that females are less aggressive than males (Maccoby & Jacklin, 1974), research on aggression *within families,* either verbal or physical, has consistently shown very similar rates for husbands and wives, and for boys and girls (Gelles, 1974; Lefkowitz, Eron, Walder, & Huesmann, 1977, Table 2.8; Steinmetz, 1977; Straus, 1974b). We interpret this as reflecting the complex social rules that govern aggressive behavior. The standard rules and expectations concerning aggression toward men and toward women apply very strongly outside the family, but apply minimally if at all inside.

A note of caution should be added. Just because husbands and wives engage in violent and abusively violent behavior in equal numbers, this does not mean that as many husbands as wives are "abused." We measured *acts* of violence, *not outcomes.* Given that a husband is typically larger and stronger than his wife, he may well do more damage than his wife would do using the same form of violence. Second, it is important to take into account the context of marital violence. Although roughly as many wives kill husbands as husbands kill wives, studies of homicide show that wives are seven times more likely to murder in self defense (Wolfgang, 1957). Lastly, "abuse" is more than being hit. The economic, social and legal constraints that bind a wife to a violent marriage are greater than the ties that bind a husband (Gelles, 1979), thus putting women in a position of having to tolerate their own victimization much more often than men.

Although most media, public, and professional attention has been directed at violence toward children and violence between spouses, these are not the only forms of violence within families. Seven hundred and thirty-three of our 2,143 respondents had two or more children aged 3 to 17 living at home. On the basis of the behavior of these 733 children (as reported by a parent) we estimate that during the course of one year, four out of five American children use one of the eight forms of violence on a sibling. More than half of the children were reported as kicking, biting, punching, hitting with an object, or beating up a brother or sister. When the rate is projected to the 36.3 million children in the U.S., aged 3 to 17, who live with siblings in the same age range, it gives an estimate of 19 million attacks on siblings. If these were committed against a stranger, they would be considered assault and battery.

If violence in the home begets violence, as many students of child abuse and family violence assume, then we should expect to find that no family relationship is free of violent behavior. We were not surprised, therefore, to find that the level of child to parent violence is also quite high. Nearly one in five children between the ages of 3 and 17 (17%) used at least one of the eight forms of violence against their parents during the survey year (as reported by the parent). Almost one in ten children (9.4%) engaged in one of the five more dangerous forms of attack. Moreover, the rate of such attacks went up in direct proportion to the frequency of attacks by parents on the child (Straus et al., 1979).

SUMMARY

As high as our figures may seem, they are probably substantial underestimates of the true level of family violence. Using parent self-reports, studying violence only toward and by children from 3 to 17 years old, and relying on parents to report child to parent and sibling violence, probably have all tended to make our data underestimates of the true level of family violence. And yet, even such underestimates are startling. If we were discussing the rate of a deadly communicable disease, or if we were reporting on violence outside of the home (for instance, school violence or violent street crime) many people would regard the rates given here as indicative of an "epidemic" of violence. Yet when we are discussing slaps, spankings and even beatings in the home, there often seems to be a tendency to downplay just how widespread, and how significant, the occurrence of family violence, including violence toward children, actually is.

DISCUSSION OF FACTORS
ASSOCIATED WITH VIOLENCE TOWARD CHILDREN

It is difficult to assess the current literature on the factors associated with violence toward children for three reasons. First, acts of severe violence are combined with nonphysical acts of maltreatment in many definitions of child abuse. Second, data gathered from samples of cases publicly labeled as "abuse" can be generalized only to populations of cases publicly labeled as "abuse," not to incidence of violence toward children. Third, some factor may seem to be associated with violence toward children, when in fact it is a spurious relationship produced by selective labeling of cases as "abuse."

The early investigations of child abuse concluded that, since child abuse occurred in all social groups, social factors were not related to parent abuse of their children (see, for example, Kempe, Silverman, Steele, Droegemueller, & Silver, 1962; Steele & Pollock, 1974). Ironically, the actual data presented by those who argued that social factors were unrelated to child abuse were reanalyzed to show that some social variables were, in fact, associated with abuse (Gelles, 1973). More recent research on abused children consistently finds social variables related to child abuse (Newberger et al., 1977; Pelton 1978). The medical-psychiatric model which dominated both the early data analyses and the early theoretical formulations of the causes of child abuse has been replaced by much more multivariate theories which try to explain child abuse on the basis of a complex of social and psychological factors.

Child Rearing Histories of Abusive Parents

So many investigators have found or have proposed that abused children grow up to be abusive parents that this proposition has become commonly accepted among professionals and the public alike. The proposition has also taken on a "deterministic" flavor. Much of the public, and some professionals, interpret it to mean that all abused children *will* grow up to be abusive parents, and that anyone who is not abused as a child will grow up to be a nonabuser.

Our national survey of family violence supports a probabilistic interpretation of the proposition that violence begets violence. We asked each of our respondents to report on how often they were physically punished when they were 13 years of age and older. Those who reported that their mothers used physical punishment more than twice a year had a rate of severe violence toward their own children far greater than the rate for respondents who reported being hit less than twice a year (18.5% vs. 11.8%). Physical punishment by fathers showed less of a difference, but was still related to abusive violence toward their own children. Respondents whose fathers hit them more than twice a year at age 13 or older had a rate of abusive violence to their children of 16.7%. The rate for those hit by father less often than twice a year was 13.2% (Straus et al., 1979).

We also found that abusive violence toward children was related to whether or not a respondent saw his or her parents engage in physical violence toward one another. Men who saw their fathers strike their mothers grew up to have a rate of abusive violence toward their own children much higher than the rate for men who reported never having seen their fathers hit their mothers (13.3% vs. 9.7%). Women who saw their mothers being hit had a rate of abusive violence toward their own children which was slightly higher than the rate for women who reported no marital violence in their families of orientation (19.7% vs. 17.4%).

Finally, there was a greater chance that, in homes where there was conjugal violence, the parents would also use severe violence toward the children (Straus et al., 1979).

Clearly it is not unreasonable to suppose that people learn to be violent by observing and experiencing violence while growing up. In many cases, there seems to be an almost undiluted "transfer," with violence learned as a child being practiced as an adult (Gelles, 1974; Gil, 1970; Palmer, 1962; Steinmetz & Straus, 1974; Lefkowitz et al., 1977; Owens & Straus, 1975).

Social Class

Early research on child abuse suggested that abuse occurred in all levels of the socioeconomic system and, therefore, that social class was not to be considered a cause of child abuse (Steele & Pollock, 1974). Pelton (1978) has called this the "myth of classlessness." He presents data from a number of investigations that demonstrate that abuse is more likely to occur in families of low socioeconomic status. Nevertheless, it could be argued that this occurs because poor people are more likely to be "caught" abusing their children, while persons from higher socioeconomic groups are insulated from the stigma of being labeled abusers.

Our national survey avoided the biases inherent in studying officially labeled cases of child abuse. We found that social status does indeed make a difference in probability of violence toward children.

There is an inverse relationship between parental income and parental violence. Those with incomes below the poverty line (less than $6,000) have the highest rates of violence (22%), while families with incomes exceeding $20,000 have the lowest rate (11%) of violence toward their children (Straus et al., Chapter 6, 1979).

Our examination of occupational status also found that parental violence is related to father's occupation. The rate of severe violence in
homes where the father is a blue collar worker is 16%, while the rate in
homes where the father is a white collar worker is 11%. Although this is a
substantial and statistically significant difference, it is smaller than the
difference typically found in examinations of official reports of child
abuse (Straus, 1979a). A reasonable interpretation is that low socioeconomic status is related to the actual incidence of child abuse, but that this
difference is magnified in the data by many studies because socioeconomic status is also related to being identified as a child abuser.

Unemployment

Some researchers have postulated that unemployment contributes to
child abuse (Galdston, 1965; Gil, 1970; Young, 1964). Many discussions
of child abuse in the mass media argue that since the rate of child abuse
has increased during times of high unemployment, unemployment must
be one of the causes of child abuse. While this position is not unreasonable,
it is a logical non sequitur. Furthermore, it is also reasonable to suppose
that the rise in the officially recorded rate of child abuse may be due to
increased media publicity, increased public awareness, and changes in
reporting laws, rather than an actual increase in the occurrence of child
abuse.

We found that in families where the husband was unemployed at the
time of the interview, the rate of physical violence toward children was
22 percent, while in families where the husband was employed full-time
the rate was 14 percent. In homes where the husband was employed
part-time, the rate was nearly double the rate of parental violence in
homes where the husband was employed full-time (27% vs. 14%). The
interpretation of these results is not completely apparent. Perhaps these
findings can be better understood in the broader context to be discussed
below.

Stress

There are a number of reasons why low socioeconomic status and
unemployment may be related to severe violence toward children. One
concept which may help account for the relationship is stress. Stress is
probably unequally distributed within the social structure with lower
socioeconomic groups probably experiencing more, or at least different
kinds of, stress. Unemployment, for example, is typically experienced as
severely stressful on the family.

There are, of course, many problems, many "stressors," that a family
can encounter. To get a more comprehensive measure of family stress, we

asked questions about which of a list of 18 problems each family had encountered in the previous twelve months. Some of these 18 problems, or stressful life events, were taken from Holmes and Rahe's "Social Readjustment Rating Scale" (1967). The items were:

1. Troubles with boss
2. Troubles with other people at work
3. Laid off or fired from job
4. Arrested or convicted for something serious
5. Death of someone I felt close to
6. Foreclosure of mortgage or loan
7. Pregnant or having a child born
8. Serious sickness or injury
9. Serious problem with health or behavior of family member
10. Sexual difficulties
11. In-law troubles
12. Much worse off financially
13. Separated or divorced
14. Big increase in the number of arguments with husband/wife/partner
15. Big increase in hours worked or responsibility on the job
16. Moved to a different neighborhood or town
17. Child expelled from school or suspended
18. Child caught doing something illegal

Among our families, experience of these 18 problems ranged from none to 13 out of 18; averaging two such stressful events during the previous year.

We found that, among the very poor and the very well-to-do, level of stress had no relationship to chances of child abuse within their families. But for middle income families (those with earnings between $6,000 and $20,000) higher levels of stress are associated with higher rates of child abuse.

We do not have a totally compelling explanation for why higher levels of stress are not associated with higher levels of child abuse for either the very low or the very high income families, but are associated with higher levels of abuse for middle income families; but we can suggest some possibilities. Perhaps being poor is itself a strong stressor condition, one not included in our index, so that, in a sense, *all* low income families are under a high level of stress. Low income families have a relatively high child abuse rate, whether they are high or low on our stress index.

The well-to-do, on the other hand, may be in somewhat the obverse situation. While they may be experiencing certain stressor conditions (i.e., conditions listed for our stress index), they are not necessarily experiencing high levels of stress because they can use their financial and other resources to avoid the stressing consequences of those stressor conditions. Just as poverty itself may be regarded as a powerful stressor condition, so relative wealth may be regarded as a powerful resource for warding off or coping with stressor conditions. So, the well-to-do may never really be very highly stressed; hence always have low abuse rates regardless of "score" on our stress index; while the poor may always really be very highly stressed hence always have high abuse rates regardless of their "score" on our stress index.

The middle income families may be well enough off to be under low-stress if other conditions (such as those on our stress index) are favorable; but not be well enough off to "ward off" the stressing effects of unfavorable conditions (such as those on our stress index). Hence, their "real" level of stress, and their consequent rate of child abuse, may vary directly with changes in circumstances such as those reflected in our stress index.

Such an explanation for the complex relationship between stress level as measured by our stress index, abuse level as measured by our Child Abuse Index, and family income level is, admittedly, speculative, and goes far beyond the evidence now at hand. But it does jibe with evidence about effects of stress in other areas; and certainly seems worthy of further investigation.

Family Size

It has often been suggested that larger families are more likely to have abused children (Elmer, 1967; Gil, 1970; Johnson & Morse, 1968; Steinmetz & Straus, 1974:146; Young, 1964), presumably because of the difficulties of coping with many children. Our results do show that violence toward children varies by size of family, but not as we expected. Parents with two children have a higher rate of violence than parents with one child. The rate does *not* increase with further increases in family size.

Social Isolation

Past studies suggest that social isolation is a major correlate of child abuse (Helfer & Kempe, 1972; Maden & Wrench, 1977; Smith, 1973). Families without continuing relationships outside the home (Young, 1964), families with few memberships in organizations (Merrill, 1962), families high in anomie (Elmer, 1967) and families without telephone (Newberger et al., 1977) have been found to have higher rates of abuse.

We found that parents who lived in the same neighborhood for less than three years had higher rates of abusive violence (18.5% vs. 11.6%) than parents who have lived in the same neighborhood for three years or more (Straus, 1979a). Participation in organizations outside the home made an even greater difference. Those who did not belong to or attend meetings of any organization (clubs, lodges, unions, church groups, etc.) had violence rates much higher than parents who belonged to or attended meetings of at least one community organization (19.9% vs. 11.6%) (Straus, 1979a).

Cultural Norms and Violence Toward Children

Edward Zigler, former head of the Children's Bureau in the Department of Health, Education, and Welfare, has compared current knowledge about child abuse to the state of knowledge about mental illness in 1948 (Zigler, Note 2). That our study and some other studies have documented the extent of violence toward children, and analyzed some of the social factors associated with what we have called abusive violence, does not contradict Zigler's assessment.

The theoretical understanding of these diverse materials is at a very preliminary stage. Gelles & Straus (1979) present an inventory of theories of violence, and offer an integrated theory of violence in the family. Our research to date, however, has convinced us that an adequate theory of violence toward children will have to take into account the structure of the society and of the family and the norms or rules of the culture.

When "violence in the family" is mentioned, it evokes the picture of a child with broken bones or a husband beating up his wife for no good reason. Such instances make up only a small part of the violence that occurs in families. Most family violence does not become a matter of public concern because it is "normal violence," in the sense that it follows the implicit rules of our culture concerning violence. Any theory purporting to explain human violence must take into account such cultural rules or norms, that specify the conditions under which violence is and is not appropriate, and the nature of the violent acts which are legitimate (i.e., which are tolerated, permitted, or required).

What are the "rules" governing the occurrence of violence within the family, and which forms are "legitimate" or acceptable? In many families the norm seems to be that if someone is doing wrong, and "won't listen to reason" it is all right to hit. In the case of parents in relation to children, it is more than just all right; many American parents see physical punishment to "teach" the child as their obligation. As we have tried to show elsewhere (Gelles, 1974; Straus, 1976; Straus & Hotaling, 1979) this norm often carries over to the relationship between husbands and wives.

In identifying a husband who beats up his wife as violent, we used the phrase "for no good reason." The implication of this phrase is that there can be situations in which there *is* "a good reason" for a husband to hit his wife, or vice versa. In fact, about one out of four Americans explicitly take that view (Stark & McEvoy, 1970).

What is a "good reason" varies from couple to couple, and from subculture to subculture. But in our culture in general, the marriage license is also a license to hit. To be sure, there are certain normative restrictions. One cannot inflict "excessive" injury even with a marriage partner.

Just how much violence is "excessive," in marriage or to discipline children, also varies with the individual couple and their subculture. Usually, there is a distinction (again, seldom made explicit) between "ordinary" spanking, pushing, and slapping, and "real" violence. At one extreme are some couples for whom even one slap is taken in the same way as it would be if one of us were to slap a department colleague. Such couples are rare. Even rarer, almost non-existent, are parents who never hit their children.

At the other extreme are couples for whom physical punishment, spanking or slapping a child, are a common occurrence. That end of the continuum is also illustrated by the so-called "stitch rule." It used to be (and still may be) an informal understanding among the police in many cities that, in cases of family fights, no arrests would be made unless there was a wound that needed stitches. The same principle, of tolerating violence, unless there is an injury, is a norm that is very widely applied to violence by parents toward children.

Family Organization and Violence

Many aspects of the way American families are organized tend to produce conflict, even though that is an unintended effect. Such conflict often—not always—leads to violence. Many such characteristics of the family are discussed in detail elsewhere (Straus & Hotaling, 1979; Gelles & Straus, 1979). A few of them are noted here.

First, the most fundamental aspect of family organization is that the family includes persons of diverse ages and both sexes. This makes the family, automatically, the locus of the "generation gap" and the site of "the battle of the sexes." Furthermore, unlike special purpose groups such as academic departments, universities, or factories, the activities and interests of a family cover just about everything. There are simply more "events" over which a dispute can develop than is true for other groups.

There is also a greater intensity of involvement in family conflict. Love, paradoxically, gives the power to hurt. So, the degree of distress felt in conflicts with other family members is likely to be much greater than if the same issue were to arise in relation to someone outside the family.

Membership in a family also carries with it both a concern for other members and a presumed right to try to influence their behavior. Consequently, dissatisfaction over undesirable activities or behavior that impinges on ones own activities is further heightened when attempts are made to change the behavior of the other.

Finally, the rules of our society make what goes on in the family strictly a private affair. This aspect of the family system insulates the family both from social controls and from assistance in coping with conflicts. Moreover, even after violence occurs, the rule of family privacy is often so strong that it prevents the victims from seeking outside help. Pizzey's well-titled book on wife-beating is called *Scream Quietly or the Neighbors Will Hear* (1974).

Few would say that these aspects of family organization should change, that, for example, the family should not consist of people of mixed age and sexes; or that it should not encompass the whole of life; or that family members should not be intensely involved with one another and committed to the family; or that family members should not have an obligation to care about and a right to try to influence other family members; or that there should be no family privacy. These are all highly desirable aspects of family organization within the context of our culture. But they are also aspects of family organization that generate a high level of conflict. And a high level of conflict increases the probability of violence, especially when much violence is supported by cultural norms.

But it is not just the high level of conflict inherent in the organization of families which produces violence. There is also a high level of conflict in other groups, for example in academic departments. Yet instances of physical violence are extremely rare in most types of groups. The most violent event that either of us can remember from 30 years in six different academic departments is a department meeting during which someone threw an eraser *at the wall.* Obviously, something in addition to a high level of conflict is involved. The high frequency of physical violence in American families is produced by the combined effects of the high level of conflict in families with two other things: (1) training (or "modeling") in violence (Straus, 1977; Straus et al., 1979); and (2) the implicit cultural norm that gives family members the "right" to hit if someone is "doing wrong" and "won't listen to reason." That combination sets the stage for a high level of violence that is endemic to American families. Such violence is, in a sense, a product of the very nature of the family itself. In our culture, the family is the locus of a relatively high level of stress and conflict. It is isolated from outside aid and intervention. Certain cultural rules make physical force permissible within it. Violence toward youth in families can be understood only in the context of the forces leading to the violence that tends to occur in all family relationships for a very large proportion of families in our society.

REFERENCE NOTES

1. American Humane Association National analysis of official child neglect and abuse reporting. *American Humane Association.* Denver. Mimeographed, 1978.
2. Zigler, Edward. Controlling child abuse in America: An effort doomed to failure. Paper presented at the First National Conference on Child Abuse and Neglect. Atlanta, 1976.

REFERENCES

Bakan, D. (1971). *Slaughter of the innocents: A study of the battered child phenomenon.* Boston: Beacon Press.

Bohannan, P. (1960). *African homicide and suicide.* New York: Athenium.

Curtis, L. (1974). *Criminal violence: National patterns and behavior.* Lexington, MA: Lexington Books.

DeFrancis, V. (1973). Testimony before the subcommittee on children and youth of the committee on labor and public welfare. United States Senate 93rd Congress, 1st Session. On S. 1191 *Child Abuse Prevention Act.* Washington, DC: Government Printing Office.

DeMause, L. (Ed.). (1974). *The history of childhood.* New York: The Psychohistory Press.

DeMause, L. (1975). Our forebearers made childhood a nightmare. *Psychology Today, 8,* 85–87.

Dexter, L. A. (1958). A note on selective inattention in social science. *Social Problems, 6,* 176–182.

Elmer, E. (1967). *Children in jeopardy: A study of abused minors and their families.* Pittsburgh: University of Pittsburgh Press.

Erlanger, H. B. (1974). Social class and corporal punishment in childrearing: A reassessment. *American Sociological Review, 39,* 68–85.

Eron, L. D., Walder, L. O., & Lefkowitz, M. M. (1971). *Learning of aggression in children.* Boston: Little, Brown and Company.

Fontana, V. J. (1973). *Somewhere a child is crying: Maltreatment — causes and prevention.* New York: MacMillan.

Galdstone, R. (1965). Observations of children who have been physically abused by their parents. *American Journal of Psychiatry, 122,* 440–443.

Gelles, R. J. (1973). Child abuse as psychopathology: A sociological critique and reformulation. *American Journal of Orthopsychiatry, 43,* 611–621. Also reprinted in S. K. Steinmetz, & M. A. Straus, (1974). *Violence in the family.*

Gelles, R. J. (1974). *The violent home: A study of physical aggression between husbands and wives.* Beverly Hills: Sage.

Gelles, R. J. (1978). Violence towards children in the United States. *American Journal of Orthopsychiatry, 48,* 580–592.

Gelles, R. J. (1979, in press). The truth about husband abuse. *Ms. Magazine.*

Gelles, R. J., & Straus, M. A. (1979). Determinants of violence in the family: Toward a theoretical integration. In W. Burr, R. Hill, F. I. Nye, & I. Reiss (Eds.), *Contemporary theories about the family.* New York: Free Press.

Gil, D. G. (1970). *Violence against children: Physical child abuse in the United States.* Cambridge, MA: Harvard University Press.

Helfer, R. E., & Kempe, C. H. (1972). *Helping the battered child and his family.* Philadelphia: Lippincott.

Holmes, T. H., & Rahe, R. H. (1967). The social readjustment rating scale. *Journal of Psychosomatic Research, 11,* 213–218.

Johnson, B., & Morse, H. A. (1968). Injured children and their parents. *Children, 15,* 147–152.

Kempe, C. H., Silverman, F. N., Steele, B. F., Droegmueller, W., & Silver, H. K. (1962). The battered child syndrome. *Journal of the American Medical Association, 181,* 17–24.

Lefkowitz, M. M., Eron, L. D., Walder, L. O., & Huesmann, L. R. (1977). *Growing up to be violent: A longitudinal study of the development of aggression.* New York: Pergamon Press.

Light, R. J. (1973). Abused and neglected children in America: A study of alternative policies. *Harvard Educational Review, 43,* 556–598.

Maccoby, E. E., & Jacklin, C. N. (1974). *The psychology of sex differences.* Stanford, CA: Stanford University Press.

Maden, M. F., & Wrench, D. F. (1977). Significant findings in child abuse research. *Victimology, 2,* 196–224.

Merrill, E. J. (1962). *Protecting the battered child.* Denver: Children's Division, American Humane Association.

Nagi, S. Z. (1977). *Child Maltreatment in the United States.* New York: Columbia University Press.

Newberger, E. J., Reed, R. B., Daniel, J. H., Hyde, J. N., Jr., & Kotglchuck, M. (1977). Pediatric social illness: Toward an etiologic classification. *Pediatrics, 60,* 178–185.

Newson, J., & Newson, E. (1963). *Infant care in an urban community.* London: Allen and Unwin.

One child dies daily from abuse: Parent probably was abused. (1975). *Pediatric News, 9,* 3ff.

Pelton, L. H. (1978). Child abuse and neglect: The myth of classlessness. *American Journal of Orthopsychiatry, 48,* 608–617.

Pizzey, E. (1974). *Scream quietly or the neighbors will hear.* Baltimore, MD: Penguin Books.

Pfohl, S. J. (1977). The "discovery" of child abuse. *Social Problems, 24*(3), 310–323.

Radbill, S. X. (1974). A history of child abuse and infanticide. In R. E. Helfer, & C. H. Kempe (Eds.), *The battered child* (2nd ed.). Chicago: University of Chicago Press.

Sears, R. R., Maccoby, E., & Levin, H. (1957). *Patterns of child rearing.* Evanston, IL: Row Peterson.

Smith, S. M. (1973). *The battered child syndrome.* London: Butterworths.

Spinetta, J. J., & Rigler, D. (1972). The child-abusing parent: A psychological review. *Psychological Bulletin, 77,* 296–304.

Stark, R., & McEvoy, J. (1970). Middle class violence. *Psychology Today, 4,* 52–65.

Steele, B. F., & Pollock, C. B. (1974). A psychiatric study of parents who abuse infants and small children. In R. E. Helfer, & C. H. Kempe (Eds.), *The battered child* (2nd ed.). Chicago: University of Chicago Press.

Steinmetz, S. K. (1977). *Cycle of violence: Assertive, aggressive, and abusive family interaction.* New York: Praeger Publishers.

Steinmetz, S. K., & Straus, M. A. (1974). *Violence in the family.* New York: Harper and Row (originally published by Dodd, Mead, and Co.).

Straus, M. A. (1974a). Foreword in R. J. Gelles, *The violent home: A study of physical aggression between husbands and wives.* Beverly Hills: Sage.

Straus, M. A. (1974b). Leveling, civility and violence in the family. *Journal of Marriage and the Family, 36,* 13–29. Plus addendum August, 1974c.

Straus, M. A. (1976). Sexual inequality, cultural norms, and wife-beating. *Victimology, 1,* 54–76. Also reprinted in E. C. Viano (Ed.), *Victims and society.* Washington, DC: Visage Press, 1976, and in J. R. Chapman & M. Gates (Eds.), *Women into wives: The legal and economic impact of marriage*. Sage Yearbooks in Women Policy Studies, Vol. 2. Beverly Hills, CA: Sage, 1977.

Straus, M. A. (1977). Wife-beating: How common and why? *Victimology, 2,* 443–458. Also reprinted in Straus and Hotaling, 1979.

Straus, M. A. (1979a). Family patterns and child abuse in a nationally representative American sample. *Child Abuse and Neglect.* (In press).

Straus, M. A. (1979b). Measuring intrafamily conflict and violence: The Conflict Tactics (CT) scales. *Journal of Marriage and the Family, 41.*

Straus, M. A., Gelles, R. J., & Steinmetz, S. K. (1979). *Behind closed doors: Violence in the American family.* Garden City, NY: Doubleday/Anchor.

Straus, M. A., & Hotaling, G. T. (Eds.). (1979). *The social causes of husband-wife violence.* Minneapolis: University of Minnesota Press, (in press).

United States Senate Hearing before the subcommittee on Children and Youth, of the Committee on Labor and Public Welfare. (1973). United States Senate, 93rd Congress First Session. On S. 1191 *Child Abuse Prevention and Treatment Act.* Washington, DC: U. S. Government Printing Office.

Wolfgang, M. E. (1956). Husband-wife homicides. *Corrective Psychiatry and Journal of Social Therapy, 2,* 263–271. Also reprinted in C. D. Bryant, & J. G. Wells (Eds.), *Deviancy and the family.* Philadelphia: F. A. Davis, 1973.

Young, L. R. (1964). *Wednesday's children: A study of child neglect and abuse.* New York: McGraw-Hill.

CHAPTER 6

CHARACTERISTICS OF PARENTAL CHILD STEALING

MICHAEL W. AGOPIAN AND GRETCHEN L. ANDERSON

Amerca is quickly learning that the family is no longer an oasis of serenity. Crime and violence between family members has become increasingly common and serious (Steinmetz and Straus, 1975; Gelles, 1972, 1979).

The dissolution of a marriage can also be characterized by conflict and violence (O'Brien, 1971). For many persons, divorce is not a resolution that immediately severs or clarifies family relationships. As Westman and Cline note:

> Divorce is an "adjustment of relationship" that does not erase the past nor create an unrelated future. For the departing husband it may mean a major change, living alone. For the wife and children life may be much the same, only more difficult. Divorce legally dissolves the marriage but it only realigns the material and intangible bonds between the affected parties [1971: 1].

The locus of control over children frequently becomes complicated when the family unit is dissolved through divorce. Problems over the custody of children when parents are divorced or separated appear even when the parties make an effort to resolve their differences amicably. One repercussion from custody disputes has been an increase in parental child stealing—legally defined as a parent abducting or detaining a child from the other parent in violation of a custody order (Agopian, 1980). Parental child stealing may occur after a divorce or during a separation prior to a divorce action. In California, the abduction of a child by a parent is a criminal act if it occurs after the implementation of a custody order (Cal. Penal Code Sec. 278.5; Agopian, 1981).

To date, no study has examined the characteristics of parental child stealing. This article will report on the frequency of parental child stealing and provide descriptive information pointing to important relationships between situational variables and the social attributes of participants in child-stealing offenses. At this stage in our research, however, we cannot directly examine the causality of parental child abductions.

This study is based upon cases screened for prosecution by the Los

Angeles County District Attorney's Office during the initial year follow-ing special legislation in California making such activity criminal — July 1, 1977, to June 30, 1978.

THE LAW AND PARENTAL CHILD STEALING

Because our research has focused on parental child stealing as a criminal offense, it should not be interpreted as a pejorative stance that child stealing is pathological "criminal behavior." First, it must be recog-nized that child stealing has evolved into a self-help method of settling custody disputes. Second, child stealing can reflect fathers' reactions to the bias of the courts in almost always favoring mothers with custody of children.

In fact, parental child stealing has been induced by incongruities within the legal process. These legal inconsistencies include: (1) the general ineffectiveness of the available statutes, (2) the failure of states to give full faith and credit to prior custody decrees, (3) the sporadic and limited practice of "clean hands,"[1] and (4) the favoring of the local petitioner in custody decrees.

Historically, child stealing has not been readily defined as a criminal act because of conflicting statutes: The welfare codes address the interests of the child, the civil laws govern the changing domestic status of the parents, and kidnapping is the concern of the criminal codes.

Recognizing this ever-increasing national problem of conflicting jurisdictional custody laws and of the dramatic increase in parental child stealing and concealments, the National Conference of Commissioners on Uniform State Laws drafted the Uniform Child Custody Jurisdiction Act which was approved by the American Bar Association in 1968. To date, the act has been adopted by 44 states and became effective as California law in 1974 as Civil Code secs. 5150–5174. Adoption of the act by states usually marks the clarification of child stealing as a prosecut-able offense and induces cooperation between subscribing states to settle custody disputes in an orderly manner in the best interests of the child.

EXTENT OF PARENTAL CHILD STEALING

There is a scarcity of accurate statistical data on the frequency of parental child stealing in America. Official figures are usually incomplete, combined within multiple offense categories, or nonexistent. The Fed-eral Bureau of Investigation does not compile information to assess the extent of parental child stealing on a national basis. Arrest Register data from the California Bureau of Criminal Statistics found 136 adults arrested during 1977, 208 arrested in 1978, and 213 arrested in 1979 for parental child stealing (Bartholomew, 1980). The Los Angeles County District Attorney reported that between January 1975 and April 1979, 400 cases of parental child stealing were screened, of which 240 were rejected for prosecution (Oghigian, 1979). The Los Angeles Sheriff's Department reported 60 parental child-stealing cases in 1977 with that figure increasing to 86 in 1978 and 65 cases in 1979 (Hess, 1980). The Los Angeles Police Department reported 163 cases of child theft for 1977 with the 1978 figure increasing to 190 cases and 179 thefts in 1979 (Smith, 1980).

There is strong reason to suspect that the official picture of parental child stealing suffers from substantial underreporting. Unofficial estimates suggest that there are 50,000 to 100,000 outright parental child thefts per year in America (Horowitz, 1977; "Abduction of own child could result in felony," 1976). When the retention of children after visitation is included, the taking of children from custodial parents may reach 400,000 cases annually ("Child stealing laws near uniformity," 1978). And some persons surmise that parental child thefts are increasing rapidly in the United States and that there are perhaps as many as 25,000 cases each year (McCoy, 1978).

The extent of parental child stealing can only be crudely estimated because law enforcement agency data are incomplete, but the potential for parental child thefts can be better gauged. Divorce is rapidly increasing in America. In 1978 Americans divorced 1,122,000 times (U.S. Bureau of the Census, 1979a:7). The rate of divorce has increased steadily, and from the 1960 rate of 2.2 divorces per 100,000 population, the rate increased in 1970 to 3.5, and in 1978 the rate of divorce peaked at 5.1 (U.S. Bureau of the Census, 1979a: 1). The number of children involved in divorce has nearly tripled between 1960 and 1976, increasing from 463,000 to 1,117,000 children (U.S. Bureau of the Census, 1979a: 8). With estimates of parental child stealing between 25,000 to 100,000, this amounts to about one child theft annually for every 22 divorces. Such a rapid increase in the divorce rate signals the potential for an epidemic of parental child stealing. Recognizing that not every divorce contains the social chemistry which spawns parental child stealing, the potential for victimization has, nevertheless, greatly increased.

The national data also note a rapid increase in the number of one-parent families between 1960 and 1978. In 1978, 19 percent of families with children were maintained by one parent—17 percent by mothers and 2 percent by fathers (U.S. Bureau of the Census, 1979a: 1). This increase of one-parent families rose from the 1960 figure of 8.5 percent—7.4 percent by mothers and 1.1 percent by fathers (U.S. Bureau of the Census, 1979a: 9). Today almost two million children live in one-parent families (U.S. Bureau of the Census, 1979a: 6). And recently, more fathers have become desirous of custody of their children (see Hanley, 1977; Molinoff, 1977). Single fatherhood increased 32 percent between 1970 and 1978 with nearly one million American children under the age of 18 living with their male parents (U.S. Bureau of the Census, 1979b: 6).

FINDINGS

In terms of the gender of offenders and custodial parents, the Los Angeles data indicate that fathers steal children more than twice as frequently as do mothers. Males were the offender in 71 percent (65) of the crimes, while females accounted for 29 percent (26) of the offenses. It must be recognized that child stealers are overwhelmingly males because custody awards almost always favor mothers as the custodial parent.

Racially, Caucasians are largely involved in parental child stealing. Caucasians comprised 68 percent (62) of the offenders and 69 percent (63) of the custodial parents in Los Angeles. Blacks made up 14 percent (13) of the offenders and 11 percent (10) of the custodial parents. Mexican-Americans comprised 17 percent of the abductors and 14 percent (13) of the custodial parents, while Orientals accounted for 1 percent of the offenders and 6 percent (4) of the custodial parents.

The age distribution of participants indicates that both offenders and custodial parents are generally young and within the same age group. Most offenders, 35 percent (32), and most custodial parents, 35 percent (30), were between 27 and 31 years of age. The next most common age group for offenders and custodial parents was between 32 and 36 years of age—25 percent (23) of the offenders and 22 percent (20) of the custodial parents. The youthfulness of participants in parental child stealing is evident since 73 percent (67) of the offenders and 76 percent (65) of the custodial parents were 36 years of age or younger. The mean age of offenders was 36 years and the mean age of custodial parents was 33 years.

The type of relationship between offenders and custodial parents in Los Angeles is predominantly that of ex-spouse as discovered in 85 percent (77) of the cases. In only 14 percent (13) of the crimes were the parties separated prior to a formal dissolution of marriage action, and one case reported a cohabitation relationship between the parties. For most participants in parental child stealing, relations are usually limited to arranging visitation periods or resolving financial support obligations.

Analysis of parental child thefts by month of year finds crimes well-distributed throughout all seasons of the year. Contrary to findings for other types of crime, parental child thefts are not highest during the warm-weather months (Falk, 1950; Wolfgang, 1958; Amir, 1971). The fall accounted for 30 percent (27) of the thefts, summer 29 percent (26), winter 22 percent (19), and the spring season 21 percent (12). April and September are the peak months for parental child snatching—each accounting for 13 percent (12) of the Los Angeles crimes. May was the least likely month for a child theft, recording only 2 percent (2) of the offenses.

Parental child stealing takes place during the weekend days. Friday was found to be the most perilous day with 21 percent (19) of the crimes, followed by Saturday and Sunday, each recording 17 percent (15) of the crimes. The days of Friday, Saturday, and Sunday accounted for 55 percent (49) of all parental child thefts. The midweek days were the safest from snatching with Tuesday reporting only 7 percent (6) and Thursday 10 percent (9) of the offenses.

The large number of parental child thefts occurring during the weekend may partly be explained by the fact that most custody decrees specify weekends as the visitation period for noncustodial parents. Although the visitation parent has guardianship over the child through the weekend, Friday may be reported as the last day the custodial parent had possession of the child. Also, offenders may find the weekend, especially Friday, particularly convenient—the child will be in transit moving openly between home and school, while the weekend provides a buffer for travel and relocation into a new community or employment for the offender.

When the period between a parental child theft and divorce was examined, it was discovered that a significant portion of parental child snatchings, 55 percent (49), are perpetrated within 18 months of a divorce. However, the single largest number of offenses, 37 percent (36), occurred after two years of the divorce action. Table 6-1 presents the distribution for parental child thefts by days between the crime and divorce.

The noncustodial parent's compliance with visitation conditions for a moderate length of time apparently enhances the success of the crime scheme. Trust of the custodial parent is gained, which may influence the custodial parent to delay reporting the crime to law enforcement agencies. Acquiring possession of the child will also be predictable and without suspicion. This period of compliance may, therefore be an essential preparatory element of the crime plan.

The location of parental child thefts provides an understanding of the circumstances surrounding the crime. An offender's actions are directed, in large part, by a crime site that affords physical access to the child. The most dangerous location for parental child snatching is the victim's residence. The home is the location of offense for 67 percent (61) of the cases, while the child's school was the crime site in 12 percent (11) of the offenses. Abductions from public facilities or outdoors accounted for 14 percent (12) of the thefts.

Table 6-1. Days Between Crime and Divorce

Days between Crime and Divorce	Number	Percent
0 to 160 days (6 months)	13	18%
181 to 365 days (12 months)	16	23
366 to 546 days (18 months)	10	14
547 to 727 days (24 months)	5	7
730 or more days (over 2 years)	26	37
Total	70*	99%**

* No information for 21 cases.
**Error due to rounding.

Communication of some form between offender and custodial parent following the crime occurred in 47 percent (43) of the 91 cases examined. Of these 43 cases, communication was by telephone in 72 percent (31), by mail in 16 percent (7), and in person for 12 percent (5) of the crimes. Communication between participants of parental child stealing takes three forms: (1) communiqués that announce the offender's intention and safety of the child, (2) communication intended to use the abduction as a mechanism to influence the relationship between the offender and custodial parent, and (3) communications that rationalize the child theft. The following verbatim accounts of communication between the parties from the crime investigation report illustrates each type (all were by telephone):

Announcement of intention and safety of child:

I've got the boys and I'm gone. Now you can think about how I've been feeling. I'll be leaving with the boys for a 35-hour bus ride in a while. You aren't going to see them again.

Mechanism to influence the relationship:

You will never find her. If you won't change your mind it won't be us that suffers, it would be the family.

Rationalization of the crime:

I am going to take my boy back to Illinois to live and you are not going to stop me. I don't want my boy raised in Los Angeles.

Table 6-2. Precipitating Circumstance to Parental Child Theft

Circumstance	Number	Percent
Day visit	11	12%
Weekend visit	30	33
Summer visit	9	10
From babysitter	15	16
Denial of visitation	7	8
Separated prior to divorce	6	7
Surprise/physical force	5	5
Other circumstances	8	9
Total	91	100%

Understanding the process that enables a noncustodial parent to seize control of the child requires an analysis of the situational elements immediately preceding the crime. Examination of the precipitating circumstances discovered that most parental child snatchings, 33 percent (30), are perpetrated under the guise of an ex-spouse exercising weekend visitation privileges. The second most popular medium for gaining physical possession of a child was from a babysitter's care, as found in 17 percent (15) of the cases. Day visitation privileges were used as part of the crime scheme in 12 percent (11) of the crimes. Table 6-2 presents the precipitating circumstances to the theft that enables an offender to take possession of the child.

DISCUSSION

The dominant characterization of parental child stealing, according to the Los Angeles data, is that the crime occurs after a divorce action and following a period of compliance with court-ordered visitation privileges. Young Caucasians are generally involved, and fathers overwhelmingly abducted children from mothers who are commonly awarded custody of children. Crimes occur equally throughout all seasons of the year. Child thefts more frequently take place during the weekend days. Children are usually snatched from their residence or school. In nearly half of the crimes, communication between the parties following the child theft occurred. Such communication generally announced the offender's intention to retain the child, attempted to influence the severed relationship between the parties, or to justify the crime. Parental child thefts most frequently are perpetrated by an offender exercising court-sanctioned visitation rights or acquiring the child from a babysitter's care.

Parental child thefts are rarely characterized by a surprise abduction and the use of force. The offender's use of court-approved visitation privileges to gain possession of the child suggests that such compliance is incorporated into the crime plan. The use of visitation privileges to snatch a child may illustrate a concern on the part of the offender not to frighten or harm the child. Such actions indicate that offenders utilize the minimum degree of force necessary to acquire the child.

The characteristics of parental child stealing that emerge from the present study suggest a desire by the offender to maintain a full-time parental relationship with the child. A tug-of-love for the child is created between parents when a divorce signals the termination of a marriage. The awarding of custody to one parent may convey a sense of failure to the noncustodial parent. The visitation parent's time with the child is carefully monitored by the guardian parent. The noncustodial parent may feel excluded from the general duties of parenting—an appendage to the new single-parent family. Recognizing that legal custody of the child has been lost, a parent may view child snatching as the remaining alternative to gain possession of the child.

The second dimension of parental child stealing indicates that the crime is intended to aid in the reestablishment of the disjointed marital relations. The abducted child becomes an agent to influence a spouse to withdraw a divorce action or bring about a reconciliation. Such instances depict a realization by the offender that the marriage is severely ruptured. The following case of a 34-year-old offender and 30-year-old custodial parent attempting to reconcile following a divorce illustrates such a case:

The R/P states that she and her husband, also the Suspect, were attempting to bring her marriage back together ever since the Court Order and that they had been living together during this time but for the past month or so, her husband had lost all interest in the children and responsibility. She advised that he is unable to hold on to any job and has no desire in helping her with the payments that come due each month. She advised that they continually fight in front of the children, therefore, she told the Suspect that she felt it necessary to recontact her lawyer to complete the divorce proceedings. She advised her husband that she was going to take the kids back to Mexico when the divorce was final for their own safety and that she would be leaving as soon as she was able to move out.

R/P states that on 9-10-77 approximately 9:00 am the Suspect told her that he was going to take the two victims sailing in Long Beach and that he would be back before long. She advised that approximately 6 to 8 hours after he left the residence he telephoned her and stated, "If you don't stop the divorce you won't ever see your kids again." R/P advised it appeared that he was calling long distance as she could barely hear his voice and he also advised her that when she recontacted her lawyer and dropped the divorce proceedings that he would send her money so that she could come and join him and his children.

These cases portray parental child stealing as symptomatic of a more serious and continuing pathology in the domestic relationship between offender and custodial parent. In such instances the offender's desire to possess the child appears secondary to restoring the marriage.

Before firm conclusions can be drawn about the patterns of parental child stealing, additional research is required that goes beyond the preliminary findings from Los Angeles. Studies using cases from various jurisdictions operating under the same sections of a criminal code as well as comparative studies from jurisdictions having different definitions of the crime are necessary.

In addition to further studies from a legalistic perspective, child stealing can and should be examined from other perspectives, such as the psychological and the ethical. One possibility is to view child stealing as a process much like the view of the "divorce process" advanced by Rasmussen and Ferraro (1979). Process perspectives such as this tend to address the problems of simplistic legal definitions of an offense, the role of agents in the justice administration system, and the ideological biases inherent in the labelling of any behavior as "criminal." It may be that to understand child stealing, one must confront the existential reality of noncustodial parents, especially fathers, who may use child stealing as an adjustment to the process of divorce. Their behavior is labelled as criminal while mothers use their legally favored position in the custodial situation for many of the same functions of adjustment to the process of divorce. The latter, of course, are not legally sanctioned. Specifically, mothers may engage in manipulations around their power of custody that are designed to (1) use the child to restore the severed relationship, (2) punish their ex-spouses, or (3) express their dissatisfaction with their new lifestyle and marital status. Expanded research using some of these alternative theoretical perspectives combined with expanded data bases can illuminate our understanding of this rapidly increasing and complex behavior.

NOTE

1. Courts violate "clean hands" when they reopen custody hearings with full knowledge that the parent who now seeks a custody decree has brought the child into court by violation of a law or by some other misconduct.

REFERENCES

Abduction of own child could result in felony. (1976, March 3). *Los Angeles Daily Journal,* 20.

Agopian, M. W. (1981). *Parental child-stealing.* Lexington, MA: Lexington Books.

Agopian, M. W. (1980). Parental child stealing: California's legislative response. *Canadian Criminology Forum, 31,* 37–43.

Amir, M. (1971). *Patterns in forcible rape.* Chicago: University of Chicago Press.

Bartholomew, D. (1980, March 12). *Personal correspondence.*

California Penal Code. (1980). St. Paul, MN: West Publishing.

Child stealing laws near uniformity. (1978, November 13). *Los Angeles Daily Journal,* 20.

Falk, G. (1952, July/August). The influence of the season on the crime rate. *Journal of Criminal Law, Criminology, and Police Science,* 199–213.

Gelles, R. (1972). *The violent home: A study of physical aggression between husbands and wives.* Beverly Hills: Sage.

Hanley, R. (1977, March 7). Fathers group to fight custody decision. *New York Times,* sec L, 57.

Hess, M. (1980, April 20). *Personal correspondence.*

Horowitz, J. (1977, March 21). The law has few answers for child-stealing cases. *Los Angeles Herald Examiner,* 8.

McCoy, M. (1978). *Parental kidnapping: Issues brief no. IB77117.* Washington, DC: Congressional Research Service.

Molinoff, D. (1977, March 22). Life with father. *New York Times,* 12.

O'Brien, J. (1971). Violence in divorce prone families. *Journal of Marriage and the Family, 33,* 692–698.

Oghigian, M. (1979, September 15). *Personal correspondence.*

Rasmussen, P., & Ferraro, K. (1979). The divorce process. *Alternative Lifestyles, 2*(4), 443–460.

Smith, J. D. (1980, April 7). *Personal correspondence.*

Steinmetz, S., & Straus, M. (Eds.). (1975). *Violence in the family.* New York: Dodd, Mead.

U.S. Bureau of the Census. (1979). *Current population reports: Marital status and living arrangements, March 1978.* Washington, DC: Government Printing Office.

Westman, J., & Cline, D. (1971, March). Divorce is a family affair. *Family Law Quarterly, 5,* 1–10.

Wolfgang, M. E. (1958). *Patterns in criminal homicide.* Philadelphia: University of Pennsylvania Press.

CHAPTER 7

RAPE IN MARRIAGE
A SOCIOLOGICAL VIEW*

DAVID FINKELHOR AND KERSTI YLLO

The subject of marital rape is cropping up with increasing frequency in the media in recent years. Yet, attention has focused almost entirely on court cases—such as those of John Rideout in Oregon and James Chretien in Massachusetts and on state legislatures, where efforts have been made to criminalize this form of sexual assault (Celarier, 1979; Croft, 1979; Laura X, 1980).

While lawyers and legislators debate the issue, those in positions best suited to understanding this form of abuse and to offering help to victims have generally remained silent. Surprisingly little attention has been paid to the problem of marital rape by researchers, counselors, therapists, and doctors. Even feminist recognition of marital rape is coming well after other types of violence against women became national concerns.

Nonetheless, public and professional awareness that marital rape exists is growing. The slowly accumulating evidence suggests that rape in marriage is not a rare crime that may blossom into a headline-grabbing trial, but that it is a persistent problem in a large number of marriages.

Prevalence of Marital Rape

Evidence about violence against wives in general leads to a suspicion that forced sex in marriage is fairly commonplace. For a long time, wife abuse also was considered a rather unusual crime, but results of recent large-scale surveys have reversed this notion. Straus, Gelles, and Steinmetz (1980) found that 16 percent of all American couples admitted to a violent episode in the course of the previous year, and for 4 percent the violence was severe enough to qualify as wife-battering.

*In D. Finkelhor, R. J. Gelles, G. T. Hotaling, & M. A. Straus, (Eds) THE DARK SIDE OF FAMILIES: CURRENT FAMILY VIOLENCE RESEARCH. Sage, 1983

Authors' Note: *Funds from NIMII grants MI115161, MI130930, and MI134109, as well as from the research office of the University of New Hampshire, helped make this research possible. Ruth Miller assisted in the preparation of this manuscript. Portions of this chapter were presented to the Society for the Scientific Study of Sex in Dallas, November 1980, and to the American Orthopsychiatric Association in New York, April 1981.*

Testimony from battered women confirms their high vulnerability to marital rape. Spektor (1980) surveyed 304 battered women in 10 shelters in the state of Minnesota and found that 36 percent said they had been raped by their husband or cohabitating partner. Giles-Sims (1979) found a similar proportion of women in shelters reporting a forced sex experience, and Pagelow (1980) reported a figure of 37 percent based on a sample of 119 women in California. Forced sex is clearly a common element in the battering situation.

Diana Russell (1980) has gathered some of the first direct evidence about the prevalence of marital rape experiences in the population at large. Russell surveyed a random sample of 930 women residents of San Francisco, 18 years and older, about any incident of sexual assault they had had at any time throughout their lives. Fourteen percent of the 644 married women in the sample reported a sexual assault by a husband. Twelve percent had been forced to have intercourse, and two percent experienced other types of forced sex. *Sexual assaults by husbands were the most common kinds of sexual assault reported, occurring over twice as often as sexual assault by a stranger.*

It is important in evaluating Russell's finding to realize that she did not ask any of her respondents whether they had been "raped," a stigmatizing term that many women are reluctant to use to describe sexual assault experiences. Instead, she asked women to describe any kind of unwanted sexual experience with a husband or ex-husband, and then only included in her tally those women who described encounters that met the legal definition of rape: "forced intercourse, or intercourse obtained by physical threat(s) or intercourse completed when the woman was drugged, unconscious, asleep, or otherwise totally helpless and hence unable to consent."

Russell's finding that marital rape is the most common kind of rape cannot thus be ascribed to semantics. She used the same definition of sexual assault in tabulating the experiences with husbands as she did with strangers.

The findings from Russell's study are bolstered by results from a survey we recently completed in Boston. In a study on the related subject of childhood sexual abuse, we also asked a representative sample of 326 women whether a spouse or person they were living with as a couple had ever used physical force or threat to try to have sex with them. *Ten percent* of the women who had been married (or coupled) answered "yes." These women, too, reported more sexual assaults by husbands than assaults by strangers (10% versus 3%). Forced sex in marriage is a frequent—perhaps the most frequent—type of sexual assault.

Wives Avoid Rape Label

Few women whose husbands have forced them to have sex define themselves as having been raped (Gelles, 1979). Most women see rape as something that primarily happens between strangers. They too share the cultural and legal assumption that there is no such thing as rape between husband and wife. Violent and unpleasant as a husband's assault might have been, most wives would resist calling it rape. No doubt raped wives, like battered wives, use many self-deceptions to avoid facing the realities of an intolerable marriage because the alternatives—loneliness, loss of financial security, admission of failure—are so frightening (Gelles, 1979).

For these reasons, asking women whether they have been raped by their husbands is an unpromising course. To use a term that more victims could identify with, we used the term "forced sex" rather than "marital rape" throughout our research.

Varieties of Coercion

Another definitional problem concerns the question of when sex is forced. It has been argued that given the power inequality in the institution of marriage, *all* marital sex is coerced (Brogger, 1976). It may be that when sex is not explicitly desired it should be considered forced. Obviously, many different sanctions and pressures are brought to bear by husbands to gain sexual access. Although all these sanctions have elements of coercion, some important distinctions can be made among them.

Four basic types of coercion can be identified. Some women submit to sex in the absence of desire because of social pressure—because they believe it is their wifely duty. This can be considered *social coercion.* Other wives comply because they fear their husbands will leave them if they do not, or because their husbands have threatened to cut off their source of money or humiliate them in some way. In these cases husbands use their resource and power advantage to force their wives. This second type of coercion, *interpersonal coercion,* refers to threats by husbands that are not violent in nature. The third type involves the *threat of physical force.* Threatened force can range from an implied threat that a woman could get hurt if she doesn't give in to an explicit threat she will be killed if she doesn't comply. For many women, the memory of previous beatings is enough to ensure cooperation.

The fourth kind of coercion, *physical coercion,* requires little explanation. Instances of physical coercion range from physically holding a woman down to striking her, choking her, tying her up, or knocking her out to force sex on her.

Focus on Physical Force

The varieties of sexual coercion in marriage would be the subject of an intriguing study; however, it is beyond the scope of this research. We have limited our study to physical force for two main reasons. First, such force is most life- and health-threatening and in that sense most extreme. Second, the presence or absence of physical threats and actual violent coercion is somewhat easier to determine empirically than is the presence or absence of other, more subtle forms of coercion. This is not meant to imply that other forms of coercion cannot be brutal or that "marital rape" can occur only when physical force is involved.

In-Depth Interviews

The following sections represent an overview of our exploratory study of marital rape from the victim's perspective. Our findings are based on 50 in-depth interviews with women whose husband or partner had used force or threat of force to try to have sex with them. Our interviewees were recruited from a number of sources. The majority (56%) were clients of Family Planning agencies in northern New England. These clinics routinely take a limited sexual history from each client. For the purposes of this study an additional question was added to the form: "Has your current partner (or a previous partner) ever used force or threat of force to try to have sex with you?" If the answer indicated that the client had had such an experience with a spouse or cohabitant, she was asked to participate in an additional interview for research purposes, for which she would be paid ten dollars.

Other interviewees (16%) were recruited through area battered wives shelters. When it was determined that a woman's violent experiences included forced sex, she was asked to participate in the research, if shelter staff felt that she was up to an interview. Additional interviewees (28%) were self-referrals. These women heard of our research in the media or through our public speaking and contacted us, offering to discuss their experiences. Finally, a few interviews (10%) were arranged as a result of an ad placed in *Ms.* magazine requesting interviews.

Although the sample is not a representative one, we do not regard this as a serious drawback because of the nature of this research. Our goal in this exploratory study was not to determine incidence rates or demographic data (our Boston survey provides such information). Rather, our purpose was to talk at length with women who were willing to discuss their forced sex experiences so that we could gain a qualitative understanding of marital rape and begin to outline issues for further research. The clinics and shelters were sites where these intimate subjects could be raised fairly easily and where intervention services could be made available to women needing them.

Three Types Uncovered

The forced sex experiences of the women we interviewed can be divided roughly into three types. One group can be described as typically "battered women." These women were subject to extensive physical and verbal abuse, much of which was unrelated to sex. Their husbands were frequently angry and belligerent to them and often had alcohol and drug problems. The sexual violence in these relationships appeared to be just another aspect of the general abuse. Along with the other kinds of anger and physical pain which these men heaped on their wives, they also used violent sex.

Let us quote briefly from a case study of one of these *"battering rapes"*:

The interviewee was a 24-year-old woman from an affluent background. Her husband was a big man, over six feet tall, compared to her 5'2". He drank heavily and often attacked her physically. The most frequent beatings occurred at night after they had had a fight and she had gone to bed. She would awaken to find him physically abusing her. Such attacks, at their worst, occurred every couple of weeks. After one incident her face was so bruised that she could not attend class for a full week.

Their sexual activities had violent aspects, too. Although they shared the initiative for sex and had no disagreements about its timing or frequency, she often felt that he was brutal in his love-making. She said, "I would often end up crying during intercourse, but it never seemed to bother him. He probably enjoyed my pain in some way."

The most violent sexual episode occurred at the very end of their relationship. Things had been getting worse between them for some time. They hadn't talked to each other in two weeks. One afternoon she came home from school, changed into a housecoat and started toward the bathroom. He got up from the couch where he had been lying, grabbed her, and pushed her down on the floor. With her face pressed into a pillow and his hand clamped over her mouth, he proceeded to have anal intercourse with her. She screamed and struggled to no avail. Afterward she was hateful and furious. "It was very violent . . .", she said, " . . . if I had had a gun there, I would have killed him."

Her injuries were painful and extensive. She had a torn muscle in her rectum so that for three months she had to go to the bathroom standing up. The assault left her with hemorrhoids and a susceptibility to aneurisms that took five years to heal.

The second group of women have somewhat different relationships. These relationships are by no means conflict-free, but on the whole, there is little physical violence. In this group, the forced sex grew out of

more specifically sexual conflicts. There were long-standing disagreements over some sexual issue, such as how often to have sex or what were
appropriate sexual activities. The following is an exerpt from a case
study of a *"nonbattering rape"*:

> The interviewee was a 33-year-old woman with a young son. Both she and her
> husband of ten years are college graduates and professionals. She is a teacher
> and he is a guidance counselor. Their marriage, from her report, seems to be
> of a modern sort in most respects. There have been one or two violent
> episodes in their relationship, but in those instances, the violence appears to
> have been mutual.
>
> There is a long-standing tension in the relationship about sex. She prefers sex
> about three times a week, but feels under considerable pressure to have more.
> She says that she is afraid that if she refuses him that he will leave her or that
> he will force her.
>
> He did force her about two years ago. Their love-making on this occasion
> started out pleasantly enough, but he tried to get her to have anal intercourse
> with him. She refused. He persisted. She kicked and pushed him away. Still,
> he persisted. They ended up having vaginal intercourse. The force he used
> was mostly that of his weight on top of her. At 220 pounds, he weighs twice as
> much as she.
>
> "It was horrible," she said. She was sick to her stomach afterward. She cried
> and felt angry and disgusted. He showed little guilt. "He felt like he'd won
> something."

In addition to the sexual assaults we classified as battering and
nonbattering, there were a handful that defied such categorization. These
rapes were sometimes connected to battering and sometimes not. All,
however, involved bizarre sexual obsessions in the husbands that were
not evident in the other cases. Husbands who made up this group were
heavily involved in pornography. They tried to get their wives to participate in making or imitating it. They sometimes had a history of sexual
problems, such as difficulty in getting aroused, or guilt about earlier
homosexual experiences. Sometimes these men needed force or highly
structured rituals of sexual behavior in order to become aroused. A case
study of one of these *obsessive rapes* is illustrative:

> The interviewee was a thirty-one-year-old marketing analyst for a large
> corporation. She met her husband in high school and was attracted to his
> intelligence. They were married right after graduation because she was
> pregnant.
>
> After the baby was born, he grew more and more demanding sexually. "I was
> really just his masturbating machine," she recalls. He was very rough sexu-
> ally and would hold a pillow over her face to stifle her screams. He would also .

tie her up and insert objects into her vagina and take pictures which he shared with his friends.

There were also brutal "blitz" attacks. One night, for example, they were in bed having sex when they heard a commotion outside. They went out in their bathrobes to investigate to discover it was just a cat fight. She began to head back to the house when her husband stopped her and told her to wait. She was standing in the darkness wondering what he was up to when, suddenly, he attacked her from behind. "He grabbed my arms behind me and tied them together. He pushed me over the log pile and raped me," she said. As in similar previous assaults, he penetrated her anally.

The interviewee later discovered a file card in her husband's desk which sickened her. On the card, he had written a list of dates, dates that corresponded to the forced sex episodes of the past months. Next to each date was a complicated coding system which seemed to indicate the type of sex act and a ranking of how much he enjoyed it.

Force and Resistance

The incidents uncovered in our study so far varied both in the amount of force used by the men and the amount of resistance offered by the women. In some cases the man applied massive force, dragging the woman somewhere, tearing off her clothes, and physically beating her. In other situations, particularly where the couple was already in bed, the force was more moderate. In several cases the women mentioned the men's weight and their persistent attempts to penetrate them as the main elements of force.

Many women said they did not put up much of a fight, however. They felt that it was no use or wasn't worth it. This is an important point to understand better, because so many victims of sexual force have been ridiculed for not meeting the masculine stereotype of how vigorously a threatened person should resist. Lack of violent resistance is often interpreted as a sign that the victims really "wanted" sex on some level or that it wasn't so traumatic.

There appear to be three main factors that inhibited the women's attempts to ward off sexual aggression from their partners. First, many of the women felt they could not ward off their partners' aggression no matter how hard they tried. They perceived their partners to be very strong. Indeed, we were struck by the large size disparity between our subjects and their partners. Women who are much smaller than their husbands may be a particularly vulnerable group, not only because they *are* weak in comparison but because they *feel* weak as well.

Second, many of the women feared that if they resisted they would be hurt even worse, especially the women who had been beaten before.

They expected that if they resisted they would be punched, bruised, and manhandled and that the sexual act itself would be more painful and damaging.

Third, many of the women believed that they themselves were in the wrong. In several cases, their husbands had convinced them that they were frigid. They believed that they were at fault for whatever marital dispute was in process, and felt responsible for their husband's mood or frustration. Although they did not want the sexual act, they were not armed with the conviction that they were *justified* in not wanting it. This made it difficult for them to put up a fight.

In general, it seemed that certain kinds of ultimate resistance tactics seemed out of the question for these women. Most did not run out of the house or physically resist by gouging at the partner's eyes or kicking him in the groin. No doubt they were hampered by their socialization not even to consider such actions. Moreover, unless they were prepared to leave, they knew that they would have to face this man later on, in the morning or the next day. Since most were not prepared to make it on their own, a central goal was "keeping the peace." They were not willing to bring out the ultimate weapons, because they had to continue living with this person. And they wanted to make things more tolerable for themselves. So appeasement rather than massive resistance appeared to be the preferable approach from their immediate point of view.

Trauma of Marital Rape

Many people fail to get alarmed about the problem of marital rape because they think it is a rather less traumatic form of rape. Being jumped by a stranger in the street, they imagine, must be so much more damaging than having sex with someone you have had sex with several times before.

This misconception is based on a failure to understand the real violation involved in rape. Those who see rape primarily in sexual terms think the degradation comes from the woman having been robbed of her reputation. Although this element can be present, what is most salient for rape victims is most often the violence, the loss of control, and the betrayal of trust.

Women raped by strangers often go through a long period of being afraid, especially about their physical safety. They become very cautious about being alone, where they go, and who they go with (Burgess & Holmstrom, 1974). Women raped by husbands, however, are often traumatized at an even more basic level: in their ability to trust. The kind of violation they have experienced is much harder to guard against, short of a refusal to trust any man. It touches a woman's basic confidence in forming relationships and trusting intimates. It can leave a woman feeling much more powerless and isolated than if she were raped by a stranger.

Moreover, a woman raped by her husband has to live with her rapist, not just a frightening memory of a stranger's attack. Being trapped in an abusive marriage leaves many women vulnerable to repeated sexual assaults by their husbands. Most of the women we interviewed were raped on multiple occasions. These women do not have the option of obtaining police protection (as do other rape victims) because these rapes are legal in most states.

The research bears out the traumatic impact of marital rape. Russell found that the marital rape victims in her study rated their experiences as having a more serious impact on their lives than did the victims of stranger rape (Russell, 1980). Other studies, too, have shown that rape by intimates in general is more, not less, traumatic than rape by strangers (Bart, 1975).

Forced Marital Sex and the Law

While research cited earlier has highlighted the high prevalence of forced marital sex, and this research has documented some of its human cost, the criminal justice system is locked in anachronistic view of the subject. As of January 1982, approximately 36 of the 50 states and the District of Columbia exempt a husband from prosecution for the rape of a wife with whom he is currently living. (An excellent review of the laws on a state-by-state basis is available from the National Center on Women and Family Law; see Schulman, 1980.) Most states have a so-called spousal exemption in their rape laws, and 13 states extend this exemption not just to husbands but also to cohabiting lovers (Schulman, 1980). Such laws effectively deny the possibility of charging a husband with rape, no matter how brutal or violent he may have been in the pursuit of sex. They also contain the implicit assumption that upon marrying a woman gives permanent and irrevocable (short of divorce) consent to any and all sexual approaches a husband wishes to make.

Changing such laws has been vehemently opposed in some quarters on the grounds that it will result in a rash of fabricated complaints or that such behavior is already adequately prohibited under existing assault laws. However, evidence from countries and states where marital rape is a crime shows that few frivolous complaints are brought (Geis, 1978). Moreover, as this and other research on rape shows, sexual assault is a crime different from other assaults, with particular motives and particularly humiliating effects on its victims. Marital rape, just like other rape, deserves special classification within the legal system (*New York University Law Review,* 1977).

Public Attitudes About Marital Rape

However, it would be naive to think that the simple removal of the spousal exemption will dramatically reduce the occurrence of marital rape. Evidence suggests that even where such laws exist, they are infrequently used (Geis, 1978). Even the minority of women who may recognize that their husbands have committed a crime against them, for various reasons—loyalty, fear, unwillingness to go through a grueling public exposure—are still extremely reluctant to press charges. The lesson of spouse abuse is that laws alone have relatively little effect (Field & Field, 1973). Physical spouse abuse is a crime and has been for many years; yet in spite of such laws, all evidence suggests that such abuse is epidemic.

The spousal exemption is merely one manifestation of a complex of social attitudes surrounding the physical and sexual abuse of wives. Until these attitudes also change, the problem will remain critical with or without a law. These social attitudes portray marital rape as acceptable behavior, at least under some circumstances, and even if sometimes objectionable, at least not very seriously so.

For insight on these attitudes, we asked groups of undergraduate students for their opinions about marital rape, and some of their replies are revealing.

Some denied entirely that the phenomenon could occur: "No. When you get married, you are supposedly in love and you shouldn't even think of love making as rape under any circumstances."

Others expressed the view that implicit in the marriage contract is an acceptance of the use of force. "Sexual relations are a part of marriage and both members realize this before they make a commitment," said one in explaining why there was no such thing as marital rape.

A number of students believed that forced sex was a reasonable solution to marital conflict. "If the wife did not want to have sex . . . after many months the husband may go crazy. [Rape] would be an alternative to seeking sexual pleasure with someone else."

"If she doesn't want sex for a long amount of time, and has no reason for it—Let the old man go for it!"

Besides expressing the opinion that force is an acceptable way of trying to salvage a marriage, such statements reveal other attitudes which work to justify marital rape: for example, the belief in a man's overpowering need for sex and the belief that women withhold sex from their husbands for no good reason. Note also the myth, discussed earlier, that forced sex is primarily a response to a woman who is denying satisfaction to her husband.

The refusal on the part of politicians and the public to see marital rape as a crime is also based on the belief that it is not a very serious offense. Peter Rossi presented a random sample of people living in Baltimore with descriptions of 140 offenses ranging from the planned killing of a policeman to being drunk in a public place. While the respondents ranked "forcible rape after breaking into a home" as the fourth most serious of all 140 offenses, just *above* the "impulsive killing of a policeman," they ranked "forcible rape of a former spouse" sixty-second, just above "driving while drunk" (Rossi, Waite, Bose, & Berk, 1974).

So while people consider some rape a serious offense, rape of a former spouse is not seen as very serious. Imagine how low the ranking would have been had Rossi asked about rape of a "current" rather than a "former" spouse. This corresponds with what we know about attitudes toward violence: The more intimate the victim, the less serious the assault is considered to be.

This can be read as rather sobering evidence that the "marriage license is a raping license." Not only is it true that by marrying, a man gains immunity (a form of license) to the charge of rape, but it also appears true that people are much less likely to disapprove of sexually violent behavior, if he directs it against a woman to whom he is married rather than some other woman.

If people do not think that spousal rape is a serious offense, it certainly contributes to a climate where husbands feel they can do it with impunity. The climate also affects the victims who conclude from such social attitudes that they are wrong to be so upset and that few people will sympathize with them, so why bring it up.

Although changing the spousal exemption law is unlikely to bring many offenders to court for their offenses, it may have some effect on the general climate of acceptance of marital rape. For one thing, the political debate should alert the community, the criminal justice system, and mental health professionals about the existence of this problem. The change in the law may also put on notice some potential husband rapists that their behavior is not generally acceptable and in fact is a crime. Finally, the change may give vulnerable women a potential tool in protecting themselves.

The deterrent effect of changing the law was illustrated in the case of one woman we interviewed. Her recently separated husband kept returning and trying to have sex with her, and he was becoming more and more aggressive in his attempts. When she told some friends about the problem, they counseled her to tell him that if he tried it again she would have him prosecuted for marital rape. Apparently the husband was familiar with the recent publicity around the marital rape trials, because after she made her threat he relented and did not molest her again. This is an encouraging incident and shows that legal changes and the public discussions they stir need not be measured merely by the number of new arrests and convictions they produce.

CONCLUSION

This review of current information about marital rape and our findings regarding wives' forced sex experiences are a first step toward a full understanding of this social problem. Our research shows that "marital rape" is not a contradiction in terms, but rather a form of violence against wives which is not rare, just rarely discussed.

The case studies and typologies developed here are intended to encourage the generation of hypotheses and further analysis of forced sex in marriage, its antecedents, consequences, and implications. As a whole, our research is intended to add to the groundswell of concern about violence against women and to signal that the time has arrived for concerted investigation and discussion of the problem of rape in marriage and for action in political, legal, academic, and clinical arenas.

REFERENCES

Bart, P. (1975). Rape doesn't end with a kiss. *Viva*, 40–42, 101–107.

Brogger, S. (1976). *Deliver us from love.* New York: Delacorte.

Burgess, A., & Holstrom, L. (1974). *Rape: Victims of crisis.* Bowie, MD: Brady.

Celarier, M. (1979, January). I kept thinking maybe I could help him. *In These Times*, 10–16.

Croft, G. (1979, September 15). Three years in rape of wife. *Boston Globe.*

Doron, J. (1980). *Conflict and violence in intimate relationships: Focus on marital rape.* Paper presented at the annual meetings of the American Sociological Association, New York.

Field, M., & Field, H. (1973). Marital violence and the criminal process: Neither justice nor peace. *Social Service Review, 47*(2), 221–240.

Geis, G. (1978). Rape-in-marriage: Law and law reform in England, the U.S. and Sweden. *Adelaide Law Review, 6,* 284–302.

Gelles, R. J. (1979). *Family violence.* Beverly Hills, CA: Sage.

Giles-Sims, J. (1979). *Stability and change in patterns of wife-beating: A systems theory approach.* Unpublished Ph.D. dissertation, University of New Hampshire.

Hunt, M. (1974). *Sexual behavior in the 1970's.* Chicago: Playboy Press.

Marital rape exemption. (1977). *New York University Law Review, 52,* 306–323.

Pagelow, M. D. (1980). *Does the law help battered wives? Some research notes.* Madison, WI: Law and Society Association.

Rossi, P., Waite, E., Bose, C., & Berk, R. (1974). The seriousness of crimes: Normative structures and individual differences. *American Sociological Review, 39,* 224–237.

Russell, D. (1980). *The prevalence and impact of marital rape in San Francisco.* Paper presented at the annual meetings of the American Sociological Association, New York.

Schulman, J. (1980a). The marital rape exemption. *National Center on Women and Family Law Newsletter, 1*(1), 6–8.

Schulman, J. (1980b). Expansion of the marital rape exemption. *National Center on Women and Family Law Newsletter, 1*(2), 3–4.

Spektor, P. (1980, February 29). Testimony delivered to the Law Enforcement Subcommittee of the Minnesota House of Representatives.

Straus, M. A., Gelles, R. J., & Steinmetz, S. K. (1980). *Behind closed doors: Violence in the American family.* Garden City, NY: Doubleday.

Wolfe, L. (1980). The sexual profile of the Cosmopolitan girl. *Cosmopolitan, 189*(3), 254–257, 263–265.

X, Laura. (nd). *The Rideout trial.* Women's History Research Center, mimeo.

CHAPTER 8

LEGISLATIVE TRENDS IN THE CRIMINAL JUSTICE RESPONSE TO DOMESTIC VIOLENCE

EVA S. BUZAWA, PH.D. and CARL G. BUZAWA, J.D.

INTRODUCTION

In the ten years from 1973–1983, forty-seven states and the District of Columbia have enacted legislation designed to modify official and societal responses to the problem of domestic violence. Such legislation, often the result of the interplay of pressure from feminist groups, actions of concerned legislators, and professionals in the criminal justice system, has markedly changed the underlying legal philosophy toward the problem of domestic violence.

Before such legislation, the statutory structure could charitably be described as benevolent neglect. To the extent that domestic violence was considered by elected officials, it was considered as one of the many "family problems." Therefore, state assistance, if any, went to traditional social welfare agencies handling a variety of family problems. The problem was not formulated as being the neglect of government institutions to perform their responsibilities in copying with domestic violence.

It is important to understand the official reaction to domestic violence in its context as one part of a spectrum of familial problems as discussed elsewhere in this book. In the nineteenth and early twentieth centuries, child abuse, unless actually leading to death, was commonly not considered to be a subject for official attention. However, by the 1920s–30s or earlier, most states enacted statutes condemning excessive violence against children and the mentally infirm. Currently, societal attention has been placed on domestic violence (discussed here) and to a lesser extent, the problem of violence against the elderly and the infirm. However, the problem of nonviolent crime within the family discussed in different chapters of this book is viewed today much like domestic violence was ten years ago. That is, if there is any concern, it is as just one more example of family problems that need not be officially dealt with by the criminal justice system.

The new statutes, while differing profoundly in their scope and limitations, have as their predominant feature the announced purpose of making structural changes in the governmental response. Such changes have primarily been concentrated in three areas: the police response to domestic violence, the judicial response to criminal forms of domestic violence, and to a lesser extent, methods of providing state funding for shelters and other direct assistance to victims of domestic violence.

The concentration here is upon the mandated changes made upon the criminal justice system's response to domestic violence. The paper shall first examine the traditional police response to domestic violence and then review the various legislative responses thereto. Following this, the prosecutorial and judicial responses to domestic violence will be reviewed. Finally, preliminary analysis will be made to determine what impact such legislation has had and what additional changes, if any, should be contemplated.

In addition to being of relevance to those studying societal responses to domestic violence, this area may also be of interest to those studying legislative efforts to meaningfully change the criminal justice system by correcting the structural deficiencies allegedly preventing its proper performance.

As was shown in Chapter 5, criminal domestic violence is not the only crime problem experienced within families. There may be difficulties with the criminal justice system that are made salient when property crime is the issue. These problems may include the rules of testimony, police reactions to family crimes, and misdemeanors. To this date, such problems have still commonly been regarded as not being fit for official attention; e.g., they are "family problems," not legitimate societal concerns.

Police

The police and local law enforcement agencies have traditionally been the primary societal institutions intervening in domestic violence. Such agencies usually have the initial contact with violence-prone families as they provide free services, are highly visible authoritative figures, maintain central dispatch and are usually the only public agency in a position to provide rapid 24-hour a day assistance. In addition, police have historically been the primary gatekeepers for victims entering the criminal justice system. They initiate arrests, file reports justifying such action, and often are consulted in the determination of the disposition in forthcoming proceedings. Finally, contact with the violent family by local public and private agencies other than the police has traditionally been largely dependent upon police referrals or the surfacing of serious child abuse rather than the infrequent initiation of contact by the victim.

Although virtually all observers acknowledge the importance of the police role, it has been widely noted that past police practices have been of limited effectiveness. While response to purely criminal problems often results in apprehension of criminals or at least cessation of criminal activity, the police have been unsuccessful in altering the cycle of battering in violence prone familial units. One Police Foundation study on domestic violence in Kansas City and Detroit between 1971 and 1973 reported that the police were called to the location of a single previous domestic assault or homicide in 85 percent of the cases and four or more incidents in 50 percent of the cases (Wilt & Bannon, 1976).

Researchers have observed several major problems with the police response. They find that police intervention has tended to be perfunctory, limited to briefly separating the assailant from the abused party and sternly warning *both* that society doesn't tolerate "disturbances to the peace" (Parnas, 1967). In addition, numerous police departments have effectively limited their involvement in domestic violence through "call screening." This is a practice in which incoming calls are given a priority and those with the lowest priority, usually including simple assaults, do not have immediate dispatch of police units (Bannon, 1974). Finally, arrests have been an infrequent occurrence estimated at between 3 percent (Langley & Levy, 1977) and 10 percent of the total reported cases of domestic violence (Roy, 1979). As researchers have noted, they are reserved primarily to cases of disrespect or challenges to police authority. The degree of actual violence or threat of violence to the victim is often only of minimal significance (Black, 1980). The majority of departments even had explicit policies against making arrests in routine cases.

There are a number of reasons why police response has been quite ineffective. FIRST, police officers lack motivation for intervention. This lack of enthusiasm is understandable.

   a. Disturbance calls tend to be quite dangerous. FBI Uniform Crime Reports have consistently reported that these calls generate approximately 30 percent of reported assaults on police officers and 20% of officer deaths.

   b. Police do not believe it is their responsibility to intervene or "resolve" marital conflicts. Officers are comfortable with the crime fighter image and have tended to resist the social worker role which encompasses family conflict intervention (Parnas, 1967).

   c. The system of police rewards may inadvertently encourage indifferent police attitudes. Patrol officer evaluations stress the quantifiable; numbers of arrests, clearances for major crimes, and other performance measures are considered to be the appropriate performance indicators. Hence, when officers or teams of officers train in crisis intervention or spend significant time attempting to resolve conflict situations, their overall evaluations may actually suffer in comparison with those who tend to treat the situation cavalierly.

d. An officer responding to a call has little opportunity to determine if a family has been involved in similar acts of violence. Most acts of family violence go unreported, or if reported, are not systematically recorded by police departments even when a conviction later occurs. Therefore, repetitive spouse abuse may be thought to be an unusual occurrence not meriting arrest.

e. Police tend to be quite worried about civil liability. They are aware that victims of abuse have later supported the abuser's claims of police brutality.

f. Finally, and perhaps most importantly, the officers are acutely aware of the few domestic violence cases which ultimately result in prosecution. Complainants, being intimately involved with their assailant, in a variety of psychological and economic ways, have a very strong tendency to voluntarily dismiss complaints. Prosecutors and judges have also tended to treat such charges lightly, often refusing to prosecute or dismissing charges. Cases are usually difficult to prove given that most acts of violence occur without the presence of non-involved witnesses.

It may be noted that many of these same arguments tend to apply in situations involving nonviolent crime within the family partially explaining why so little official attention has been placed on that area.

SECOND, the sheer volume of domestic violence cases often represents a challenge to chronically understaffed, overworked departments. Disputes and disturbance calls are the single largest category of calls that police receive. Also, they tend to occur nights or weekends when criminal activity and traffic responsibilities invoke their greatest demands. As a result, it is not surprising that recurrent spouse abuse calls receive lower priority in such circumstances, at least absent knowledge of imminent threats to the victim's life.

THIRD, police have historically had little training on the causes or control of domestic abuse or the optimal police response to disturbance calls. For example, a study surveying police crisis intervention training, disclosed that in the late 1970s such training tended to be superficial and rudimentary, usually being restricted to one day of lectures for the entire topic of social conflicts including hostage situations, handling the mentally disturbed, coping with alcoholics, suicide, and child abuse as well as spousal violence (Buzawa, 1976). In one case, this single day's lecture was the only real exposure to all such topics in the entire six to eight week training program. In addition, until the late 1970s, virtually no police department had any continuing in-service training in this area.

FOURTH, police officers have had limited powers in handling domestic violence. One severe handicap facing officers was the statutory restriction that peace officers only had authority to make arrests for misdemeanors upon prior issuance of an arrest warrant or where the misdemeanor was committed in the officer's presence. This contrasted to statutes that authorized warrantless arrests where the officer had probable cause to believe a felony had been committed even though the officer was not present. Domestic violence has been usually characterized as simple assault, a misdemeanor, unless accompanied by aggravating circumstances such as use of a weapon, intent to commit murder or inflict grievous bodily harm, or sexual assault. As a result, police officers could not legally make an arrest unless violence continued in their presence or a previously existing warrant had been issued. Prior issuance of arrest warrants was never widely used to prevent future acts of domestic assault since they were tied to specific past conduct, were only valid for a short time, and required victim initiation and subsequent visits to the prosecutor's office to sign complaints.

Changes in the Police Response

As a result of growing awareness that police had been unable to cope with domestic violence, the statutes affecting their response have changed rapidly. Five such innovations have become widely instituted in recent years. FIRST, in many states *police powers have been increased.* They have been granted the authority to make misdemeanor arrests upon a determination of probable cause that a person committed certain illegal acts. Ten years ago, virtually no state gave officers such powers. However, by 1980, 23 states did and by 1983, 33 states and the District of Columbia had statutes broadening arrest powers (Lerman, et. al., 1983). Twenty-eight states currently allow an arrest under certain circumstances if there is probable cause to believe that the person committed a misdemeanor assault. Nineteen states permit a warrantless arrest with probable cause that a temporary restraining or protective order (described below) has been violated.

Although designed to correct the same statutory and behavioral deficiencies, such statutes vary considerably.[1] Six states provide for

---

[1]The scope, limitations and citations for such statutes are reported in greater detail in Lisa Lerman and Franci Livingston, "State Legislation on Domestic Violence," *Response,* Vol. 6, No. 5 (September/October, 1983).

mandatory arrest under certain circumstances such as violation of a temporary restraining order (TRO) or upon the probable cause that an aggravated assault had occurred. The other statutes give the officer discretion to make arrests if deemed appropriate. The legislative disparity in the mandating of arrests reflects the substantial dispute in existing literature as to the proper role of arrests in the overall police response to domestic violence. Sociologists who concerned with societal reaction (labeling) suggest that an undue emphasis on arrests may exacerbate abusive tendencies. As a result, the development of family crisis intervention teams tacitly urging mediation and discouraging arrests has been advocated (Bard, 1970). However, feminist groups have stated that such efforts failed to treat domestic violence as the criminal act that it would be treated as in any other context thus trivializing profoundly destructive antisocial behavior.

The only empirical study of the effect of postlegislation police practices was recently reported by Sherman and Berk (1983) as part of a Police Foundation study. Their preliminary analysis was that arrested individuals exhibited markedly less recidivism than those ordered to separate or those merely advised of their rights. However, such results are only preliminary at this time and in any event, rely upon official measures of recidivism. Such measures have historically been considered highly unreliable due to inconsistent police reporting practices. In addition, domestic violence cases may present an insurmountable problem for the use of official statistics. Many victims whose spouses or cohabitants were arrested may be reluctant to report further violence due to fear of even greater abuse or the very real economic risk they may face if an arrest ultimately results in a fine or jail sentence of the abuser.

A SECOND change, less widely adopted, has been to *increase the responsibility of police* when handling domestic violence calls. Eighteen statutes now require officers to inform the victim of her legal choices including the option of pressing arrest charges. Eleven require the police to transport the victim to the hospital or shelter if circumstances so require. Five statutes provide that the officer should stay until the victim is no longer in physical danger.

THIRD, there is a growing recognition that officers have legitimate reason to *obtain protection from civil liability* when handling domestic violence cases. Currently, seventeen states provide a certain degree of statutory immunity from suits for actions taken in good faith to enforce domestic violence statutes.

FOURTH, most new statutes address the real problems that police had in not knowing whether they were *responding to a chronically abusive family member* or a first offender. Twenty-nine states now provide for TROs to be automatically sent by the courts to the police department. Eighteen states further require the police department to formulate some procedure to inform the officer of the TROs, thereby identifying recidivistic families. In addition, eight states now require the development and maintenance of statistical reports on the incidence of domestic violence. Such reports are extremely useful to police departments in understanding the magnitude and severity of family violence in their service community.

FIFTH, fourteen states have mandated or "encouraged" the development or implementation of police domestic violence training programs. However, in our experience, the actual content of such training programs is not usually specified in any meaningful way, instead being left to the discretion of the training administrator. It appears that the content of the training program has a direct impact on the potential attitude change of officers. Unfortunately, our correspondence with program coordinators have found that many programs have continued to reflect traditional police biases against active police involvement in domestic violence and have spurned the assistance of feminist groups, those with different professional expertise (such as doctors, social workers, or executives from shelter programs) and those whose views challenge current police practices. As a result, there is the potential in many areas for such training to reinforce preexisting attitudes rather than effect actual change.

Behavioral Change by Police

It is difficult to determine whether police behavior has actually changed as a result of implementation of domestic violence statutes. There are few studies directly measuring behavioral change, and such results would be difficult to interpret since changing victim and societal attitudes toward family violence may profoundly affect arrest rates or other measure of police performance.

However, on the research arrest practices of the Detroit Police Department, before and after implementation of the Michigan domestic violence legislation (which removed impediments to misdemeanor arrest, encouraged greater police involvement, increased police training, made TROs available, etc.) found that while the officers expressed a growing willingness to arrest domestic violence offenders and a high awareness of their new ability to do so, this was not translated to any higher rate of arrest (Buzawa, 1982). In fact, departmental records indicated that officers responded to fewer domestic violence-related runs after the statute was enacted and made correspondingly fewer arrests. This was true even though available evidence did not suggest that the rate of incidence of domestic violence was decreasing. A companion attitudinal study showed that only those officers that had attended an intensive 24-hour training program expressed high levels of confidence in handling domestic violence or in the expressed willingness to make arrests in such cases.

This result has been supported by subsequent research in the State of New Hampshire where the key determinant of police attitudes appeared to be the quality of in-service training. In Michigan, a comprehensive in-service training program was developed through the joint efforts of numerous professionals in the field. The training program once developed, was enthusiastically supported by the administration of the Detroit Police Department. The reverse was generally true in New Hampshire Training which appeared to be primarily conducted by individuals either inexperienced with the criminal justice response to domestic violence or those holding nonsupportive views. In this context, unlike Michigan, training had little positive impact. Absent such training, most officers rejected the basic tenets of New Hampshire's new domestic violence statute. From this, the authors concluded that the removal of structural impediments to police performance or rudimentary training do not of themselves predict that actual behavior will markedly change (Buzawa and Buzawa, pending).

Prosecutorial and Judicial Response

Societal response to abusive families has also been limited by problems with the use of prosecutorial and judicial discretion to screen out domestic violence cases from the criminal justice system. Prosecution of arrested abusive individuals constitutes society's strongest intervention in abusive situations. When such stern measures are not followed, abusive individuals rapidly realize that the criminal justice system is not really concerned with their conduct. Several problems in this area have been isolated.

A. In the past, most domestic violence complaints have been voluntarily dismissed by prosecutors. For example, in Detroit in one year, out of 4,900 warrants issued for cases of domestic assault, fewer than 300 were ultimately tried (Bannon, 1975). A considerable number of these cases were admittedly dropped because of reconciliation, reformation of an abuser, or a plea negotiation in which the prosecutor extracted promises of future good conduct. However, according to Bannon, a significant reason for the marked attrition appears to have been prosecutorial antipathy toward these cases.

In addition, prosecutorial and judicial personnel have informally disposed of cases by delaying processing. For example, one practice has been the routine mandating of a cooling-off period before issuing a warrant. This mandatory period, often of two to seven days, tended to screen many cases before arrest warrants were even issued. After this, preliminary arraignments often took place much later, sometimes weeks after a complaint. For example, in one state preliminary arraignments regularly took place 6 to 8 weeks after the complaint was filed. A hearing was then held at least a month after the preliminary arraignment. The delay was at least partially intended to facilitate reconciliation and voluntary complaint withdrawal. The resulting procedure would then not be shown as a voluntary dismissal by the prosecutor even though prosecutorial actions greatly influenced the outcome.

Prosecutors have taken such actions for a variety of compelling reasons.

FIRST, there is a strong systemic bias towards diverting or dismissing new cases from the criminal justice system. Court dockets are overcrowded and prosecutorial staffs are overworked and underfunded. Domestic violence-related offenses constitute a major part of such workload. In fact, in one major city, Detroit, most of the warrant requests of the Misdemeanor Complaint Bureau were generated from acts of domestic violence (*Parnas*, 1967). Consequently, there has been a strong tendency to divert such cases. While this may be justifiable for many offenses, it is less so in the context of domestic violence since an individual that is arrested is rarely being arrested for his first offense.

SECOND, prosecutors along with police, know that a very high percentage of complaints are dismissed by victims during the course of prosecution. This tends to rationalize the prevalent cynicism often noted.

THIRD, prosecuting a criminal action is extremely difficult in domestic assault. Evidence proving beyond a reasonable doubt the unprovoked occurrence of an assault is difficult to obtain. Such conduct usually occurs at night when no other witnesses are present. If children do observe abuse, prosecutors and judges are reluctant to reveal testimony to spare them further trauma.

FOURTH, many prosecutors along with police question the underlying mandate of court action. They often express the belief that courts should not ordinarily intervene in family disputes. Such attitudes are not necessarily a chauvinistic denial of the pain that an abused victim feels. Instead, often there is a recognition that in many circumstances, arresting an abuser exacerbates an existing problem. Prosecutors have told us that on some occasions, husbands have become so enraged at a spouse or cohabitant initiating his arrest that the victim received an aggravated level of abuse despite police warnings, arrests, or even court orders to the contrary. The result is then an economically or psychologically dependent victim who has to resume living with an even angrier violent person. In addition, many prosecutors believe that processing such charges can have a dramatic deleterious effect on other family members.

FINALLY, because domestic violence cases are routine misdemeanors, prosecutors know that proper handling of such cases are not likely to enhance advancement. In fact, the reverse is often true. To the extent that a prosecutor with a mixed caseload spends time to adequately handle domestic violence cases, he/she will not be able to devote scarce resources to preparing more publicly visible cases or more serious (felony) offenses.

B. There has been a well noted inflexibility of the judiciary to adequately respond to those few cases that were reported and were ultimately scheduled for trial. Customarily, judges would dismiss or continue the case, issue a fine, or at most sentence the offender to a short period of probation. Customarily, there was little judicial cognizance of the need for rehabilitation programs and other non-criminal alternatives to supplement traditional criminal penalties or to deter future violence in families that had already initiated divorce proceedings.

This inflexibility is extremely significant due to the high esteem accorded by criminal justice professionals to the opinions of the judiciary. Early in the career of virtually every police officer and prosecutor, they have found cases dismissed or sanctions imposed for failing to accurately predict judicial attitudes. Thus such attitudes have tended to enforce existing attitudes and procedures of the police and prosecutors and encourage resistance to change.

Changes in the Legislative Response

Several legislative responses have been adopted to cope with the perceived problems with judicial functions including the widespread development of injunctive relief to prohibit future violence, the broadening of available remedies in domestic violence cases, and less often, measures to limit prosecutorial discretion.

One of the primary legislative changes in the response to domestic violence has been the development of statutorily authorized TROs. The ability to grant such orders has been a modern statutory innovation. Before the new domestic violence statutes were enacted, virtually no states granted injunctive relief prior to formal judicial proceedings. This was due to a historic reluctance to grant ex parte relief (relief when only one party to a dispute is present). The TRO lasts for a short duration — three days to ten days and in any event terminates when the other party has notice and an opportunity for hearing. By 1980, thirty-four states allowed judges to grant injunctive relief in abusive situations. By 1983, forty-three states and the District of Columbia allowed such relief.

The grounds for granting a TRO naturally vary greatly. However, three grounds have been adopted in virtually all modern statutes, orders for the defendant to: stop continued beating; stop threats of physical abuse; and temporarily move out of a common residence. The last order may be the most significant as it forces the abuser rather than the victim to bear the burden of finding another residence and establishes a clearly enforceable right, the violation of which may be easily documented.

In addition (as more fully described in Lerman, et al., 1983), TROs have been granted in several other circumstances: attempted physical abuse in 28 states and the District of Columbia; child custody and visitation rights in 33 states; temporary support, attorney fees or temporary division of property in 28 states; orders for the defendant to enter counseling in 23 states; and to prevent the abuser from contacting his victim in 16 states.

However, certain inexplicable restrictions on the use of protective orders that have often been adopted. For example, 14 statutes pertain only to spousal abuse, e.g., not covering common law marriages or cohabitation. This limitation is extremely serious. A recent study of 600 severely battered women found that 73 percent of the victims studied were single, divorced, or separated at the time of hospital admission (Stark, 1983). In addition, the degree of specificity of the procedure to issue, enforce and publicize the existence of TROs appears to vary greatly. It has been noted that the greater the degree of specificity, the more likely that law enforcement and judicial personnel treat the existence of the remedy seriously (Lerman, et. al., 1983).

SECOND, a number of states have broadened judicial powers to grant alternative sentences. In some legislation, the traditional reluctance of the judiciary to send abusive individuals to jail or prison has been directly addressed by adopting formal diversion programs. The archtypical procedure provides for several hearings. At the first hearing, the offender is admitted to the program and release is conditioned upon making various promises or paroles for future behavior. Mandatory psychological counseling of the individual or family unit is then provided as an adjunct. In the second hearing, the offender's compliance with diversion program requirements is determined, and if met, the offender's record is expunged. Typically such programs are only for offenders who consent and have no prior arrest record, the victim consents, and the court counselor believes the offender will benefit from treatment. In addition, other states have developed mediation systems or the use of warning letters explaining that complaints were received of illegal behavior and threatening prosecution upon recurrence.

THIRD, formal changes to criminal codes have been adopted in a few states. While every state generally prohibits assault and battery, eleven states now make spouse abuse a separate criminal offense. This was adopted to make court personnel more cognizant of the real differences between spousal violence and other assaults. It also allows the state to keep a better record of the incident of domestic violence. By differentiating domestic violence from other assaults, law enforcement personnel will hopefully be able to have greater knowledge of previous offenses and perhaps encourage more explicit and hence effective charges.

Finally, limits on the prosecutorial discretion have been imposed in several contexts. In most states that have adopted domestic violence statutes, requests for TROs or "protective orders" may be filed by the victims themselves. This attempts to indirectly address the problem of inappropriately exercised prosecutorial discretion. In addition, eleven states mandate that court personnel assist the victim in filing petitions while nineteen require a preparation of forms usable by law people. Finally, to prevent unnecessary delays, several states have given requests for TRO's priority over other civil actions expressly addressing past procedures that deliberately delayed hearings.

Despite this, few states have imposed mandatory duties on the prosecutor or judiciary in domestic violence cases. Where available, these have been limited to the highly specialized situations of handling claims of violations of existing TROs, providing assistance in preparing summons or arrest warrants, informing victims of their legal rights or forbidding "discouragement" of a person from filing a petition or signing a complaint. Only in the states of Washington and Utah has the inappropriate use of prosecutorial discretion been directly addressed. In these states, prosecutors must quickly notify victims of whether they will prosecute and of the availability of initiating private complaints.

At this time, there is no empirical study of whether the prosecutorial or judicial response has changed as a result of the new legislation. Unfortunately, we believe that such changes have not been widely accepted. Prosecutors still are subject to a crushing caseload burden, have little exposure to in-service training on domestic violence and, in conversations with us, continue to express substantial doubt as to the efficiency of criminal justice responses to the problems of spousal violence.

In addition, we have spoken with numerous directors of domestic violence shelters and state agencies in charge of coordinating official responses to domestic violence. They have stated that one continuing obstacle to achieving prosecutorial effectiveness is the traditionally high turnover of assistant district attorneys or prosecutors. This position has traditionally been occupied for several years by new attorneys prior to starting their primary career. This turnover, in addition to affecting overall competency, means that few have the ability to effectively assimilate the entire criminal code at the same time they are learning criminal procedure, effective trial tactics, etc. The result appears to be a tendency to concentrate on familiar and easier to prosecute offenses. Finally, this turnover minimizes the impact of any in-service training program, since unlike the police, it would need to be constantly repeated to cover all new prosecutors.

The logical method of handling the problem of excessive prosecutorial turnover (in the absence of a far reaching effort to cut turnover) would be the instituting of a career type position of staff paralegal or legal assistant specializing as a victim advocate. This person would then not only serve as an invaluable resource in the handling of cases, but could also serve as an effective vehicle for raising the consciousness of the relevant court officers.

CONCLUSION

There is currently a multiplicity of state statutes attempting to change the criminal justice system's traditional response to domestic violence. While six states have no modern statutes, others have enacted a variety of innovations, often with seeming unnecessary restrictions on their use. This confusing structure and the underlying failure to develop a national consensus as to the proper method of responding to domestic violence has perhaps encouraged criminal justice professionals to refuse to change previous ingrained behavior. Instead of focussing attention on the implementation of statutes in each state, it would appear to be preferable to enact federal domestic violence legislation, perhaps under the auspices of the recently created National Commission on Domestic Violence. Alternatively, we would advocate the establishment of a uniform or modern state domestic violence statute (presumably avoiding unnecessary restriction and incorporating the best features of the different statutes). Such efforts might encourage the development of a unified agency response to domestic violence.[2]

---

[2]It is the authors' understanding that currently Lisa Lerman is drafting a proposed model state code. This proposed code is presently scheduled to be published in the *Harvard Journal on Legislation*, pending, 1984.

Finally, the authors of the new statutory framework have generally provided an adequate understanding of existing structural impediments to agency action. In addition, the statutes have usually provided a high degree of understanding of what role the criminal justice system should play in the societal effort to limit domestic violence. However, the crucial missing ingredient appears to be the failure of such statutes to provide for an incentive structure or training that will bring about actual behavioral change. Such incentives might be placed in the statute or may be the practical outcome of sustained pressure by concerned professionals and/or feminist groups unwilling to accept token efforts at compliance or possible threats of lawsuits by legal advocacy groups. Absent such incentives, the crucial variable in actual behavior would be the attitudes of agency personnel. If these are not currently adequate, systemic change would be best effected in the long run by comprehensive preservice and inservice training programs, and as a necessary correlate, consistent support from the heads of the effected agencies.

REFERENCES

Bannon, J. (1974). *Social conflict assaults: Detroit, Michigan.* Unpublished report for the Detroit Police Department and the Police Foundation.

Bannon, J. (1975, August 12). *Law enforcement problems with intra-family violence.* Speech delivered to the American Bar Association, Montreal, Canada.

Bard, M. (1970). Training Police as specialists in family crisis intervention. *U. S. Department of Justice.*

Black, D. (1980). *The manners and customs of the police.* New York: Academic Press.

Buzawa, C., & Buzawa, E. (1979, May). Legislative responses to the problem of domestic violence in Michigan. *Wayne Law Review.*

Buzawa, E. (1976). *Survey of police crisis intervention training.* Unpublished manuscript.

Buzawa, E. (1982, December). Police officer response to domestic violence legislation in Michigan. *Journal of Police Science and Administration, 10*(4).

Langley, R., & Levy, R. C. (1977). *Wife beating: The silent crisis.* New York: E. P. Dutton.

Lerman, L. G. (1981). *Prosecution of spouse abuse: Innovations in criminal justice response.* Washington, DC: Center for Women Policy Studies.

Lerman, L. G., & Livingston, F. (1983, September/October). State Legislation on domestic violence. *Response, 6*(5).

Parnas, R. (1967). The police response to the domestic disturbance. *Wisconsin Law Review, 914,* 946.

Roy, M. (Ed.). (1977). *Battered women.* New York: Van Nostrand Reinholt Co.

Sherman, L. W., & Berk, R. A. (1980). Police responses to domestic assault: Preliminary findings. *Police Foundation Working Paper.*

Stark, E., & Flitcraft, A., et al. (1981). *Wife abuse in the medical setting.* A monograph published by the Office of Domestic Violence Department of Health and Human Services.

Wilt, M., & Bannon, J. (1976). *Domestic violence and the police: Studies in Detroit and Kansas City.* Washington, DC: The Police Foundation.

Part III
CRIME BY THE FAMILY

Whenever two or more members of the same family act together while committing an illegal act they are demonstrating what we have called crime *by* the family. In some cases the action may involve just two members of the family acting in consort while in other instances the entire family may be active participants. Crime by the family also varies in terms of its frequency. In some families the criminal behavior may be a one time occurrence—several members being drunk and disorderly following a wedding reception. At other times the criminal behavior may be repeated on a regular basis—two brothers involved in selling drugs. In extreme cases the family may resort to crime as their total means of livelihood.

This is not a new phenomenon. Although systematic research on the full range of these problems has been scanty, there have been some good historical and case materials. The tales of family crimes often are gruesome, including deeds such as those described by Brown (1969).

> ...there have been many examples of freelance multiple murderers in American history. The annals of crime in the United States abound with them. Among the earliest were the brutal Harpe brothers, Micajah (Big Harpe) and Wiley (Little Harpe), who in 1798–99 accounted for anywhere from about 20 to 38 victims in the frontier States of Kentucky and Tennessee. Dashing babies' brains against tree trunks. . . .
>
> Numerous freelance multiple murderers crop up, in the 19th century. Among them was the evil Bender family of southeastern Kansas. The Benders from 1871 to 1873 did away with at least 12 unwary travelers who had the bad judgment to choose the Bender roadside house for a meal or lodging. Eventually the Benders were detected but seem to have escaped into anonymity one jump ahead of a posse.

Brown describes these family generated crimes as freelance murders. That is, the perpetrators were not linked to any political or social organizations which facilitated their actions. Other historical examples include the "family feud" common to the southern Appalachian regions and the southwest. At times these feuds lingered for several generations involving dozens of participants and resulting in many casualties. Again, according to Brown (1969:46–7):

> The great feuds of Texas and the Southwest were strikingly similar to those of the southern Appalachians, were about as well known in their own day, and had similar origins. . . . not even the Hatfield-McCoy feud exceeded the length, casualties, and bitterness of the great Sutton-Taylor feud (1869–99) of DeWitt and Gonzales Counties, Texas. Among the major feuds of Central Texas were the Horrell-Higgins feud of Lampasas County (1876–77), the Jaybird-Woodpecker feud of Fort Bend County (1888–90), and the Stafford-Townsend-Reese-Hope feuds of Colorado County (1890–1906).
>
> One of the most devastating of family feuds involved the Graham and Tewksbury families of Arizona. This feud between "cattle men" and "sheep men" was "fought, like the title phrase from Zane Grey's novel of the vendetta, "to the last man." Only with the lone survivor of the two families did it come to an end.

Although we are treating feuding in Part III, which is on crimes *by* the family, feuds also illustrate the topic of Part IV—crimes *against* a family. Family feuds were classic examples of activities in which most or all family members participated. Several generations would at times be involved. This pattern of multigenerational criminal activity still exists in areas other than feuding. A recent case in point involves the arrest of three generations of a family on drug charges:

> An ailing 86-year-old man known as "Gramps" and two members of his family pleaded innocent yesterday to charges they sold marijuana to supplement their Social Security income.
>
> "We had no choice. They were dealing and we had to arrest them just like anyone else," said Lt. Richard Sproules, who added that the suspects were treated "with respect" because of their advanced age.
>
> Arthur of 9 Harrison Ave., his daughter Jean, 63, and her 18-year-old son, Walter, were arrested at their home Saturday. Police allege they netted about $200 a week from sales of the illegal weed to eke out their social security benefits.
>
> Jean said in interview Monday that she couldn't live on her $400 Social Security check, and said they were under other pressures as well (AP, 1/18/83). (Last names have been deleted.)

CHAPTER 9. The first chapter in this section "The family as a criminal group" again uses data generated by the authors' surveys of college students. This portion of the data describes the delinquent and criminal activities of the respondent committed along with another family member. Like the drug case described above, we found both same-generation and multigeneration activity. While it is true that more deviance tended to occur with friends than with family members, a substantial amount of illegal behavior was committed by family members acting together.

CHAPTER 10 deals with the relationship between the amount of violence within the home and the rate of crime and violence outside the home. Straus's study of a student sample, and also a large and nationally-representative sample, show that children (particularly boys) who were hit by their parents tended to have higher rates of vandalism and violence outside the home. The importance of both the modeling effect of violence as well as the experience of being a victim are considered. In either case, socialization into patterns of violence appears to be significant.

CHAPTER 11. Cressey's early (1930s) research on the "Criminal Tribes in India" also highlights the socialization process as well as the salience of structural features of a society. This study is important because it shows that "crime may be a problem not of individual demoralization, but of group traditions. These tribes are hereditary groups that specialize in different types of crime." Cressey provides a description of the different types of criminal tribes and their activities.

Perhaps the best known early study of criminal families is Dugdale's famous study of the Jukes family, done in the mid 1870s. This study is particularly interesting because it also illustrates the fact that descriptive research, although an essential starting point, cannot substitute for research which tests a hypothesis by experimentation or by correlational methods. Without the latter type of analysis (which is what distinguishes modern social science from the work done earlier), there is no reasonable way to decide between various explanations of the high rate of criminality in the Jukes family:

> Dugdale conducted a study of county jails in the state and was struck by the frequency with which he encountered a certain family name. Dugdale expanded his study, gathering what data he could concerning the background of this family—christened Jukes for the sake of anonymity. He concluded that the congenital inadequacy of this family—its immorality, criminality, idiocy, and insanity—had cost the state of New York over a million and a quarter dollars. But to Dugdale and most of his contemporaries, these alarming results did not provide a brief for eugenic marriage laws or compulsory sterilization. They made, on the contrary, an urgent plea for environmental reform. That the Jukes's antisocial traits could be inherited dramatized the need for immediate reform of the conditions in which they lived; otherwise, drinking, narcotics addiction, poor moral and hygenic surroundings would not simply menace one generation but would contaminate as well all succeeding generations.

By the 1880s and early 1900s, however, this attitude had begun to change.

Dugdale's optimistic use of hereditarian arguments to bolster his melioristic position had been transformed into a defensive and hostile emphasis on the deterministic aspects of heredity. But a few short decades after Dugdale's work, many students of heredity were calling for the sterilization of the unfit—and no longer with enthusiasm for environmental reform (Rosenberg, 1966).

CHAPTER 12. Dugdale's attempt to show the family link with crime was not only of passing historical interest. Recent studies, using more sophisticated methods, also examine this relationship. In the Farrington et al. chapter on "The Familial Transmission of Crime," the records of young males were examined over a period of years to see if "criminal records run in families." The importance of having a parent with a criminal record, a sibling with a criminal record, and the clustering of crime with certain families were examined. Various explanations for the positive findings included closer surveillance by police once a family member was convicted and the possibility that older siblings serve as models for younger siblings. The first explanation points to the importance of societal reactions to crime as a determinant of subsequent crime, while the latter emphasizes the socialization process and the dynamics of the family itself.

REFERENCES

Brown, R. M. (1969). Historical patterns of violence in America. In Graham, & Gurr, *Violence in America.* New York: Signet Books.

Rosenberg, C. E. (1966). Science and American social thought. In D. Van Tassel, & M. G. Hall (Eds.), *Science and society in the United States* (pp. 137–184). Dorsey, 1966.

Rosenberg, C. E. (1966). Scientific theories and social thought. Reprinted in B. Barnes (Ed.), *Sociology of science*, 1972, Baltimore, MD: Penguin Books.

CHAPTER 9

THE FAMILY AS A CRIMINAL GROUP

MURRAY A. STRAUS AND ALAN JAY LINCOLN

The chapters in section II clearly show that a great deal of crime goes on within families. In fact, as we said there, if one is going to be a victim of a criminal act, the chances are much greater that the "criminal" will be another member of your own family than a stranger.

This chapter is concerned with another way that families might be involved in crime. It reports a study of the extent to which families, *as a group,* carry out crimes against people *outside* their family. This may seem like such a rare and odd event that it raises the question of why we thought it was worth investigating. There are at least three reasons.

The most general reason is the skeptical view that sociologists tend to adopt toward all social institutions. Being skeptical about things that are usually taken for granted is part of the professional heritage of the discipline. Rather than relying on "common sense" (which is another way of saying "relying on the established way of looking at things"), sociologists try to look beneath the surface to see if they can discover important aspects of an institution such as the family that are not what they might seem to be.

A second reason for deciding to investigate crimes carried out by families is the idea that the family, like other institutions of a society, tends to reflect and reinforce key aspects of the society. Thus, if the society tends to be bellicose and violent, this point of view leads to the hypothesis that the family will also be violent. This is clearly consistent with the findings of the research on family violence, including cross-cultural research (Archer and Gartner, 1984; Montague, 1978; Straus, 1977). Similarly, if crimes against strangers are common in a society, that suggests the possibility that the family will also be engaged in crime against strangers or acquaintances.

A final reason why it might be useful to study the family as a criminal group is that people tend to look to other members of their family for companionship and aid in whatever they are doing. It is widely believed that you can trust another member of your own family more than you can trust anyone else. So if someone is looking for a trustworthy person with whom to engage in a new business, it seems reasonable to think that family members will be high on the list, regardless of whether that enterprise is legal or illegal.

THE METHODS USED TO LOCATE AND STUDY "CRIMINAL FAMILIES"

The Families Studied

The data on criminal activities of families in this chapter is based on information about the same 437 families described in Chapter 4. The questionnaire described earlier covered several topics, including a series of questions about crimes the students who completed the questionnaire engaged in during the last year they lived at home before going to college.

"Self-report" studies of juvenile delinquency were pioneered by Nye and Short in the 1950s (Nye and Short, 1957). The idea of getting information about delinquency by having children complete a questionnaire was an important technical innovation in criminology, and there have been many "self-report" studies of juvenile delinquency since Nye and Short's pioneering work (Hindelang, Hirshi, and Weis, 1981).

Self-report studies of crime have two main advantages. First, they include crimes that only the person committing the crime knows about. Official statistics on crime, with the possible exception of murder and auto theft, are always incomplete because a large percentage of crimes never get reported to the police. The second advantage of interview data on crime arises because, even when a crime is reported to the police, information about the person committing the crime is usually sketchy or nonexistent. But self-report studies almost always include detailed information about the person who completed the questionnaire. This makes it possible to investigate many more questions about what factors are related to criminal behavior than can be investigated using official crime statistics.

How Crimes by Families Were Identified

The questionnaire included the usual social background information about the respondent. In addition, the study we are describing is unique because, for each crime in the questionnaire, we asked whether it had been committed together with someone else, and who that person was. When the person was a member of the same family as the respondent, we counted that an instance of a family group engaging in crime (see Chapter 1 for a discussion of the pros and cons of this procedure).

The questionnaire included a list of 18 criminal acts. The list is deliberately diverse. Some of them—such as "Stole money using force"—

are serious crimes. They are classified as felonies, and conviction can result in a prison sentence. Others, such as "used illegal drugs," are the subject of considerable controversy. In some states they are classified as among the most serious crimes, and in other states they are classified as a minor crime. In all states there is wide disagreement over whether to classify drug use as a crime; and about how serious a crime.

HOW OFTEN DO FAMILY MEMBERS COMMIT A CRIME TOGETHER?

Criminals All?

Ninety six percent of the students in this sample reported committing one or more of the 18 crimes in our list. Looking down the first column of figures in Table 9-1 shows that the more serious the crime, the less often it occurred. That is hardly surprising. What is surprising is how many of the students in this sample committed *serious* crimes. The second row of Table 9-1 shows that just over one out of three of the college students in this sample had engaged in one or more of the five serious crimes listed at the end of Table 9-1.

We consider these to be extremely high rates for three reasons. First, even though we promised anonymity, it would be remarkable if everyone who answered these questionnaires "told all." Second, these rates are many times greater than the rates for crimes known to the police (as given in the Uniform Crime Reports) for the comparable crimes such as rape ("Forced someone to perform sexual acts") and robbery ("Stole money using force"). Third, these were crimes committed by a group of which is generally regarded as least prone to delinquency—high school seniors from unbroken homes who intend to go to college. Finally, we asked only about crimes committed during the senior year in high school. Had we asked whether the crime had ever been committed, the rate might have been considerably higher.

Although the high rate of crime by these students is important, we will not consider it further because we want to turn to the main focus of this chapter: crimes committed by a family *group*.

Crimes with Other Family Members

The second and third columns of Table 9-1 give the data on the key issue of this chapter: what is the extent of crime carried out by family groups? These two columns use somewhat different methods to answer this question.

PERCENT OF ALL STUDENTS OR FAMILIES. The first method, as given in the middle column of Table 9-1, takes as the starting point all

Table 9-1. Crime Rates, Overall, With Family Members,
And Percent That Crime By Family Groups Is of All Crimes Reported.

Crime	% Of Students Who Offended Once Or More	% Of Students Who Offended Jointly With Family Member	% Of Offenders Who Offended Jointly With Family Member*
Any of the 18 crimes	95.7	55.8	58.3
Serious crimes only	34.3	5.7	16.6
Drove without a license	63.5	27.2	42.8
Drinking while under age	87.6	48.5	55.4
Used illegal drugs	57.2	18.5	32.4
Altered or used false ID	31.3	6.6	21.1
Skipped school	68.9	12.8	18.6
Violated traffic law	66.1	29.3	44.3
Punched non-family member	38.9	7.6	19.5
Made obscene or threatening phone calls	15.8	3.2	29.3
Intentionally damaged property	35.9	4.6	12.8
Stole something worth less than $50	40.3	6.4	15.9
Stole money without using force	19.5	1.4	7.2
Signed someone elses name to something	35.2	6.0	17.0
Beat up non-family member	22.2	4.1	18.5
Forced someone to perform sexual acts	3.4	0.2	5.9
Stole something worth more than $50	7.8	0.5	6.4
Stole money using force	0.7	0.0	0.0
Sold property respondent had stolen	7.3	0.7	9.6
Broke into a building	14.6	0.9	6.2

* The figures in this column are the percent that the rates shown in the middle column is of the rates given in the first column.

the students who participated in the survey. The figures in this column are the percent of all students who had engaged in a crime together with another member of their family. Since each student represents a family, this method can also be thought of as measuring the percent of families who engage in crime, but that is an underestimate because it leaves out crimes by family groups which did not include the student—crimes committed jointly by the parents, for example.

PERCENT OF OFFENDERS. The column on the right side of the table takes offenders as the starting point, i.e., only the part of the sample who committed the crime. The figures in this column are the percent of offenders who committed the crime jointly with another member of their own family. This was computed by dividing the middle column of Table 9-1 by the first column. The resulting figure is the percentage of youthful offenders who carried out the crime jointly with another member of the same family.

If everyone in the sample had committed the crime, then the middle column and the right hand column would be identical because, since everyone is an offender, there would be no difference between the number of students and the number of offenders. This is very nearly the situation in respect to the first row of the table ("Any of the 18 crimes") since just about everyone in the sample had committed at least one of these crimes. However, the "Serious crimes" tabulated in the second row were committed by "only" 34 percent of the sample, so the percentages in the middle column and the right column can and do differ. The middle column shows that 5.7 percent of the students in this sample had engaged in a serious crime together with another member of their family. The right-hand column shows that, of those who engaged in a serious crime, 16.6 percent did it together with another member of their family.

INCIDENCE RATES. Our hypothesis was that the rate for crimes carried out by family groups would be high, although we had no basis for predicticing how high. The actual figures turned out to be extremely high. The first row of Table 9-1 shows that a majority of the crimes carried out by high school seniors are family crimes in the sense that they were committed by a group who were members of the same family.

SERIOUS CRIME. Of course, most of the family crimes, like most of the nonfamily crimes committed by these students, were petty crimes; and some of them are crimes which criminologists already know are often done as part of a group (such as underage drinking and driving without a license). Therefore, the more unique and important data are to be found in the second row of Table 9-1, and in the last six rows of that table. These give the figures on serious crimes.

The last six rows of the table show the rates separately for each of the serious crimes included in the survey. All but the rate for assault ("beat up nonfamily member") are low.

The second row of the table summarizes the rates for the six serious crimes in a single index. The summary index shows that about one out of 20 of these students (5.7%) had committed a serious crime in collaboration with another member of their own family. Of those who committed a serious crime, about one out of six (16.6%) did so as part of a family group.

The rates for serious crimes by the family, although low relative to other crime, should not be regarded as trivial because they are high in an absolute sense, and high relative to the rate for crimes reported in the National Crime Survey (NCS), and even higher when compared with the Uniform Crime Reports (UCR) of crimes known to the police. For example, the NCS reports a rate of 9.6 per 1,000 for aggravated assault, whereas the rate shown in Table 9-1 for the closest equivalent—"Beat up"—is 4.1 percent, which is the same as 41 per 1,000, and is therefore over

4 times greater than the NCS rate. Similarly, the incidence of rape is 1 per 1,000 in the NCS, but the students in this survey forced sex on someone in collaboration with another family member at double that rate. However, it is important to remember that, for the reasons given in Chapter 4, it is not possible to make precise comparisons between the rates from this study and either the NCS or the UCR. For example, as pointed out earlier, the rates in Table 9-1 are more like rates for *criminals*, rather than for *crimes* (as in the NCS and UCR), because we counted families in which these acts occurred rather than the number of times they occurred.

SERIOUS CRIME RELATIVE TO ANY CRIME. Although the previous paragraph indicates that serious crimes carried out jointly with other family members cannot be dismissed as inconsequential, the contrast between the rates for "Any of the 18" crimes and serious crimes also needs to be emphasized. The much lower rate for serious crimes reflect two things. First and most obviously, there is less serious crime by anyone, and this applies to both crimes carried out by individuals and family groups. Second, and more important for the purpose of this book, the lower rate of serious crimes by family groups is not just a reflection of the fact that serious crime occurs less often than petty crime. The rate for serious crime in general (34.3) is about a third of the rate for "any crime" (95.7). But the rate of serious crime by family groups (5.7%) is only a tenth of the rate for any crime (55.8%).

The right hand column of Table 9-1 indicates still more clearly that family groups have an even lower rate of serious crime than do individuals. Of the total number of serious offenders in the sample, only 16.6 had committed the offense in collaboration with other members of their family. Overall, the findings in Table 9-1 lead to the conclusion that there is a very high rate of crime carried out by the family—both minor crime and serious crime. However, Table 9-1 also shows that crimes by family groups tend to be less serious types of crime as compared to crimes by individuals, and that puts a different light on the "criminality" of family groups.

WHO ARE THE PARTNERS IN CRIME?

Up to this point we have used the terms "crimes by the family" and "crimes committed in collaboration with other family members" without indicating who those other family members are. Our hypothesis is that siblings would predominate, and especially same-sex siblings. But, as Table 9-2 shows, no one predominates. We find it startling and remarkable that parents and children are jointly involved in crime as often as these figures indicate, and regard this as an issue which urgently needs to be studied.

Table 9-2. Sex Differences In Family Group Crime.

Other Family Member Involved	Percent Of:	
	males	females
Brother	41.2	38.1
Sister	36.8	45.1
Father	39.5	45.1
Mother	33.8	44.4

SOCIAL CLASS AND SEX DIFFERENCES IN CRIME BY FAMILY GROUPS

Social Class

Official statistics based on crimes known to the police show that far more crimes are committed by and against low socioeconomic status (SES) persons than those higher in SES. As we pointed out in Chapter 4, there is considerable controversy over whether those statistics accurately portray the situation. There is evidence that the police are more likely to arrest or report crimes by low status persons than by high status persons. To the extent that this is true, the social class difference in official crime statistics reflect a difference in the behavior of the police more than a difference in the criminal behavior of people in different SES groups. Our study of crimes *within* the family (see Chapter 4) is consistent with that point of view because we found no differences between SES groups in the rate of within-family crime.

Does this also apply to crimes *by* family groups? Just because there are no important SES group differences for crimes within the family does not necessarily mean that there are no class differences in respect to crimes by family groups. The two situations are different. For example, people tend to be more tolerant of violent acts between family members (such as a husband slapping his wife) than they are of violent acts between unrelated people (such as one professor slapping another). Despite this possibility, we found no consistent or important differences between social class groups in respect to the percent of the sample who engaged in a crime jointly with another member of his or her family. This applies to both petty crime and serious crime.

Sex Differences

Comparing the males in this sample with the females, we found remarkably few differences. Taking all crimes, both petty crime and serious crime, committed jointly with another member of the family, the percentages are the reverse of those for crimes known to the police since they show a higher rate for the females: 52 percent of the male students as compared to 61 percent of the female students. Thus females have a rate that is about 17 percent *higher* than the rate for the males in this sample, but this is not a large difference and it is not statistically significant ($p < .07$). On the other hand, if the comparison is restricted to *serious* (the six crimes listed at the bottom of Table 9-1), the rates are four and a half times higher for the males than the females: 9 percent of the males, compared to two percent of the females, engaged in one or more of these crimes jointly with another member of their family, and the difference is statistically significant ($p < .01$). This sex difference is almost entirely due to a greater tendency of males to engage in violence (beating up, or forcing a sex act on a nonfamily member) in collaboration with another family member.

Sex by Class Interactions

We also compared low, middle, and high socioeconomic status group families to see if the same pattern of sex differences prevailed within each of the three SES groups. The results for the middle and high SES groups are essentially the same as for the sample as a whole—much higher rates of serious violent crime by males, but except for those crimes, no important differences between males and females in respect to the percentage who committed crimes together with another member of their family.

For the low SES part of the sample, however, there were a number of differences in the rates for the males as compared to the females. These are shown in Table 9-3. Since the sample included only 38 males and 20 females from low SES families, there was no point to computing tests of significance because, with those small numbers, none of the differences would be statistically reliable. Instead, we decided to include in Table 9-3 any nonserious crime, provided the rate for one sex was at least ten percentage points higher than the rate for the other sex, or was at least double the rate for the other sex.

As already noted, because of the small number of cases, none of these differences are statistically reliable when taken one by one. This means that we cannot have confidence in the differences because, with a small sample, there is too great a risk that the differences between the males

Table 9-3. Sex Differences In Family Group Crime, For Low SES Families.

Crime	Percent Of:	
	males	females
Drinking while under age	39.5	50.0
Used illegal drugs	31.6	15.0
Altered or used false ID	10.5	5.0
Skipped school	13.2	5.0
Violated traffic law	26.3	15.0
Punched non-family member	10.5	0.0
Intentional damaged property	7.9	0.0
Stole something worth less than $50	10.5	0.0
Stole money without using force	2.6	0.0

and females could occur by chance. However, the sex differences shown in Table 9-3 follow such a consistent pattern that they are worth considering further. Let us assume then that these are real differences (as compared to just random fluctuations). What could account for the fact that we find a pattern of sex differences among students from low SES families, but little or no difference between the sexes among students from middle and high SES families?

One possible explanation is based on the fact there is a greater "differentiation of roles" between the sexes in lower SES families as compared to middle-class families (Blood and Wolfe, 1960; Rubin, 1976; Scanzoni, 1980; Young and Wilmot, 1973). In lower-class families, there is a greater tendency for men to associate with men and women with women; and a greater tendency for activities to be divided up into things that "men do" and that "women do," as compared to activities that either might do, or joint activities. Thus, more middle-class than working-class men share in traditional female household tasks, and conversely, politics (a traditional male sphere) is more often an interest of middle-class women than working-class women. This pattern of sex role differentiation may apply to crime as well as to housework and politics. Traditionally, crime rates for men are many times greater than those for women. As in other spheres of life, it seems that working-class families adhere more closely to those traditional sex roles in respect to crime as well as in respect to other activities.

SUMMARY AND CONCLUSIONS

This chapter gave the results of an exploratory study of crimes carried out by groups of family members. Whenever two or more members of a family committed a crime together, we counted that as an instance of crime *by* the family. Using this definition, over half of the families of the 437 students we studied can be said to have committed a crime. Most were minor rather than serious crimes, and some were "status offenses" such as skipping school (13%), underage drinking (49%), or driving without a license (27%). Other crimes which were often done as a member of a family group, while not felonies in most instances, are less easy to dismiss. They include vandalism (5%), obscene phone calls (3%), theft of less than $50 (6%), and forgery (6%). Finally, during the year they were high school seniors, about 6 percent of the students in this sample had committed a serious crime in collaboration with another family member. The most common serious crime by a family group was assault (4%), but the list included rape and theft of more than $50, sale of stolen property, and breaking and entering.

In addition to getting a rough idea of how much crime is committed by family groups, we looked into who made up these groups, and into differences in the rates for males and females. Our hypothesis was that the family groups engaging in crime together would mainly be siblings, and especially those of the same sex; and that male students would have a higher rate of crime in collaboration with other family members than females. However, to our surprise, neither of these hypotheses was supported. Siblings of the opposite sex, and even parents, were involved in crimes with our sample about as often as siblings of the same sex. Although the males had a much higher rate of carrying out assaults together with another family member than did the females in this sample, there were no important differences between the sexes in respect to the other crimes.

Finally, we tested the hypothesis that the lower the socioeconomic status of the family, the greater the tendency to engage in crime together with another family member. This hypothesis was also *not* supported. However, we did find that when the SES of the family is taken into consideration, an important sex difference is revealed. The hypothesis of greater male than female criminality was found to characterize the low SES families, but not the middle and the high SES families. It seems that working-class families are characterized by traditional sex roles in respect to crime as well as in respect to other activities.

REFERENCES

Archer, D., & Gartner, R. (1984). *Violence & crime in cross-national perspective.* New Haven: Yale University Press.

Blood, R. O., & Wolfe, D. M. (1960). *Husbands & wives: The dynamics of married living.* Glencoe, IL: Free Press.

Hindelang, M. J., Hirschi, T., & Weis, J. G. (1981). *Measuring delinquency.* Beverly Hills: Sage.

Montague, A. (1978). *Learning non-aggression.* Oxford: Oxford University Press.

Nye, F. I., & Short, J. F. (1957). Scaling delinquent behavior. *American Sociological Review, 22,* 326–331.

Rubin, L. B. (1976). *Worlds of pain: Life in the working-class family.* New York: Basic Books, Inc.

Scanzoni, J., & Szinovacz, M. (1980). *Family decision-making.* Beverly Hills: Sage.

Straus, M. A. (1977). Societal morphogenesis and intrafamily violence in cross-cultural perspective. *Annals of the New York Academy of Sciences, 285,* 717–730.

Young, M., & Wilmont, P. (1973). *The symmetrical family.* London: Routledge & Kegan Paul.

FOOTNOTES

[1]However, these figures may be underestimates because the data was gathered for only one member of the family: a child that happened to be in college. We have information about criminal acts by other members of these families only if they were committed with the student who answered our questionnaire. For example, a crime that a brother committed with another brother, or with the father or mother would not be included in our questionnaire.

We did not include questions on crimes by other members of the family for two reasons. First, it would make an already long questionnaire intolerable. Second, and more important, the data would be highly questionable. Criminal acts are often carried out secretly. We did not think it was reasonable to expect that the students we surveyed would know about crimes committed by their parents or their brothers and sisters, unless the student was a participant in that crime.

CHAPTER 10

FAMILY TRAINING IN CRIME AND VIOLENCE*

Murray A. Straus

FAMILY PATTERNS AND DEVIANT BEHAVIOR

It is a cliche to point out that society depends on families to adequately socialize each new generation. It is almost as much of a cliche to point out that some families fail to train their children to be adequate members of society. The idea implicit in the second of these statements is what can be called a "socialization deficit" theory of deviance. That is, children "go wrong" because of things that families have NOT done or done poorly; for example, not enough love or not enough guidance.

Important as socialization deficits may be in explaining deviance, they are far from the whole story. There are a number of other ways in which family experience can lead to deviant behavior. For example, the level of conflict in some families (even those providing adequate food, clothing, shelter, love, and guidance) may be demoralizing. Or families may present the child with such contradictory expectations that he or she can only escape through schizophrenic fantasy—the famous "double bind" theory of schizophrenia. In these two examples, it is not what families do not do, but what they do, that makes for deviance.

Families can also provide role models for deviant behavior, or sometimes even explicitly teach deviance. The so-called "criminal castes" of India are a clear, even if somewhat unusual, example. These are castes which had a specific type of crime as their hereditary occupation. At the other extreme are situations in which modeling of deviant behavior is unintentional and not even realized by the parents.

The analysis to be presented in this paper is based on the assumption that the use of physical force by parents in dealing with children, and by spouses in dealing with each other, inadvertently trains the participants in such a family to engage in violence and other criminal acts outside the family. This assumption is consistent with the early work of Glueck and Glueck (1950). However, subsequent research has produced inconsistent results. Some studies find little or no relationship between child abuse and aggression or delinquency (for example, Elmer, Evans and Reinhart,

164

1977; Morse, Sahler and Friedman, 1970). Other research suggests that some abused children become withdrawn rather than aggressive (George and Main, 1979; Martin and Beezley, 1974). It is very likely that the link between family violence and criminal behavior is contingent on a number of other factors (Bolton, Reich and Gutierres, 1977; McCord, 1979). Clearly this is a complicated and important issue that needs further investigation.

SAMPLE AND METHOD

Hypothesis

This study to be reported used survey data to test the hypothesis that there is a correlation between the amount of violence within the family and the rate of crime and violence outside the family. It is important to note that if the hypothesis is supported, it strengthens the case for the underlying theory from which the hypothesis was derived, but does not prove it, since the same results could be produced by other causal processes.

Method

The method to be used to test the hypothesis is a secondary analysis of data from two cross-sectional surveys. In both surveys the independent variables (family violence) and the dependent variables (nonfamily violence and crime) are for the same one year referent period. Consequently, although the data can be used to test the hypothesis that persons from violent families have a higher crime rate than others, as indicated above, the causal processes and the causal direction (if any) underlying such a correlation cannot be established. Despite this limitation, the importance of the issue, combined with the paucity of previous research, and the contradictory findings of what little research there is, makes it worthwhile to examine the issue with this data.

Different methods were used to obtain the data on family violence and on crime in the two studies. If these different methods were to be described at this point, the details of each procedure would be difficult to recall when the results are presented. Consequently, it is probably best to simply indicate that all data come from either interviews or questionnaires, and that the specific techniques will be described in the sections of the paper where the incidence rates for each aspect of crime and violence are presented.

Samples

STUDENT SAMPLE. The data for the first study was obtained through questionnaires distributed in introductory sociology and anthropology classes at a state university in New England. The questionnaire asked about family characteristics and about conflict in the family that occurred during their senior year in high school (which in many cases was only two months earlier). The questionnaire was anonymous and voluntary (although completed during the class period). Of the 583 questionnaires distributed, 95.2 percent or 555 were completed. However, the number of cases for analyses which require data on both parents is 385 because the remaining students were not living with both parents that year. Data is available for this sample on intrafamily violence by both the parents and the respondents (see Straus, 1974), but the crime data is restricted to the respondents.

An obvious limitation of the student sample is that it describes only unbroken families with a child in college. Such families and their children are far from representative. For example, since all are attending college, they may be more adequately functioning individuals and families than a representative cross section. Consequently, descriptive statistics on intrafamily violence and on crime by these students are likely to be underestimates. Nevertheless, a great deal of family violence and nonfamily crime was reported. Moreover, the central issue of this paper is not the amount of family violence or the amount of crime, but the question of whether these are correlated. Consequently, since a correlation is not affected by the absolute level of the two variables, valid results are possible, even if the two variables are each severely underestimated (Straus, 1970: 572–573), provided there is no "interaction" between the reasons for the underestimate and either the independent or dependent variable.

THE NATIONAL SAMPLE. Data for the second study come from personal interviews with a national probability sample of 2,143 families. This is also not entirely representative of American families because single parent households were excluded. However, comparison with census data on husband-wife families show a close correspondence.

The respondent was the husband for a random half of the national sample, and the wife for the other half. Contrary to our original expectations, the rates of family violence based on interviews with husbands corresponded almost exactly with rates computed from data from interviews with wives. Further information on the characteristics of the sample, and a table showing correspondence between husband and wife data for a number of variables is in Straus, Gelles, and Steinmetz, 1980.

INCIDENCE OF FAMILY VIOLENCE

Measures of Family Violence

The student sample data on violence was obtained using an early version of the Conflict Tactics Scale (CTS). The national sample data is based on a revised version. The later revision includes additional items designed to measure serious assaults; specifically beating up, and use of a knife or gun. Consequently, for the national sample, two violence rates will be reported: a minor violence rate and a severe violence rate. The former is roughly comparable to simple assault, and the latter to aggravated assault. However, for the student sample, only an overall violence rate will be reported. A complete description of the CTS, including the items in both versions, scoring methods, and reliability and validity data is given elsewhere (Straus, 1979; 1981a).

Intrafamily Assault Rates

In view of the space limitations of a journal article, and in view of the fact that most of the data on family violence in these two samples has been reported elsewhere (Straus, 1974; Straus, Gelles, and Steinmetz, 1980), only a brief summary will be presented.

COUPLE VIOLENCE. The spousal violence data in the first two columns of the first row of Table 10-1 show that, irrespective of whether the data come from interviews with the husbands and wives themselves, or from questionnaires completed by a child in college, there is agreement on a remarkably high annual incidence of violence. Rates of 161 and 156 per 1,000 mean that amost one out of eight couples experienced one or more violent incidents during the year.

The next two rows of Table 10-1 show that both the spouses themselves and their children agree in reporting that violence by wives against husbands is about as common as violence by husbands against wives.[*1]

SEVERE COUPLE VIOLENCE. The severe violence measure can be thought of as roughly comparable to aggravated assaults in the UCR or the National Crime Survey. It is available only for the national sample. The rates on "severe violence" are shown in the right column of Table 10-1.

The UCR aggravated assault rate is approximately 190 per 100,000, and the National Crime Survey rate is about 2,600. But the severe violence rate for the national sample (after multiplying by 100 to make it per 100,000) is 6,100 or about two and a half times higher than even the National Crime Survey rate.

VIOLENCE BY TEENAGERS. The data on intrafamily violence by teenage children in the national sample are not directly comparable to the

Table 10-1. Intra-family Violence Rates per 1,000 Couples or Children

	Annual Violence Rate*		
Family Relationship	Student Sample: Total	National Sample: Total	Severe
Couple	161	156	61
Husband-to-wife	108	120	38
Wife-to-husband	107	115	46
Parent-to-child**	293	337	57
Child-to-parent**	135	91	34
Child-to-child**	563	571	308

* The "total" violence rate was computed by counting as violent anyone who engaged in one or more of the violent acts in the Conflict Tactics Scale (Straus, 1979; 1981). The "severe violence" rate was computed in the same way, but is restricted to violent acts which were judged to carry with them a high risk of producing serious injury (see text). Consequently, the two should not be added because the severe violence incidents are already included as part of the total violence index.

** For the student sample, the data refer to children in their senior year of high school. For the national sample the data are restricted to children age 13 through 17. The rates are much higher for younger children. For example, 97 percent of three year olds in this sample were hit by their parents (Straus, 1981).

data in the student sample. First, as previously noted, slightly different versions of the CTS were used. In addition, the ages differ (high school seniors for the student sample, and 15 through 18 for the national sample). Moreover, for the national sample, the data are restricted to violent acts known to the parents, whereas the student data is self-reported. Because of these differences, the rates shown in the "Student" rows of Table 10-1 often differ from those in the "National" rows.

On the other hand, despite these differences, both the student sample and the national sample data show similar patterns in respect to violence in different family roles. For example, both are consistent with other studies in showing that parents are more violent to their children than to each other (roughly double the violence rate). This is a point that will be explored in detail later. The data in the last row of Table 10-1 documents a fact that almost everyone "knows" but whose significance is generally ignored: the high frequency of both minor and serious assaults between siblings. This is most dramatic in the case of the student sample because they are the oldest and (by virtue of the fact that they have succeeded in entering a university with relatively high admission standards) the most stable group. Yet, these rates show that over half had hit a sibling during their senior year in high school, and 30 percent severely assaulted a sibling that year.

Overall, the data in Table 10-1 show that violence is frequent in American families. In fact, these figures are part of the evidence which suggests that the family is the most violent group or institution that a typical citizen is likely to encounter over his or her lifetime. The question to be addressed in this paper is whether this high level of violence within the family is related to violence outside the family, and to nonfamily crime.

INCIDENCE OF NONFAMILY VIOLENCE AND CRIME

Measures of Nonfamily Violence and Crime

The focus of both the studies from which this data is drawn was on intrafamily conflict and violence, rather than on nonfamily crime. Consequently, the data on crime and violence outside the family are limited, but still useful.

STUDENT SAMPLE. The questionnaire used to gather the data on family violence also included a ten item version of the Short-Nye self report delinquency scale, and a series of questions on violent acts by the respondent against persons outside his or her family. The specific questions are given in Table 10-2.

NATIONAL SAMPLE. The interview included a question which asked if, during the previous year, the respondent had been "arrested or convicted for something serious." The response to this item permits computing an annual incidence rate. Clearly this is a very crude measure of the criminal activity of the sample because, among other limitations, it does not provide information on what the crime was, and it omits crimes for which the respondent was not arrested or convicted.

In respect to juvenile crime, two questions are available for analysis. Each parent in the national sample was asked if a child had been "kicked out of school or suspended," and whether a "child got caught doing something illegal." These items share the inadequacies of the adult crime question. In addition, there is a further loss of data on crimes that the child got caught doing, but which were not known to the parents.

Table 10-2. Incidence per 1,000 of Delinquent and Violent Acts

Delinquent/Violent Act	Incidence For:	
	Males	Females
A. DELINQUENCY SCALE ITEMS (Student sample)		
Driven a car without a license or permit	236	196
Taken little things (worth $2 or less) that didn't belong to you	486	285**
Purposely damaged or destroyed public or private property	388	93**
Had sexual intercourse	502	268**
Taken things of large value (worth $50 or more that didn't belong to you	65	7*
Used drugs to get high	321	378
Defied your parents authority to their face	53	63
Been regarded as a discipline problem by school authorities	201	85**
Gotten kicked out of school for getting into trouble	61	3**
Been picked up or questioned by the police	325	136**
B. NON-FAMILY VIOLENCE ITEMS (Student sample)		
Hit or tried to hit another person, but not with anything	366	97**
Hit or tried to hit another person with something hard	63	15*
C. DELINQUENCY ITEMS (child 15-17, National Sample)* **		
Child got kicked out of school or suspended	67	
Child got caught doing something illegal	23	
D. ADULT CRIME ITEM (National Sample)		
Got arrested or convicted for something serious	19	9*

* = p for sex difference <.05; ** = p<.01
*** This data is not available by sex. In addition, the figures are not incidence rates becasue they refer to any of the respondent's children, rather than to one randomly selected "referent child" used for all other data on children in the national sample study.

Incidence Rates

STUDENT SAMPLE. Since, as noted above, the student sample is not representative of high school seniors, no commentary will be offered on the incidence rates for delinquent and violent acts in part A of Table

10-2. However, the sex differences and the correspondence with national sample data are pertinent.

There are statistically significant differences between the male and female students on seven of the ten items. All indicate higher delinquency for male high school seniors than female. The largest difference is in respect to vandalism. Very few girls engaged in vandalism (93 per 1,000), as contrasted with more than one out of three boys (389 per 1,000). In part B, there is a similar difference in respect to violence against nonfamily members.

The three delinquency items on which boys and girls did not differ significantly are also important because they provide indirect evidence that the differences on the other items are not simply a function of a greater tendency of girls to avoid reporting socially disapproved acts.

Overall, it is clear that even in this somewhat selective sample of students, there was a large amount of delinquency and violence, especially among the boys. The question to be addressed in subsequent sections of the paper is whether those who engaged in such acts came from families with higher levels of violence than did the nondelinquent and nonviolent students.

NATIONAL SAMPLE TEEN AGERS. Part C of Table 10-2 gives the delinquency rates for the 15- to 17-year-olds in the national sample. They are not directly comparable to the student sample data because of the age difference and because (as explained in the table footnote) we could not get separate data for boys and girls. Nevertheless, it is interesting that the rate of being expelled from school for the boys in the student sample is almost identical with the rate in the national sample (61 versus 67). On the other hand, there is a huge difference between the two samples in respect to involvement with the police—a rate of only 23 per 1,000 15- to 17-year-olds in the national sample, versus 325 for boys and 136 for girls in the student sample (last row of part A). One possible explanation is that the difference is because the national sample data was obtained from the parents, whereas the student sample is self-report. Consequently, part of the difference might be due to police involvements that were not known to the parents. The age difference might also be a factor.

NATIONAL SAMPLE ADULTS. Part D of Table 10-2 reports on the indicator of adult crime available in this study. It is difficult to compare the 19 arrests per 1,000 men and 9 arrests per 1,000 women with the arrest data collated by the FBI. The rates for this survey are substantially lower than the official rates. However, when allowance is made for the different bases for the statistics, there may be little difference. Specifically, the rates from this survey are based on interviews with married couples, who are a group that is likely to have been involved in less criminal activity than the population as a whole. In addition, the official rates use the arrest as the unit of tabulation, whereas the rate given in Table 10-2 uses persons (some of whom may have had multiple arrests or convictions) during the year. But even assuming that these are accurate figures, they present a methodological problem. Specifically, the adult crime rates shown in Table 10-2 are based on only a small number of cases, raising questions about the reliability of any findings. In addition, the highly skewed distribution limits the statistical techniques that can be used. Had this been the only crime data, it would probably have been unwise to proceed. However, since it will be analyzed along with the more adequate juvenile crime data, the results can be judged as part of an overall pattern of findings.

CRIMINAL CORRELATES OF PARENTAL VIOLENCE

This section examines the question of whether there is a link between the use of violence by parents and the criminal behavior of children. Two aspects of criminal behavior will be considered: violence against persons outside the child's family, and various indicators of juvenile delinquency. The data on nonfamily violence by children is available only for the student sample. Delinquency data is available for both samples.

Nonfamily violence

Previous reports on the national sample have shown a high correlation between parental use of violence and intrafamily violence by children: the more children are hit by their parents, the higher the rate at which such children hit their brothers and sisters and their parents (Straus, 1981b; Straus, Gelles and Steinmetz, 1980). These results were interpreted as indicating that, in addition to securing compliance to parental wishes, physical punishment teaches (usually inadvertently) the child to be violent.

However, it has been argued that any such learning is not a general prescription for violence. Rather, according to this argument, the child models only the specific behavior of the parent. Consequently, any unintended lesson applies only to similar situations. In the case of parental use of physical punishment, since the parents are engaged in socially accepted acts, usually for some desirable purpose such as enforcing rules of proper behavior, there should be little or no relationship between violence by parents and violence by the child outside the family.

Our view, however, is that even though most children will model only the type of violence to which they have been exposed, an important fraction of children will generalize to nonfamily situations. The lines labeled A and B in Figure 10-1 provide evidence on this issue from the student sample.

Lines A and B in the left half of Figure 10-1 show that for boys there is clearly a link between having been hit by ones parents that year and assaults on nonfamily members. For girls (lines A and B in the right half of Figure 10-1), there is only a slight tendency in this direction. However, even these small differences may be important because of their consistency with the findings for the boys. That is, taken together, all four comparisons using variables A and B show that the rate of nonfamily violence is greater for students whose parents had hit them compared to students whose parents had not. Consequently, the data in Figure 10-1 is much more consistent with the hypothesis that parental violence generalizes to nonfamily relationships than it is with the idea that only the specific behavior of the parent is learned.

Delinquency

STUDENT SAMPLE. The data on delinquency for the student sample is shown in Figure 10-1 by the lines labeled C (vandalism), D (theft involving $50 or more), and E (the overall delinquency scale). Two of the six comparisons of students who had been hit with those who had not been hit show statistically significant differences on these variables. However, all six of the comparisons are in the same direction, i.e., indicating that students who have been hit by their parents have a higher rate of engaging in delinquent acts than children who had not been hit.

The sex differences are again striking. The relationship between parent-to-child violence and vandalism and theft is much weaker for girls than for boys. The relationship of parental violence with the total delinquency scale is greater, but still less than for the boys.

Even though the differences are small for girls, the consistency of the findings suggests that there is truly a link between the use of physical force by parents on children and delinquent behavior by children. However, since these are cross-sectional data, the causal interpretation is open to question. By labeling the violence of the parents as the independent variable, and the violence and criminal behavior of the child as the dependent variables, it is clearly implied that parent-to-child violence is criminogenic. But the causal direction could be entirely opposite. Specifically, it may be that it was the violent and criminal acts of the children which led the parents to hit them. A longitudinal study would provide the best data on this issue. In the meantime, these findings must be interpreted with caution.

NATIONAL SAMPLE. Because the revised version of the Conflict Tac-

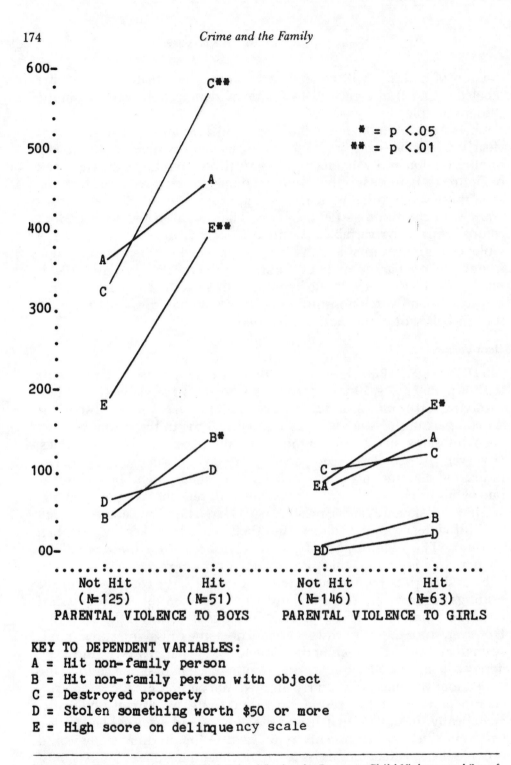

Figure 10-1. Delinquency Rate of High School Seniors by Parent-to-Child Violence and Sex of Child (Student Sample).

tics Scales was used for this sample, it is possible to divide the children who were victims of parental violence into two groups: those who experienced what we have called "ordinary" violence and those who experienced a severe assault (punching, kicking, biting, hitting with an object, beating up, attacks with a knife or gun). The latter group are, fortunately few in number, but of sufficient importance to be worth distinguishing despite the small number of cases.

Figure 10-2 shows that there is a considerable difference between boys and girls in the extent to which parental violence is related to delinquency. For the girls, this is essentially no relationship. But for the boys, ordinary violence is associated with a slightly higher rate of delinqency; and severe violence is associated with a dramatically higher rate of delinquency.

CRIMINAL CORRELATES OF COUPLE VIOLENCE

In this section the focus shifts from violence by parents towards their teenage children to violence between the spouses themselves. The dependent variables are the violence and delinquency of the children and also the criminal involvement of the husbands and wives. Because of the relatively low N's for more extreme acts of violence, it was not possible to make separate comparisons for the "ordinary violence" of married life (i.e. pushing, slapping, shoving, throwing things) versus more severe assaults.

Nonfamily Violence

Lines A and B in the left half of Figure 10-3 show that boys growing up in families where there is physical fighting between the parents were much more likely to be assaultive to persons outside the family.

This finding also helps clear up questions about the interpretation of the similar data linking parent-to-child violence and violence outside the home. When those data were presented, it was with the caution that the parent-to-child violence might be a reaction to the violent behavior of the child, rather than a cause of the child's violence. But it is very unlikely that the violence between the parents in this sample was in reaction to the nonfamily assaultive behavior of their children. Consequently, although it certainly does not prove that there is a causal relation between the parent-to-child violence and the child's violence, the fact that violence between the COUPLE is associated with violence by the child, strengthens that interpretation for parent-to-child violence.

The data on nonfamily violence by the girls in this sample, however, shows only slight and inconsistent relationships with violence between their parents (lines A and B in the right half of Figure 10-3). This is also

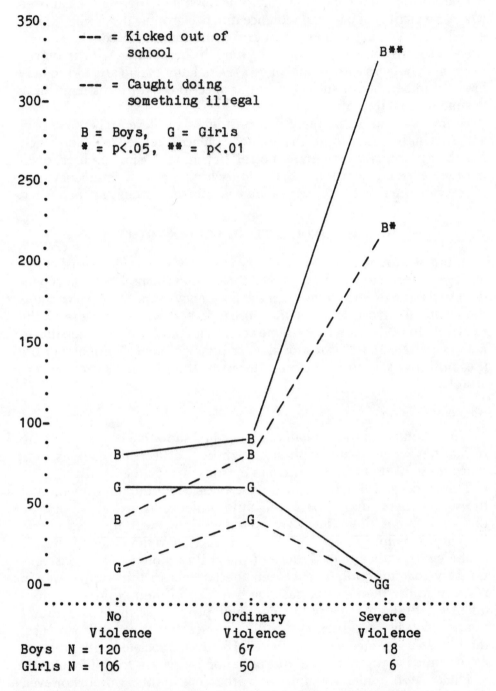

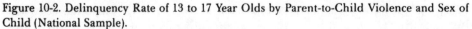

	No Violence	Ordinary Violence	Severe Violence
Boys N =	120	67	18
Girls N =	106	50	6

Figure 10-2. Delinquency Rate of 13 to 17 Year Olds by Parent-to-Child Violence and Sex of Child (National Sample).

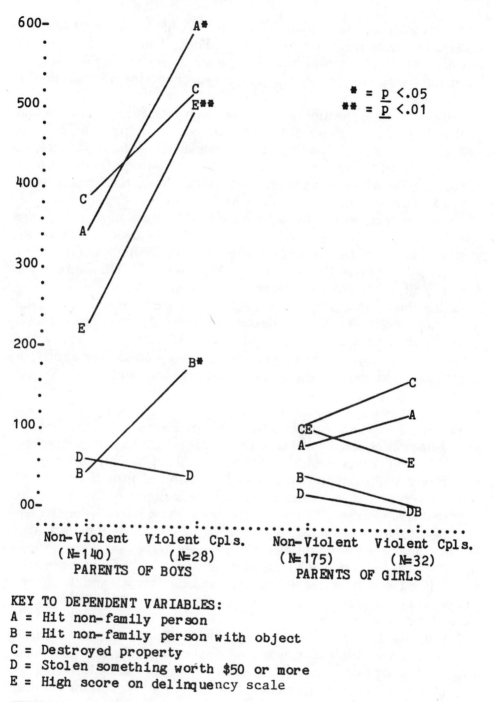

Figure 10-3. Delinquency Rate of High School Seniors by Couple Violence and Sex of Child (Student Sample).

consistent with the data reported on the link between parent-to-child violence and nonfamily violence by girls. Those data showed only small and nonsignificant relationships. It therefore seems to be the case that intrafamily violence has little or no carryover to violence outside the family for girls.

The near zero association for girls between intrafamily violence and nonfamily violence is also noteworthy because it helps explain (or at least is consistent with) some puzzling facts about violence by women: (1) In contrast to the findings just presented, data reported elsewhere (Straus, 1981b) shows that for girls as well as boys, the more parent-to-child violence, the higher their rate of INTRA-family violence. (2) Consistent with this is the fact that, WITHIN the family, women are assaulted by other family members, and themselves assault other family members, at about the same rate as men (Straus, 1980). (3) On the other hand, it is well known that violence by women OUTSIDE the family is only a small fraction of the violence rate of men.

Taking these three propositions together, it seems that what enables the third proposition to be true, despite the first and second propositions, is the findings shown in Figures 10-1 and 10-3—that intra-family violence does not carry over to violent behavior outside the family by women to anywhere near the extent that it does for men.

Delinquency

STUDENT SAMPLE. Lines C, D, and E in Figure 10-3 represent the same three delinquency indicators used for the analysis in which parent-to-child violence was the independent variable. The only difference is that Figure 10-3 compares students whose parents hit each other with those who reported no violence between their parents. The results for boys (left side of Figure 10-3) show that boys whose parents were violent had higher rates of vandalism (C) and a higher overall delinquency score (E), but that there was essentially no difference in the rate of engaging in theft. For girls (right side of Figure 10-3) there are no significant differences, and in fact, two of the three delinquency indicators (theft and the overall delinquency scale) reveal lower rates on the part of girls whose parents were violent to each other.

NATIONAL SAMPLE. There are only two delinquency items available for the national sample teen agers, but the findings (Figure 10-4) consistent in showing that teen agers whose parents were violent during the year of the survey had higher rates of delinquency than did the children of nonviolent couples.

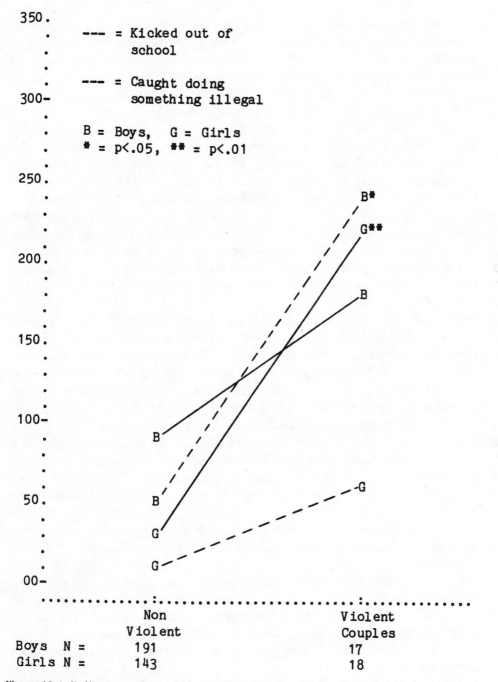

Figure 10-4. Delinquency Rate of 13 to 17 Year Olds by Couple Violence and Sex of Child (National Sample).

Family Violence and Adult Crime

Finally we come to the issue which may be the most unique contribution of this paper—the extent to which violence within the family is associated with criminal behavior outside the family. As pointed out earlier, the data on nonfamily crime is limited. It consists of a single question on whether the respondent had been "arrested or convicted for something serious" during the previous 12 months.

Although the indicator is limited, the number of cases available includes almost all the 2,143 families for which there is data. This is because it was not necessary to exclude the large number of couples who had no teen age children living at home, as was the case when parent-to-child violence was used as the independent variable and child's violence and delinquency as the dependent variables. Consequently, there are enough cases to let us compare couples whose violence was restricted to minor acts of violence (the "ordinary violence" group) with those whose violence included one or two serious assaults during the year of this survey, and those who experienced three or more such violent incidents during the year.

PARENT-TO-CHILD VIOLENCE. The result of this tabulation can be quickly summarized. For both fathers and mothers there is no association whatsoever between engaging in either minor or severe violence against children and being arrested or convicted during the year of this survey.

MARITAL VIOLENCE. It is fortunate that there are enough cases to permit a distinction to be made on the basis of the seriousness and frequency of marital violence because Figure 10-5 shows that for both men and women, a high rate of serious marital violence is associated with a high arrest and conviction rate. For women, there is a steady increase in this indicator of criminal behavior as the amount of marital violence increases. For men, however, there is little difference between the nonviolent and those who engaged in minor violence or "only" one or two incidents of severe violence. Thus, marital violence is closely linked to crime on the part of women, but for men it is linked only at the extreme.

Since the marital violence categories used in Figure 10-5 do not indicate who is carrying out the assault, the analysis was also run using violence by the husband as the independent variable, and then violence by the wife. These are not plotted because the addition of four lines would make Figure 10-5 too difficult to read. But the results can be easily summarized.

For violence by husbands, the plot has essentially the same shape as that shown in Figure 10-5, but the rates are higher for those who seri-

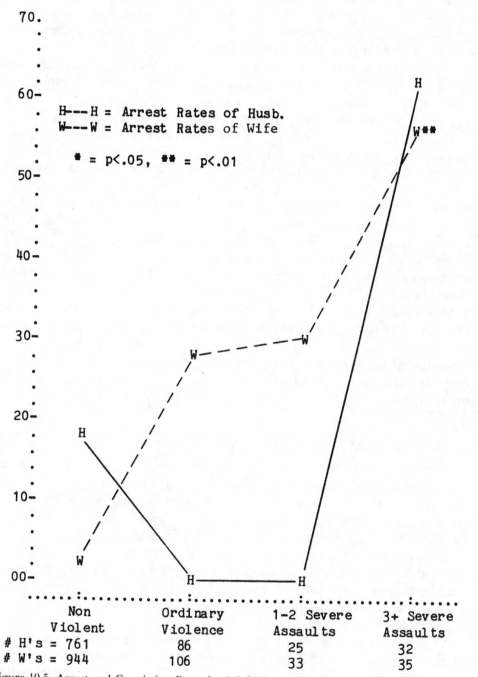

Figure 10-5. Arrest and Conviction Rates for Adult National Sample by Amount of Marital Violence and Sex.

ously assaulted their wives (16 for the 1–2 serious assault group, and 143 for the 3+ serious assault group). The same applies to women who were assaulted by their husbands, i.e., the same shape curve, but a higher rate for those assaulted 3 or more times (91). For violence by wives, the plot of the arrest rate for men is again similar to that shown in Figure 10-5, but in this case the men seriously assaulted three or more times had a lower arrest rate (40). The same applies to the arrest rate of women who assaulted their husbands. It reaches a peak of 42 (rather than 57 as shown in Figure 10-5) for those who engaged in three or more such assaults.

The results in Figure 10-5 and those given in the two previous paragraphs can be summarized using gamma coefficients. For husbands, the minimal associations are shown by the gammas of .07 for couple violence (Figure 10-5), .15 when husband-to-wife violence is the independent variable, and −.27 when wife's violence is the independent variable. For wives, the close association of marital violence with this indicator of criminal behavior is shown by the gammas of .78 for couple violence, .76 when the husband-to-wife violence is the independent variable, and .69 when wife-to-husband violence is the independent variable. All of these figures indicate that marital violence and crime are much more closely linked to crime for women than for men, and that this applies irrespective of whether the woman is the victim or the aggressor in marital violence. The intriguing question—but one which cannot be investigated with the data from these two studies—is why marital violence is linked to criminality so much more closely for women than for men.

SUMMARY AND CONCLUSIONS

This study tested the hypothesis that intrafamily violence is associated with nonfamily violence and crime. The hypothesis was tested using data from two surveys: a nationally representative sample of American couples (N = 2,143), and a sample of families of students in a New England state university (N = 385). The results indicated that:

(1) Teenage boys who had been hit by their parents during the year covered by this survey have a higher rate of violence against nonfamily members than other boys. However, for girls there is essentially no correlation between parent-to-child violence and their own violence outside the family.

(2) Boys, and to a lesser but still significant extent girls, who were hit by their parents have higher rates of vandalism and theft, and a larger proportion had high scores on the Short-Nye delinquency scale than did children who had not been hit by their parents that year. The boys (but

not the girls) also had a higher rate of being expelled from school.

(3) Violence between the husbands and wives in this sample was also found to be correlated with nonfamily violence and delinquency by teenage boys, but not by girls.

(4) Parents who severely and repeatedly assaulted their children did not have a higher rate of arrest or conviction than other parents.

(5) Couples who engaged in violent acts against each other had higher rates of criminal involvement than nonviolent couples. However, for husbands, the elevated crime rate occurred only for those who repeatedly and severely assaulted their wives. Ordinary minor violence, and even occasional severe assaults made no difference for the men. For the women, irrespective of whether they were the victims or the aggressors, the more marital violence, the higher the crime rate.

In general, the results summarized above are consistent between the two different studies analyzed, thus lending confidence to the conclusion that intrafamily violence is linked to nonfamily violence and crime. Moreover, certain internal comparisons suggest that the causal direction goes from intrafamily violence to the nonfamily violence and crime, rather than the reverse.

Assuming for the moment that family violence is criminogenic, the crucial question is what social and psychological processes produce this effect. The role model provided by violent parents is probably one factor, but it cannot explain the correlation with theft, vandalism, and other nonviolent delinquent acts. Another part of the linking process may be the experience of being a victim.

The victimization explanation is consistent with previous research (Owens and Straus, 1975) and with some of the findings of this study. For example, it is the teenagers who have been assaulted by their parents who exhibit elevated rates of nonfamily violence and crime, not the parents who carried out the assaults. And it is wives in violent marriages, rather than their husbands, who have higher crime rates. Since it is wives who are the predominant victims of marital violence (even when they themselves are violent to their husbands), this is consistent with the victimization explanation. Victimization can be criminogenic because it tends to undermine the faith in the efficacy and fairness of the world that is conducive to conforming behavior.

Probably other factors, in addition to role modeling and victimization, are also important. As stated in the introduction, the link between intrafamily violence and nonfamily violence and crime is a complicated and important issue on which previous research has shown conflicting results. The findings in this paper, by helping to establish the basic issue of just what aspects of family violence are linked to nonfamily violence and crime, pave the way for research to test theories concerning the underlying causal processes.

REFERENCES

Bolton, R. G., Reich, J. W., & Gutierres, S. E. (1977). Delinquency patterns in maltreated children and siblings. *Victimology, 2,* 349–357.

Elmer, E., Evans, S., & Reinhart, J. (1977). *Fragile families, troubled children.* Pittsburgh: Pittsburgh University Press.

George, C., & Main, M. (1979). Social interactions of young abused children: Approach, avoidance, and aggression. *Child Development, 50,* 306–318.

Glueck, S. & Glueck, E. (1950). *Unraveling juvenile delinquency.* Cambridge, MA: Harvard University Press.

Martin, H. P., & Beezley, P. (1974). Prevention and the consequences of abuse. *Journal of Operational Psychiatry, 6,* 68–77.

McCord, J. (1979). Some child-rearing antecedents of criminal behavior in adult men. *Journal of Personality and Social Psychology, 37,* 1477–1486.

Morse, C. W., Sahler, O. J. Z., & Friedman, S. B. (1970). A three-year follow-up study of abused and neglected children. *American Journal of Diseases of Children, 120,* 439–446.

Owens, D. M., & Straus, M. A. (1975). The social structure of violence in childhood and approval of violence as an adult. *Aggressive Behavior, 1,* 193–211. Also reprinted in I. H. Hyman and J. H. Wise (Eds.), *Corporal punishment in American education: Readings in history, practice and alternatives* (pp. 107–125). Temple University Press, 1979.

Straus, M. A. (1969, May). Phenomenal identity and conceptual equivalence of measurement in cross-national comparative research. *Journal of Marriage and the Family,* 233–241.

Straus, M. A. (1974, February). Leveling, civility and violence in the family. *Journal of Marriage and the Family, 36,* 13–29. Plus addendum August, 1974. Also reprinted in R. W. Cantrell and D. F. Schrader (Eds.), *Dynamics of Marital Interaction.* Kendall/Hunt, 1974, and in K. C. W. Kammeyer (Ed.), *Confronting the issues: Sex roles, marriage and the family.* Boston: Allyn and Bacon, 1976.

Straus, M. A. (1977, March 12). *Normative and behavioral aspects of violence between spouses: Preliminary data on a nationally representative USA sample.* Paper read at the Symposium on Violence in Canadian Society, Simon Fraser University.

Straus, M. A. (1979). Measuring intrafamily conflict and violence: The Conflict Tactics (CT) scales. *Journal of Marriage and the Family, 41,* 75–88. Also in Victims and aggressors in marital violence. *American Behavioral Scientist, 23,* pp. 681–704. 1980, May/June.

Straus, M. A. (1981a, July). *Re-evaluation of the Conflict Tactics Scale.* Paper presented at the National Conference for Family Violence Researchers, University of New Hampshire.

Straus, M. A. (1983). Ordinary violence versus child abuse and wife beating: What do they have in common? In D. Finkelhor, R. J. Gelles, G. T. Hotaling, and M. A. Straus (Eds.), *The dark side of families* (chap. 13). Beverly Hills, CA: Sage.

Straus, M. A., Gelles, R. J., & Steinmetz, S. K. (1980). *Behind closed doors: Violence in the American family.* New York: Doubleday/Anchor.

FOOTNOTES

*Paper presented at the 1981 annual meeting of the American Society Of Criminology under the title "Family Violence And Non-Family Crime And Violence." This paper is one of a series of publications of the Family Violence Research Program at the University of New Hampshire. The program is supported by the University of New Hampshire and by NIMH grants MH27557 and T32 MH15161.

1. It is important to note that the measure of violence used here is assaults carried out, and not injuries produced. If the latter is the criterion, the situation is far from equal since, for a variety of reasons, wives are injured much more often than husbands. See Straus, 1977; Straus, Gelles, and Steinmetz, 1980: 43).

2. The data on delinquency was restricted to these three items because presenting all eleven would make it very difficult to read Figures 10-1 and 10-4. The vandalism and theft items were selected because they are the most comparable to adult crimes. The others are status offenses (e.g., had sexual intercourse), so-called victimless crimes (e.g., used drugs), or a crime that does not have the same meaning when carried out by an adolescent as compared to an adult (car theft). However, the delinquency indicators not analyzed separately are included as components of the delinquency scale.

CHAPTER 11

THE CRIMINAL TRIBES OF INDIA

PAUL FREDERICK CRESSEY

The criminal tribes of India illustrate the extent to which crime may be a problem not of individual demoralization, but of group traditions. These tribes are hereditary groups that specialize in different types of crime. Their criminal activities, which furnish their chief means of support, are handed down from generation to generation. Each tribe has its own traditions, as well as a distinct name, and its existence is frankly recognized by the general public.

The population of these criminal tribes has been variously estimated at from one to four million people.[1] Many individual tribes have a population of 100,000 or more. These large tribes are divided into a number of subgroups, many of which have abandoned criminal activities and become quite law-abiding. No exact total can be given of the population actively engaged in crime because of the difficulty in distinguishing between the groups which have become peaceful and those which are still criminal.

The number of different criminal tribes is also unknown. The same tribe may be referred to by a variety of names in different language areas. Thus the tribe known as Kaikadi or Kaikari in Bombay is called Kuraver and Erukala in South India and elsewhere is spoken of as Korwa. This tribe is divided into scores of subdivisions, located in different parts of India, and having local names which completely disguise their relationship.[2] Sixty different criminal tribes are mentioned in Edwardes' *Crime in India*, but this is only a partial list, for many important tribes are omitted.[3] A study of the chief criminal tribes in Bombay Presidency lists 23 tribes who are known by 102 different names, and this does not include any of their subdivisions. Twelve of these tribes had a population in the province of Bombay, in 1901, of approxi-

---

[1]Sir George MacMunn, *The Underworld of India* (London, 1933), pp. 144, 151. Sir John Cumming (ed.), *Modern India* (London, 1931), p. 113.

[2]Michael Kennedy, *Criminal Classes in Bombay Presidency* (Bombay, 1908), pp. 63–83.

[3]S. M. Edwardes, *Crime in India* (Oxford Press, 1924), p. 164.

mately a million people, but many of the subdivisions of these tribes were not actively criminal.[4]

Criminal tribes are widely distributed throughout India, the largest number being in the provinces of Bombay, the Punjab, and Madras. Bengal has the smallest number. A good many live in the native states, where police surveillance is usually more lenient, and from which states they make forays into British territory. They are not native to Burma or Ceylon, though occasionally Indian bands visit these countries.

The origin of these tribes is lost in antiquity, many of them having apparently existed for centuries. Some entered India as camp followers with the armies of the Mogul Emperors. The gradual decay of the Mogul Empire and the wars connected with the British conquest of India produced a century and a half of disorder during which the activities of these tribes greatly increased. Before the days of the railway two tribes, the Banjara and the Uppu Kuraver, acted as common carriers in different parts of India, using large caravans of bullocks or donkeys. The railways destroyed their occupation and both groups gradually turned to criminal pursuits, developing traits which probably were already latent among them as wandering caravan drivers.[5] Some criminal tribes may be related to the pre-Dravidian races of India, although the aboriginal groups which still exist are not hereditary criminals. Attempts have been made to show a relationship between European gypsies and some of the wandering criminal tribes of India. There are superficial similarities, such as their migratory life, petty pilfering, fortune telling, and dancing by the women, but there is no evidence of any historic connection between the two groups.

Most criminal tribes are Hindu, with recognized places in the Hindu caste system. Their status varies all the way from such groups as the Mona Bhatras, who wear the sacred thread and claim to be Brahmins, to the Pardhis and Mangs, who are members of the outcaste, or depressed classes. Probably the majority of the criminal tribes are of relatively low caste standing, with a considerable minority who belong to the depressed classes. In many of the larger tribes the distinctions between the various subdivisions are so strict that members of different divisions will not intermarry or even eat together. In North India there are a good many Mohammedan criminal tribes, and two or three are Sikh.

All criminal tribes have their special religious traditions and patron gods. Many tribes have particular shrines to which they go on pilgrim-

---

[4]Kennedy, *op. cit.*

[5]N. R. Cumberlege, *Some Account of the Bunjarrah Class* (Bombay, 1882), pp. 14, 32.
   Hatch, *op cit.*, p. 218.

ages and where they make offerings to insure good luck in their professional activities. After a successful exploit they generally sacrifice a part of their loot as a thank offering to their protecting deity. Special rites and omens are observed and there are strict religious oaths which they keep. Among these people crime is not a matter of personal disorganization, but represents the normal integration of the individual in the life of his group. They regard their activities as perfectly moral, sanctioned as they are by tribal traditions and religious beliefs.

Social status within a tribe depends upon a successful criminal career. Among such tribes as the Bhamptas and Mang-garudis it is reported that a man may not marry until he has proved himself a proficient thief.[6] In numerous tribes an individual must commit at least one theft a year in order to maintain good standing in his caste. In a particular cattle-stealing tribe a youth has to go bareheaded until he qualifies himself for manhood by committing a daring theft. Leadership in a group goes to the cleverest and most successful criminal.

Each criminal tribe tends to specialize in a specific type of crime. This specialization is bound up with their caste rules and religious traditions. Thus the Bauriahs, following their tribal mores, engage only in house burglary and cattle stealing at night during the dark half of the moon, and they avoid all crimes in the daytime. The Oudiahs, on the other hand, engage in housebreaking and theft only during the day. The Soonarias, who are daytime pickpockets and petty thieves, take an oath to the goddess Devi never to engage in any other type of crime. The Berads follow a cycle of criminal activities which changes with the seasons of the year. Other tribes display equally interesting types of specialization.

In the face of changing economic and industrial conditions there have been modifications in the traditional activities of some tribes. The railways have presented new opportunities for crime and several tribes have developed a talent in this field, some concentrating on stealing from freight cars and others specializing on passenger trains. The Bhamptas, who have become the most important group of passenger thieves, usually disguise themselves as well-to-do travelers, stealing the baggage of their fellow passengers when the latter are asleep and throwing it off the train at prearranged points where their confederates are waiting. They are traditional pickpockets and find the trains a profitable place for this older profession as well. Formerly, the Bhamptas were only daytime thieves, but with the growth of their railway activities these old prohibitions have broken down.[7] Changes in traditional criminal mores are

---

[6] E. J. Gunthrope, *Notes on Criminal Tribes* (Bombay, 1882), p. 104. Kennedy, *op. cit.*, p. 21.

[7] Kennedy, *op. cit.*, p. 26.

reported for many other tribes, in which the strict taboos seem to be disintegrating in the face of new conditions. The older members of the tribes often bemoan the passing of the hereditary tribal standards, complaining that the younger generation is becoming nothing but common thieves and criminals.

Each tribe has its own traditional methods of carrying out its criminal activities. Police who are familiar with the *modus operandi* of different criminal tribes are able to determine, in the case of any particular crime, the type of criminal tribesman involved by the characteristic way in which the act was committed. Different tribes of house burglars use different methods of breaking into a house, and use different types of tools. Highway robberies are carried out differently by various tribes. In each tribe there is usually a specialized vocabulary and a series of secret signs dealing with their criminal activities. It is often possible for such tribesmen to carry on a confidential conversation in public places and give warning to each other without arousing the suspicion of intended victims. Certain traditional disguises are also adopted by some tribes when traveling. Children undergo a long period of training in order to master the technique of their tribal profession.

Criminal tribesmen always operate in organized gangs, with a definite leader and a considerable division of labor in carrying out their exploits. The members of the gang act together in common defense, they share equally in the disposition of the spoils, and they care for the families of any members who may be imprisoned or killed. In numerous tribes the women act as spies in locating possible loot. They gain access to prosperous looking houses by telling fortunes, begging, or selling baskets, herbs, or trinkets.

In addition to their criminal activities most tribes engage in some other, ostensible means of support. These are generally of a rural character as criminal tribesmen are not traditionally city dwellers. Some own small plots of land which they cultivate, or they hire themselves out as field laborers or herdsmen. Others act as watchmen, in which capacity they justify the old proverb "Set a thief to catch a thief," for they are quite loyal to their employers. Among the more nomadic tribes there are cattle traders, musicians, fortune tellers, some who exhibit trained monkeys and snakes, and others who do tattooing. The manufacture of baskets, brooms, ropes, and mats is quite common, as is the collection of forest products, and hunting. One tribe makes and repairs household grinding stones and another produces cheap toys for children. Begging, particularly in the guise of a holy man, is a respectable activity in India and is resorted to on occasion by many criminal tribes.

Three main types of criminal tribes may be recognized: those that are nomadic, those that are settled but go on extensive criminal expeditions, and those that, being settled, engage only in local depredations. Most tribes fall clearly into one or another of these types, but in the case of some nomadic tribes certain subdivisions of the tribe have settled down to permanent residence. Also some settled tribes are only relatively stable, moving occasionally from village to village within a given district.

The nomadic, gypsy-like tribes carry all their household possessions with them as they move from camp to camp. Individual gangs vary in size from three or four families to several score. They usually erect temporary grass huts at each camp, though some tribes have reed shelters which they carry with them when they move. During the monsoon season they generally remain more or less stable. There are many different kinds of wandering criminal tribes: some are petty pilferers, others cattle thieves, burglars, highway robbers, or counterfeiters. Behind the cover of some reputable occupation they carry on their criminal activities anywhere within a radius of twenty or thirty miles of their encampment, often returning from some foray at night so as to escape observation. The village nearest their camp is usually exempt from their activities, thus giving the local villagers a certain protection in return for the latter's toleration of their camp. However, if they spot any rich loot in such a village they may return to capture it after having moved on some ten or fifteen miles. Among the most important wandering tribes are the Sansis, Kuravers, Mang-garudis, Waddars, and Pardhis.

Numerous other tribes engage in extensive criminal expeditions while maintaining a settled residential base. Their expeditions are usually seasonal, the gangs leaving home after certain religious festivals in the fall and returning late in the following spring. The women and children remain at home in their villages while the able-bodied men go on tour, often taking with them a few adolescent boys as apprentices. In one or two tribes some of the women may accompany the men, but this is not usual. One of the most common disguises of the men while traveling is that of holy men on a religious pilgrimage. There is an endless movement of *saddhus* and *fakirs* throughout India, whose coming and going are never questioned and who are supported by the alms of the orthodox. Many criminal tribesmen find this type of disguise very helpful. Other tribesmen pose as prosperous business men or high caste travelers. No section of India is immune from the visits of these imposters. Not infrequently they keep in touch with their families by mail and remit the profits of their exploits by postal money orders. Among this class of criminals there are pickpockets, railway thieves, counterfeiters, burglars, robbers, and swindlers who take up collections for nonexistent charities. They are quite law-abiding in their home villages, and often share a part of their profits with village officials to insure local protection. The most important tribes of this type are the Bauriahs, Oudhias, Bhamptas, Chapparbands, Harnis, and Minas.

The third type of criminal tribe is that which has a settled place of residence and confines its activities to its immediate neighborhood. Usually not more than one or two families will live in a given village, where they make a pretense of having some ordinary occupation. They maintain contact, however, with fellow tribesmen scattered through other villages, and gangs can be rapidly gathered for any large scale operation. Their activities are usually confined within a radius of thirty or forty miles, which distance they are often able to walk in a single night. Their own villages are free from their activities, save for occasional cases of petty stealing. Different tribes specialize in such activities as the theft of crops, stealing cattle, sheep, or goats, robbery, or burglary. A form of blackmail is practiced by some tribes who demand employment from shopkeepers and farmers as watchmen. If such employment is refused they retaliate in their traditional manner. The best known tribes of this class are the Banjaras, Berads, Mangs, Ramoshis, and Maghaya Doms.

There are several other criminal groups in India which are sometimes confused with the criminal tribes. Some of the aboriginal peoples, as the Bhils and Kolis, occasionally turn to crime under the economic pressure of crop failures or avaricious money lenders, but they are not habitual or professional criminal tribes. There are also numerous secret criminal groups or fraternities, membership in which is obtained by individual initiation. The most famous of these fraternities, that of the Thugs, was suppressed early in the nineteenth century, but its name has remained as a synonym for the most brutal type of robber.[8] Such secret fraternities of criminals are not biological or caste groups and so are to be distinguished from the hereditary criminal tribes.

The reformation of these criminal tribes is a particularly difficult problem. Ordinary penal methods have proved quite futile in dealing with them, but newer methods of restraint and supervision are gradually bringing about their rehabilitation. These problems will be discussed in a subsequent paper under the title, "Reforming the Criminal Tribes of India."

REFERENCES

Cumberlege, N. R. (1882). *Some account of the Bunjarrah class* (pp. 14, 32). Bombay.
Cumming, Sir J. (Ed.). (1931). *Modern India* (p. 113). London.

---

[8]Col. Meadows Taylor, *Confessions of a Thug* (first published, 1839; reprint Oxford Press, 1916).

Edwardes, S. M. (1924). *Crime in India* (p. 164). Oxford Press.
Gunthrope, E. J. (1882). *Notes on criminal tribes* (p. 104). Bombay.
Hatch, W. J. (1928). *Land pirates of India* (pp. 19, 63, 218, 233). London.
Kennedy, M. (1908). *Criminal classes in Bombay presidency* (pp. 21, 26, 63–83). Bombay.
MacMunn, Sir G. (1933). *The underworld of India* (pp. 144, 151). London.
Taylor, Col. M. (1839, reprinted in 1916). *Confessions of a thug.* Oxford Press.

CHAPTER 12

THE FAMILIAL TRANSMISSION OF CRIMINALITY

D. P. FARRINGTON, GWEN GUNDRY, and D. J. WEST

THE PREVALENCE OF CRIMINAL RECORDS

The Criminal Record Office of Scotland Yard maintains files that provide a more or less comprehensive register of all persons who have been convicted of criminal offences in England and Wales in modern times. By searching for the names of a sample of young persons and their parents it is possible, in principle, to ascertain the prevalence of individuals with criminal records, and to investigate the extent to which criminal records run in families. Until now, no systematic inquiry along these lines has been published in this country. Since some older studies were reviewed by Wootton (1959), the extent to which criminality runs in families has been a neglected topic of research.

The present investigation is based on 394 young males (born 1951–4) whose names, together with those of their parents, brothers and sisters, have been searched for repeatedly in the Criminal Record Office as part of a delinquency research project known as the Cambridge Study in Delinquent Development (West, 1969). The sample, recruited at age 8–9 years, comprised all the boys in the second forms of 6 state primary schools situated in a working-class area of London, and was thus an unselected group of males of that particular generation and neighborhood. The original sample included 411 boys, but 14 were older brothers of other boys in the sample, and 3 moved abroad permanently at age 13 or earlier, and so hardly had time to acquire a criminal record. These 17 boys have been eliminated from the sample for the purposes of the present analysis.

The 394 boys and their families have been under research scrutiny for some 12 years, and the boys themselves have been interviewed on a number of occasions. A considerable amount of social data is available to supplement the statistics reported in the present paper (West and Farrington, 1973). In order to obtain particulars for searching, the full name and date of birth of each family member, including the mother's maiden name, was sought during interviews. These data were checked against, and in some cases supplemented by, information from medical and social service records and from birth certificates and marriage certificates obtained at Somerset House. Of the 394 males in the sample, 356 of their fathers, 374 of their mothers, 310 of their brothers and 329 of their sisters were identified and searched for at the Criminal Record Office. A criminal record was located for 27.9 percent of the original sample of 394 'target' boys, 26.4 per cent of their fathers, 13.4 per cent of their mothers, 36.5 per cent of their brothers and 7.6 per cent of their sisters. In all, of a total of 1763 persons belonging to 394 different families, 392 have so far (up to and including the year 1973) acquired a criminal record, an average of almost one person per family of 4–5 persons.

These figures necessarily exclude certain family members. Only biological parents who lived with the boy during the whole of his first 3 years were counted. This led to the exclusion of 20 fathers (5 of whom died and 15 deserted or had no contact with the boy during his first 3 years) and 6 mothers (2 of whom died and 4 deserted). Eighteen other fathers and 14 other mothers had to be excluded because their records were unsearchable. They came to England after the age of 25, which meant that during their most delinquent-prone years they had no opportunity to acquire a criminal record in this country. One father who arrived after 25, but acquired a criminal record here, was counted. Only the (ostensibly) full brothers or sisters of the 394 target boys were counted, and only if they were born before 1 September, 1956 and had not died or moved abroad before the age of 16.

The figures in this paper include only entries actually found at the Criminal Record Office, and exclude any findings of guilt which would not normally be recorded in the case of a first offender. Most minor nonindictable offences, especially motoring offences, are therefore excluded. Breaches of probation and other court orders, and a few convictions that were known to the research workers but not contained in central records, were not counted. Findings of guilt under the age of 10 were not counted, neither for the 394 target boys, nor for their siblings, because the change in the age of criminal responsibility from 8 to 10, which took effect in February, 1964, meant that not all of them were at risk of prosecution for the whole period between their eighth and tenth birthdays. The figures quoted in this paper are the result of repeated name searches over an extended period. Repetition was advantageous because files not found on one occasion were located on another, and because full identifying particulars, such as maiden names, were not always known when the research began and were obtained later.

It may seem curious that the prevalence of a criminal record in the original sample of 394 target boys (27.9 per cent) was less than that among their brothers (36.5 per cent). Most of the brothers, however, were older, and hence had been exposed to the risk of prosecution for a longer time. Furthermore, and perhaps more importantly, since all brothers belonged, by definition, to families with at least 2 sons, they tended to come from the larger-sized families among the sample. In this, as in other surveys, members of larger families more often had criminal convictions than those from smaller families.

The prevalence of criminal records among both target boys and their (predominantly) older brothers was greater than that among their fathers, in spite of the fact that their fathers had been at risk much longer. This result undoubtedly reflects the great increase in the incidence of criminal convictions that has taken place from one generation to the next. In contrast, the prevalence of criminal records among sisters was less than that among mothers, probably because females tend to have first convictions later in life than males. Unlike the mothers, the sisters, at the last time of searching, had not yet passed beyond the years of greatest risk for acquiring a criminal record. Whereas the majority of males who are found guilty at some time in their lives are first found guilty at age 20 years or less, the majority of convicted females are first found guilty at age 25 or later (McClintock and Avison, 1968).

THE INFLUENCE OF A PATERNAL CRIMINAL RECORD

Among the 356 target boys whose fathers' records were searched, the likelihood of acquiring a criminal record, and especially the likelihood of becoming a recidivist (i.e., having 2 or more criminal record entries) was significantly increased if the father had a record. Table 12-1 displays the relationship. Nearly half of the boys with criminal fathers (46 out of 94) acquired records, compared with less than one-fifth (48 out of 262) of those with noncriminal fathers. Those who became recidivists were more than twice as likely to have criminal fathers as those so far convicted only once (34 out of 56, as opposed to 12 out of 38).

The influence of a father's record became even clearer when target boys and their brothers were considered together. Of the 94 criminal fathers, 62.8 per cent had 1 or more delinquent sons. Of the 262 noncriminal fathers, only 27.1 percent had 1 or more delinquent sons. Admittedly, criminal fathers had more sons on average than noncriminal fathers (2.15 as opposed to 1.64), but for any given number of sons at risk in the family the presence of a criminal father increased the prevalence of delinquency among them. Where only 1 son in the family appeared in the analysis, 35.3 percent of the sons of criminal fathers had criminal records,

Table 12-1. Criminality of Father and Delinquency of Target Boy

Criminality of Father	Delinquency of Target Boy							
	Not Found Guilty		One Finding of Guilt		Two or More Findings of Guilt		Total	
	Percent-age	Number	Percent-age	Number	Percent-age	Number	Percent-age	Number
Not convicted	81.7	214	9.9	26	8.4	22	100	262
Not more than 1 adult conviction or found guilty as juvenile only	50.0	28	16.1	9	33.9	19	100	56
Two or more adult convictions	52.6	20	7.9	3	39.5	15	100	38
Total	73.6	262	10.7	38	15.7	56	100	356

Significance test: Dividing fathers into convicted and not convicted, and boys into found guilty and not found guilty, $x^2 = 31.8$ with 1 degree of freedom, $P<0.001$.

in comparison with only 18.8 percent of the sons of noncriminal fathers. With 2 sons in the family, the figures were 51.7 percent and 15.9 percent. With 3 or more sons, the figures were 57.3 percent and 32.8 percent.

The more seriously criminal fathers were no more likely to produce delinquent sons than those with less serious records (see Table 12-2). Of the target boys whose fathers were adult recidivists (i.e., having at least 2 adult conviction entries), about half (18 out of 38) became delinquents. However, an equally high proportion of boys (28 out of 56) whose fathers had slight records (defined as not more than 1 adult conviction or juvenile findings of guilt only) became delinquents. Even among the boys with the most persistently criminal fathers (i.e., having 4 or more adult convictions) the proportion becoming delinquents was still only half (7 out of 14). Confirmation that the degree of seriousness of the paternal record had little influence was obtained by combining the statistics of the target boys and their brothers. Of the 56 fathers with slight records, 62.5 percent had at least 1 delinquent son. Of the 38 adult recidivist fathers, 63.2 percent had at least 1 delinquent son.

Most of the factors of family adversity associated with delinquency were particularly evident among boys first convicted at an early age, but this was not true of paternal criminality. Among the 356 target boys whose fathers' records were searched, about half of those first found guilty under age 15 years (19 out of 41) had a criminal father. Among those first found guilty at age 15 or later, a similar proportion (27 out of 53) had a criminal father. Again, adverse family influences are normally most prevalent among juvenile recidivists, rather than among those who have only 1 juvenile conviction, but this was not the case in regard to paternal criminality (West and Farrington, 1973). In fact, boys who became recidivists as juveniles were significantly less likely to have criminal fathers than those who did not become recidivists until they were young adults (13 out of 29, as opposed to 21 out of 27; $\chi^2 = 5.06$ with 1 d.f., $P < 0.025$).

It might be expected that the influence of paternal criminality would weigh most heavily upon the oldest son in a family, but no evidence emerged to support this. The question was investigated by considering families with at least 2 sons in the analysis, and comparing the oldest son (whether or not he was one of the target boys) with the younger sons. Of the oldest sons, 56.7 percent of those with criminal fathers acquired a record. Of the younger sons, the corresponding figure was 54.6 percent.

A father's criminal record also had an effect on his daughters. Considering only fathers with 1 or more daughters, 9 out of 149 noncriminal fathers (6.0 percent) had at least 1 criminal daughter, in comparison with 10 out of 57 criminal fathers (17.5 percent).

THE INFLUENCE OF MATERNAL CRIMINALITY

Boys with criminal mothers were more likely to acquire criminal records than those with noncriminal mothers. As many as 54.0 percent of the 50 target boys with criminal mothers had records, in comparison with only 22.8 percent of the 324 boys with noncriminal mothers. This was a statistically significant difference ($\chi^2 = 19.8$ with 1 d.f., $P < 0.001$). Because of the tendency of criminal mothers to be married to criminal fathers, maternal and paternal influences were difficult to disentangle. Of the total of 50 criminal mothers, 27 were married to criminal fathers, and a further 7 came from families in which the father had to be excluded from the analysis (e.g., due to death, desertion, etc.).

Of the 16 boys with a criminal mother married to a noncriminal father, 5 (31.3 percent) acquired records, whereas of the 244 boys with neither parent criminal 43 (17.6 percent) acquired records. Seven out of the 16 families with a criminal mother and a noncriminal father (43.8 percent) included at least 1 delinquent son (i.e. the target boy and/or 1 or more of his brothers), in comparison with 63 out of the 244 families with neither parent criminal (25.8 percent). This suggests that a criminal mother had an effect on her sons even when the father had no criminal record. Where the father had a criminal record, the likelihood of delinquency in the sons was increased if the mother also had a record. Of the 27 target boys whose parents both had criminal records, 17 (63.0 percent) became delinquents. In contrast, of the 64 boys with criminal fathers and noncriminal mothers, 26 (40.6 percent) became delinquents.

Maternal criminality also had an effect upon daughters. Considering only mothers with 1 or more daughters, 10 out of 36 criminal mothers

(27.8 percent) had at least 1 delinquent daughter, in comparison with only 9 out of 176 noncriminal mothers (5.1 percent). Although the figures are sometimes small, they suggest that criminal mothers had more effect than criminal fathers on the delinquency of their daughters. However, in the case of sons criminal fathers had, if anything, a slightly greater influence. Considering only those families in which one parent was criminal and the other noncriminal, 7 out of 16 criminal mothers (43.8 percent) had 1 or more delinquent sons, compared with 35 out of 64 criminal fathers (54.7 percent). In these families with at least 1 daughter, 4 out of 13 criminal mothers (30.8 percent) had at least 1 delinquent daughter, compared with only 4 out of 35 criminal fathers (11.4 percent).

THE INFLUENCE OF CRIMINAL SIBLINGS

Table 12-2 shows that 115 target boys had 1 or more brothers and none with a criminal record. Only about one-fifth of these 115 were delinquents, whereas of the 80 boys who had 1 or more brothers with findings of guilt against their names exactly half were delinquents. There was evidence to show that this effect could not be explained by the fact that delinquents had more brothers than nondelinquents, since the difference occurred regardless of the number of brothers in a family. For example, among boys with only 1 brother, 41.4 percent (12 out of 29) of those with a delinquent brother were delinquents, in comparison with only 19.5 percent (17 out of 87) of those with a nondelinquent brother. Again, of those with 2 delinquent brothers, 60 percent (6 out of 10) were delinquents, compared with 40.9 percent (9 out of 22) of those with 1 brother delinquent and the other nondelinquent, and only 23.8 percent (5 out of 21) of those with 2 nondelinquent brothers.

Delinquent brothers had an effect whether or not the father had a record. Among boys with criminal fathers, 40.9 percent (9 out of 22) of those with only nondelinquent brothers were delinquents, in comparison with 65.8 percent (25 out of 38) of those with 1 or more delinquent brothers. Where the father had no criminal record, only 10.8 percent (9 out of 83) of those with nondelinquent brothers were delinquents, in comparison with 37.5 percent (9 out of 24) of those with delinquent brothers.

An attempt was made to determine whether the influence of older brothers was greater than that of younger brothers, by considering middle sons in families of 3 or more sons. In point of fact, the proportion of delinquent middle sons was almost the same in families with a convicted oldest son as in families with a convicted youngest son (64.8 percent of 54, as opposed to 63.9 percent of 36).

Table 12-2. Delinquency of Target Boy and of his Brothers

	Delinquency of Target Boy							
	Not Found Guilty		One Finding of Guilt		Two or More Findings of Guilt		Total	
Delinquency of Brothers	Percent- age	Number	Percent- age	Number	Percent- age	Number	Percent- age	Number
No brothers included in analysis	75.9	151	12.6	25	11.6	23	100	199
One or more brothers none found guilty	80.9	93	9.6	11	9.6	11	100	115
One or more brothers found guilty	50.0	40	13.8	11	36.3	29	100	80
Total	72.1	284	11.9	47	16.0	63	100	394

Significance test: Dividing boys according to whether or not they have convicted brothers, and according to whether or not they themselves have been found guilty, $x^2 = 23.0$ with 1 degree of freedom, P<0.001.

Delinquency among the 394 target boys was also associated with delinquency among their sisters. Considering only boys with at least 1 sister, 57.9 percent (11 out of 19) of those with 1 or more delinquent sisters were delinquent, in comparison with 30.5 percent (62 out of 203) of those with only nondelinquent sisters.

A FAMILY PROPENSITY TOWARDS CRIMINALITY

It follows from the significant association between criminality among the target boys and criminality among their parents and siblings that persons with a criminal record are not randomly distributed in the population. Certain families have much more than their fair share of convicted persons. In the present analysis, 44 out of the 394 families (a minority of 11.2 percent) accounted for something approaching one-half (184 out of 392) of all the convicted individuals. Even more strikingly, 17 families (a minority of 4.3 percent) accounted for nearly one-half of all the recorded convictions (561 out of 1197).

Although criminal families tend to be larger than average and hence to have more members exposed to the risk of conviction, this by no means accounts for the uneven distribution of convicted persons. Regardless of family size, the risk of an individual acquiring a criminal record increases considerably if another member of the family has a conviction. In Table 12-3 the families are classified according to the number of members included in the analysis, apart from the target boy. It can be seen that, for every size of family, the likelihood of a target boy acquiring a criminal record is significantly increased by the presence of other family members with convictions. For example, in large families (i.e., 5

Crime and the Family

or more persons in addition to the target boy) the likelihood of acquiring
a record is substantial even when no other family member has a conviction (6 out of 23, or 26.1 percent). However, if 1 or more other persons in
the family have convictions, the likelihood is increased considerably (29
out of 52, or 55.8 percent).

Table 12-3. Delinquency of Target Boy and Convictions of other Family Members

Number of Other Family Members	Number of Other Convicted Persons							
	0		1		2 or More		Total	
	Percent-age	Number	Percent-age	Number	Percent-age	Number	Percent-age	Number
1 or 2	19.2	14/73	33.3	8/24	*	0/1	22.4	22/98
3	9.6	9/94	31.3	10/32	46.7	7/15	18.4	26/141
4	17.5	7/40	47.8	11/23	53.8	7/13	32.9	25/76
5 or more	26.1	6/23	40.0	8/20	65.6	21/32	46.7	35/75
Total	15.7	36/230	37.4	37/99	57.4	35/61	27.7	108/390

Notes: The figure given is the percentage of target boys who are delinquents. Four of these boys (including
2 delinquents) were in families with no members included in this analysis.
*Figures too small to give meaningful percentage.

Table 12-4. Official Delinquency of Target Boy,
According to his Self-reported Delinquency Criminality

	Percentage of Target Boys Convicted at Different Levels of Self-reported Delinquency							
	Low		Low Average		High Average		High	
	Percentage	Number	Percentage	Number	Percentage	Number	Percentage	Number
Father not convicted	5.0	60	14.1	92	22.2	72	42.1	38
Father convicted	23.5	17	37.5	24	38.1	21	78.1	32

EXPLANATIONS OF THE FAMILIAL PROPENSITY TO CRIME

The results show that crime runs in families, but they provide no
explanation. The figures could conceivably reflect police activity rather
than family deviance. The risks of detection and prosecution might
increase for all members of a family, regardless of any real increase in
misconduct, once any of them acquires a record. Antisocial behavior
among the target boys, which had not necessarily come to the notice of
the police, was investigated by means of self-admissions during interviews at ages 14–17 years. These admissions were used to grade the boys
on a scale of self-reported delinquency (West and Farrington, 1973). It

can be seen from Table 12-4 that, at all levels of misbehaviour, the presence of a criminal father substantially increased the likelihood that a target boy would be convicted. For example, in case of the low-scoring (i.e., well-behaved) boys the likelihood of conviction increased over four times (from 5.0 percent to 23.5 percent) if the father had a record.

The target boys were reclassified according to admissions made at 18–19 years and the analysis was repeated, with similar results.

While these findings point to the importance of police selection, they also show that this is not the only factor. The totals in Table 12-4 show a steadily increasing conviction rate for the entire sample as behavior, according to self-report, worsens. It could be argued that the selection process is more apparent than real, providing that self-reports are not valid measures of behaviour. In general, research has shown that self-admissions do provide a valid assessment of antisocial conduct (Farrington, 1973), but it is conceivable that boys with criminal fathers are peculiar in tending to conceal their delinquencies and to make themselves appear better than they really are. However, no direct evidence of this was found when boys' known conviction records were compared with their accounts of court appearances during interviews. An explanation based on concealment by boys from criminal families was rendered even less plausible when similar results emerged from an analysis in which the boys' levels of antisocial behavior ('troublesomeness') were estimated from the reports of peers and schoolteachers when they were aged 8 and 10 years (Table 12-5).

Table 12-5. Official Delinquency of Target Boy,
According to his Rated Troublesomeness and his Father's Criminality

	Percentage of Target Boys Convicted at Different Levels of Troublesomeness							
	Low		Low Average		High Average		High	
	Percentage	Number	Percentage	Number	Percentage	Number	Percentage	Number
Father not convicted	8.9	112	14.1	71	30.8	39	40.0	40
Father convicted	35.7	14	42.3	26	45.0	20	61.8	34

One possible explanation of the familial incidence of delinquency is that older males transmit criminal habits to younger males by direct example. However, the bad example of older brothers was not the crucial factor, since, as previously mentioned, the presence of convicted younger brothers was just as deleterious as that of convicted older brothers. If paternal example was especially important, it might be expected that

Table 12-6. Official Delinquency of Target Boy, According to his Self-reported
Delinquency and the Recency of his Father's Convictions

| | Percentage of Target Boys Convicted at Two Levels of Self-reported Delinquency | | | |
| | Below Average | | Above Average | |
	Percentage	Number	Percentage	Number
Father not convicted	10.5	152	29.1	110
Father last convicted before target boy's birth	31.3	16	65.2	23
Father last convicted when target boy aged 0-9 years	30.8	13	36.4	11
Father last convicted after target boy aged 10 years	33.3	12	73.7	19

criminal fathers whose convictions ceased before their sons' births would
have less influence than those convicted during their sons' formative
years. This was not the case. The prevalence of delinquency among
target boys was not significantly greater for those whose fathers were
convicted after their tenth birthdays than for those whose fathers were
last convicted before they were born. The actual figures were 18 out of 31
(58.1 percent) and 20 out of 39 (51.3 percent) respectively.

Table 12-7. Official Delinquency of Target Boy, According to his Self-reported
Delinquency and the Criminality of his Father and Brothers

| | Percentage of Target Boys Convicted at Two Levels of Self-reported Delinquency | | | |
| | Below Average | | Above Average | |
	Percentage	Number	Percentage	Number
No criminal father or brother	9.0	145	29.3	92
Criminal father, no criminal brother	21.4	28	53.6	28
No criminal father, at least 1 criminal brother	31.3	16	38.3	26
Criminal father and at least 1 criminal brother	53.8	13	72.0	25

The evidence quoted earlier showing that the persistence of paternal convictions was not related to the likelihood of delinquency in sons also casts doubt on the assumption that a father's criminality is transmitted to his sons in any direct way. Whether or not the father has a record seems to be important, rather than the quality of the record.

It might be thought that such a finding fits the hypothesis of police selection, if the existence of any kind of paternal criminal record influences the police in their handling of a young offender. In practice, however, the local police are unlikely always to know about, or to search systematically for, stale paternal records. Nevertheless, as shown in Table 12-6, a paternal record, even when the father was last convicted before his son's birth, has the effect of trebling the likelihood of conviction for comparatively well-behaved children (i.e., those below average on self-reported delinquency). The reason for this might be that boys with convicted fathers tend to have convicted brothers, and that the local police are very likely to know about a young offender's convicted brothers. However, Table 12-7 shows that a criminal father and a criminal brother independently increase the likelihood of conviction of a target boy, for both the comparatively well-behaved and the comparatively badly-behaved.

It is possible that the communication of criminality from fathers to sons takes place indirectly, perhaps by means of transmission of anti-authority attitudes which lead to delinquent behavior or antagonize the police. The target boys were presented with a questionnaire about the police at ages 14 to 17 years, and it was found that those with official convictions expressed particularly hostile opinions. Although they were not tested, it is likely that criminal fathers were also hostile to the police, in which case their sons might be expected to acquire similar opinions. Indeed, a somewhat higher proportion of target boys with criminal fathers expressed more than usually critical opinions of the police than of those with noncriminal fathers (56.4 percent of 94, as opposed to 43.1 percent of 262; $\chi^2 = 4.36$ with 1 d.f., $P < 0.05$). Bearing in mind the earlier evidence (West and Farrington, 1973) that critical attitudes tended to develop after the experience of being prosecuted and convicted, it seems likely that the sons of criminal fathers are more critical of the police primarily because they are more likely to have been convicted. Considering only the target boys who were free from convictions, those with criminal fathers were not significantly more critical (41.7 percent expressing more than usually critical opinions, in comparison with 38.3 percent of those with noncriminal fathers).

The suggestion that criminal fathers might encourage delinquency in sons by an attitude of tolerance towards lawbreaking was contradicted by the impressions of the social workers, who felt that criminal parents were no less critical than other parents of delinquency in their children. This point was investigated during interviews with the target boys when they were aged 18–19. Nearly all the boys with criminal records admitted having been convicted, and all those who admitted convictions were asked about their parents' reactions to them. An analysis of their reports showed that target boys with criminal fathers described attitudes of condemnation at least as frequently, if not slightly more frequently, than boys with noncriminal fathers.

Against the idea that criminal parents directly inculcate their children in crime, or teach them criminal techniques, only 4 criminal fathers and 2 criminal mothers were convicted for offences with 1 or more of their children. In contrast, nearly half of the criminal sisters (10 out of 25) had at least 1 conviction sustained with another member of the family (usually a brother), and the same was true for 42 of the 223 convicted target boys and their brothers.

It may be that families in which there is a convicted parent are distinguished by some subtle difference in home atmosphere, or in child-rearing standards, which affects the likelihood of delinquency among children. In this research, parents were rated on their attitude and behavior towards the target boy. These ratings, which were derived from social workers' reports when the boys were aged 8–10 years, were combined into a single global assessment of 'poor parental behaviour', which took into account unfavourable parental attitudes, harsh or unsatisfactory discipline, and family disharmony (West and Farrington, 1973). It emerged that target boys with criminal fathers were not, to any significant extent, more likely than those with noncriminal fathers to have been exposed to 'poor parental behaviour' (26.1 percent of 92, as opposed to 22.1 percent of 249). On the other hand, boys with criminal mothers were frequently said to have suffered poor parental behaviour (46.9 percent of 49, as opposed to 20 percent of 310; $\chi^2 = 15.5$ with 1 d.f., P < 0.001). It was also found that boys with a criminal father and boys with a criminal mother were particularly likely to have experienced 'poor parental supervision,' according to the social workers' assessments. However, the presence of a criminal parent increased the likelihood of delinquency in the target boy at all grades of parental supervision, so poor supervision on the part of criminal parents was unlikely to have been the sole reason for delinquency in their sons.

These results are difficult to interpret. As far as general parental behaviour is concerned, it seems that criminal mothers are deviant but criminal fathers are not. This could be because criminality in women, being more unusual than criminality in men, is more likely to be accompanied by other forms of deviance. On the other hand, the social workers had less contact with fathers than with mothers, and it may be that their ratings of some aspects of parental behavior were less accurate in relation to fathers than to mothers. The degree of watchfulness and supervision exercised by the parents was a relatively easy matter to observe, and in that respect both criminal fathers and criminal mothers had lower than average standards. At the time they made their assessments, the social workers knew of the criminality of certain fathers, and it could be argued that their unfavorable opinions were biased by this knowledge. The connection between maternal conviction and parental behavior could not have been caused by such bias, because few of the mothers' conviction records were available at the time. So the results do, after all, point to some differences in performance of parental functions by criminal and noncriminal parents. Although the differences were not of the most obvious and expected kind, they may have contributed to the increased risk of delinquency among the offspring of criminal parents.

Since criminal parents tend to belong to the lower classes, and to pass on their low social status to their children, it could be argued that the transmission of criminality is merely one aspect of the transmission of low social status. The relevant data did not support this interpretation. As an index of social class, the families were graded according to income when the target boys were aged 8–9 years. At all income levels, poor, adequate and comfortable, the presence of a criminal parent increased the likelihood of delinquency in the target boy. In other words, criminal parents had some criminogenic influence regardless of their social status.

Finally, it is conceivable that a predisposition to crime is transmitted genetically. This view has to be taken more seriously since Hutchings and Mednick (1973) showed that the delinquency of adopted sons in Denmark bore a closer relationship to the criminality of their biological fathers than to that of their adoptive fathers. In so far as the findings of the present inquiry suggest that fathers pass on criminal tendencies to their sons without any direct inculcation of antisocial attitudes or habits, they are consistent with a genetic mechanism. Unfortunately, the data did not permit any further investigation of this possibility.

Conclusion

If 1 or more other members of his family have a criminal conviction, an individual has a considerably increased risk of acquiring a criminal record himself. The evidence obtained in this research points to the existence of particularly vulnerable families, but does not fully explain how this vulnerability is transmitted from one family member to another. Selective prosecution of persons from families in which someone has a record appears to be an important factor.

REFERENCES

Farrington, D. P. (1973). Self-reports of deviant behavior: Predictive and stable? *Journal of Criminal Law and Criminology, 64,* 99–110.

Hutchings, B., & Mednick, S. A. (1973). Major issues in juvenile delinquency. In *World Health Organization Symposium.* Copenhagen: WHO Regional Office.

McClintock, F. H., & Avison, N. H. (1968). *Crime in England and Wales.* London: Heinemann.

West, D. J. (1969). *Present conduct and future delinquency.* London: Heinemann.

West, D. J., & Farrington, D. P. (1973). *Who becomes delinquent?* London: Heinemann.

Wootton, B. (1959). *Social science and social pathology.* London: Allen & Unwin.

Part IV
CRIME AGAINST THE FAMILY

The previous sections examined a variety of crime problems that occur within the family, or are committed by family members acting together. The focus in this final section is on crime directed *against* the family as a group. That is, crimes which target several members of the same family, occur in family territory, or involve family property (see Chapter 1). The variety of criminal activities against families is enormous. The impact of these varied actions depends in part upon the nature of the crime. The losses of property or life, or the seriousness of the injury, affect the immediate impact of crime on the family. But as we saw in Chapter 2, indirect costs also can be significant, and may in fact be greater than the direct costs. It appears that many people are far more concerned about violent crime than they are about property crime, even though the violent crimes are much less likely to occur.

Incidence Rates

What factors have been shown to affect the likelihood of victimization against families? Chapter 13, "Households Touched By Crime," suggests that family income, place of residence, and race are important factors to consider. These national data suggest that nearly 24 million households (27%) of the total, were victimized by a crime of violence or theft. Roughly 5 percent of households experienced a violent crime—rape, personal robbery, or assault. In contrast nearly 20 percent reported an episode of larceny.

These percentages are important both for what they say about the frequency of household victimization in America, and also for what they tell us about the need to view all crime statistics with caution and skepticism. The problem is illustrated by comparing the National Crime Survey data in Chapter 13 with the data from the survey of families of students in Chapter 5. The student family study found that more than half of the children had been the perpetrator of an assault against a sibling. This is substantially higher that the National Crime Survey data which was intended to examine crimes by *both* family and nonfamily members. Similarly, the student family data on larceny (Chapter 4) also shows higher rates of crime within the family than appear in the national victimization surveys. Most of these episodes obviously were not reported to any criminal justice agency, nor to the National Crime Survey interviewer.

Protective Reactions

It appears that at least one quarter of all families experience crime during a given year (many more using our data). One frequent response to crime is a desire to increase the ability to protect the home. Protective responses include the use of security devices such as intrusion alarms and area alarms as well as trained dogs. Neighborhood watch patrols have become more common in many locations. At times these patrols are initiated following a single violent crime. In other cases, the groups form in reaction to continuing high levels of crime in the area. This was the case in one northern New England community in which residents formed "crime watch" operations. Homeowners and renters set up a system for watching for strangers and unfamiliar cars in their neighborhood.

Another common response to crime that threatens the home and family is to pass laws thought to increase safety. Attempts to change or add legislation allowing homeowners greater protection rights have been initiated in many states. These are often referred to as "deadly force" laws. Usually there are several components to these laws. They include the right to use necessary force to protect one's own or family's safety, or property. The conditions under which this force can be used often is spelled out as well. Typical of these concerns was the debate over such legislation in Maine.

> Property owners should be allowed to shoot trespassers and should not have to give a warning if it would endanger them, supporters of measures to toughen property owner's rights say ... bills he is sponsoring would allow deadly weapons to be used to defend personal property and again make trespassing on posted property a crime. Under current law, a person may use deadly force to protect himself or another person from death or against a person committing a kidnapping, robbery or sexual attack under any circumstance. Inside a home, a person may shoot an intruder to protect himself or others from injury providing that he gives prior warning, unless giving a warning would endanger him. (New) proposals would allow a person to shoot a trespasser anywhere on his property. . . . (Fosters Daily Democrat, Dover, NH, 3/29/77).

Similar legislation was introduced in Massachusetts:

Gov. Edward J. King yesterday signed legislation instituting the so-called
"Castle Doctrine" in Massachusetts by allowing residents of a dwelling to use
deadly force to defend themselves from a criminal intruder.

Signing his third anticrime bill in as many days, King said the measure
"returns to homeowners the rights that they should have had all along"
but lost when the state Supreme Judicial Court ruled in 1975 that, whenever safely possible, Massachusetts residents must take every opportunity to
retreat or leave their home before confronting an intruder with deadly
force.

King said that until yesterday, Massachusetts was the only state in the
country not to have such a law. The statute takes effect in 90 days.

Discussing the deadly force bill at a State House news conference, King
stressed that "one's home is one's castle."

" ... (Yet) unbelievable as it may sound, until today, a criminal intruder
could break into your home or my home, rob, assault or threaten you or your
family, and you may have had the legal duty to retreat even to the point of
leaving your home."

"Let the word go out to everyone home owner or apartment dweller
alike. The Castle Doctrine is today secure in Massachusetts" (Boston Globe,
12/25/1981:4).

Sometimes the pressure to increase protection of the home is less
subtle. While some legislation *allows* homeowners to use force to protect
their home other approaches may encourage or even require forceful
action. Several communities in 1983 passed legislation *requiring* homeowners to keep a gun in the home for protection. Other communities
passed or considered legislation "encouraging" homeowners to arm
themselves.

An ordinance here that "encourages" townspeople to have a gun in their
homes has prompted a showdown between some sportsmen and some residents who are outraged by the suggestion.

A special town election—the first in two years—has been scheduled for
Thursday night, when the 2250 registered voters in this northeastern Vermont
town will be asked whether they want to keep the measure that was approved
by selectmen in July. . . . The controversial ordinance begins by reassuring
residents of their constitutional right to bear arms. Opponents have no
problems with that part.

It's the second section they object to. This section states: " ... Every citizen,
especially every head of household has the responsibility and duty to self,
family and country to possess firearms and acquire the necessary knowledge
for the safe and judicious use of said firearms; and they are encouraged but
not required to do so," the ordinance says (Boston Globe, 10/9/83).

Psychological Effects

Following the material on Households Touched by Crime, Chapter 14 and 15 describe reactions to crimes against families. In Chapter 14, Allodi examines the intense problems that affect the victim of systematic torture and the families of these victims. From the mid to late 1970s about 7000 political refugees from Latin America resettled in Canada. Many had been the victims of torture. Allodi focuses upon the physical and psychiatric effects of this treatment. Particular attention is paid to the children of the victims. The problems of treatment and rehabilitation are pursued.

Chapter 15. The reactions of burglary victims are described by Waller and Okihiro. Their study of burglary victims in Toronto covers the problems of the immediate reactions of those confronted by an intruder, the emotional reactions of those who were confronted directly and not confronted, and the victim's preferred form of punishment. Waller and Okihiro also compare the patterns of nonreporting of victims which were very similar to the reactions of burglary victims in the United States. Finally, the prevention strategies adopted by victims are discussed.

Burglary and larceny are not the only way families can be the victims of property crimes. Numerous schemes and "cons" are directed against the unsuspecting.

Although serious confidence schemes usually are not life-threatening, unfortunately, in some societies life-threatening attacks or crimes against selected families may be commonplace. For example, in the last ten years there have been over 500 kidnappings for ransom in Italy.

(Rome) The recent severing of a kidnap victim's ear by his captors has shocked Italy and focussed attention on the continuing kidnapping problem.

Sixteen-year-old Giorgio Calissoni's severed right ear was found in a Rome trash can on Dec. 18. The act by what is believed to be a band of Sardinian criminals was the first time since 1973 that Italian kidnappers had mutilated a prisoner. . . . Ever since June 1960, when a wealthy Sardinian was kidnapped and held for ransom, Italian criminals have used kidnapping as a lucrative and relatively safe enterprise. Although it began in the South, by the 1970s the phenomenon had taken increasingly firm root in the more developed—and therefore wealthier—industrialized North. The peak year was 1977, when at least 75 persons were kidnapped for ransom. Last year there were 50, and the toll for this year stands at 39. . . .

Analysts here agree on several of the causes and aggravating factors. Families often interfere with police operations, and there are no laws permitting systematic searching of the large, international transport trucks kidnappers are believed to use. And police are often ill-equipped to follow the kidnappers into the mountains of Sardinia and Calabria, where 60 percent of those kidnapped are taken.

Finally, poor economic conditions in the South continue to make it easy for criminal organizations to recruit kidnappers among unemployed youth (Boston Globe, 12/26/83:16).

Attacks against families are not only motivated by financial interests. Harassment and persecution may be based on ethnic or racial hatred, political beliefs, or religious differences.

CHAPTER 13

HOUSEHOLDS TOUCHED BY CRIME,
1983 BUREAU OF JUSTICE STATISTICS

The proportion of the Nation's households touched by a crime of violence or theft fell in 1983 to 27 percent from the previous year's level of 29 percent. This is the lowest level in the 9-year period for which these data are available (Table 13-1). The percent of the Nation's households touched by crime has been declining slowly since 1975, but the 1982–83 change was the largest year-to-year decrease to date. A household is considered "touched by crime" if during the year it experienced a burglary, auto theft, or household larceny, or if a household member was raped, robbed, or assaulted or was the victim of a personal larceny.

The percentage of households victimized fell substantially in 1983 for virtually every type of crime. This represents a shift from the experience of previous years, when declines were caused primarily by a decrease in the percentage of households touched by personal larceny without contact (theft from a place away from the home, such as an office or restaurant) (Figure 13-1). Only rape and simple assault did not decline significantly in 1983, while personal larceny with contact (purse snatching or pocket-picking) decreased marginally.

Although the percentage of households touched by crime was lower than in previous years, a substantial portion of Americans felt the impact of serious criminal victimization in 1983. One household in every five was the victim of personal or household larceny, and one household in ten either suffered a burglary or had a member who was the victim of a violent crime committed by a stranger. Also, 4 percent of U.S. households were victims of *both* personal and household crimes, and about 1.5 percent experienced both personal theft and violence.

Changes and Trends

Three of the most serious crimes were among those that underwent dramatic decreases from their 1982 levels. The proportion of households touched by robbery dropped by 19 percent; for aggravated assault and burglary the proportions dropped 9 percent and 11 percent respectively (Table 13-1).

The proportion of U.S. households touched by robbery reached a

213

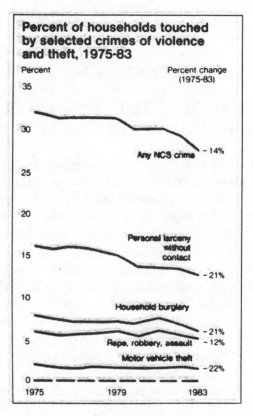

Figure 13-1.

level (1.1%) equal to the previous record low established for the crime in 1978. The percentage of households touched by burglary declined sharply in 1983, reaching the lowest level ever for that crime. In fact, while the total number of households in the Nation in 1983 was 18 percent larger than in 1975, the number of households burglarized was 7 percent below the 1975 figure.

As in prior years, suburban households were somewhat less vulnerable to crime than urban households, but more vulnerable than rural households. It appears, however, that the vulnerability to crime of households in suburban areas, although still generally closer to the higher risk associated with urban households, was moving toward the lower level of risk associated with rural households (Figure 13-2). Personal larceny without contact, which in the 1970s was the only crime affecting a higher percentage of suburban homes than urban homes, occurred in both urban and suburban households with the same frequency in 1983. The nearly identical percentages victimized by this crime in urban and

Table 13-1. Households touched by crime, 1983 and relative percent change since 1982

	1983		1982[1]		Relative percent change 1982-83[2]
	Number of households	Percent	Number of households	Percent	
Total	**86,146,000**	**100.0%**	**85,178,000**	**100.0%**	–
Households touched by					
All crimes	23,621,000	27.4	24,989,000	29.3	-7
Violent crime	4,400,000	5.1	4,776,000	5.6	-9[3]
Rape	128,000	0.1	136,000	0.2	-6[3]
Robbery	981,000	1.1	1,196,000	1.4	-19
Assault	3,620,000	4.2	3,835,000	4.5	-7
Aggravated	1,301,000	1.5	1,415,000	1.7	-9[3]
Simple	2,568,000	3.0	2,712,000	3.2	-6[3]
Larceny	16,983,000	19.7	17,835,000	20.9	-6
Personal	11,230,000	13.0	11,821,000	13.9	-6[3]
With contact	533,000	0.6	574,000	0.7	-7[4]
Without contact	10,836,000	12.6	11,381,000	13.4	-6
Household	7,706,000	8.9	8,181,000	9.6	-7
Burglary	5,268,000	6.1	5,865,000	6.9	-11
Motor vehicle theft	1,193,000	1.4	1,358,000	1.6	-13
Crimes of high concern[5]	7,681,000	8.9	8,521,000	10.0	-11

NOTE: Detail does not add to total because of overlap in households touched by various crimes. Percent change is based on unrounded figures.
[1]Recalculated estimates—See Methodology section for explanation.
[2]All differences are statistically significant at the 95% level except those noted by asterisks.
[3]The difference is not statistically significant at the 90% level.
[4]The difference is statistically significant at the 90% level.
[5]Rape, robbery, assault by strangers or burglary.

suburban areas may result, in part, from daily population movement patterns in metropolitan areas, because personal larceny without contact is, by definition, a crime that occurs away from the home. The vulnerability of urban, suburban, and rural households to burglary decreased at comparable rates between 1975 and 1983.

The gap between the percentages of white and black households touched by crime widened in 1978 and again in 1981, because of differences in the vulnerability of black and white households to violent crime (Figure 13-3). In 1983, the difference between the percentages of white and black households touched by crime was about the same as in the previous two years.

The percentages of families with incomes over $15,000 that are touched by personal larceny in a given year has fallen sharply since 1975.

DETAILED FINDINGS

In 1983, as in previous years, black households, households with higher incomes, and households in central cities had the greatest vulnerability to criminal victimization (Table 13-2).

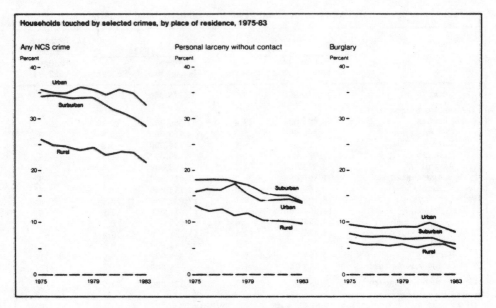

Figure 13-2.

Race of Household Head

• 4.6 percent of all black households had members who were victims of serious violent crime (rape, robbery, or aggravated assault), almost twice the percentage for white households (2.4%).

• Black households were more vulnerable than white households to burglary (8.5% vs. 5.8%).

• About the same percentage of white households as black households suffered thefts of objects from places away from the home (at work, in restaurants, etc.); however, a higher percentage of black than of white households suffered thefts of objects from around the home (excluding burglaries).

Family Income

• The fraction of all families touched by a crime of violence or theft varied by size of income; about a fourth (26%) of all low income families were victimized compared with about a third (35%) of all high income families.[1]

• Households with annual incomes of $25,000 or more a year had the greatest risk of being touched by crimes of theft. A fourth (25%) of these

----

[1]In this report households with annual incomes of less than $7,500 are considered low-income households; those with incomes of $7,500–$14,999, medium; $15,000–$24,999, medium high; and $25,000 or more, high.

households suffered thefts during 1983, compared with 16 percent of households with incomes under $7,500.

Place of Residence

• For most personal crimes, the aggregate victimization experience of suburban households was closer to that of urban households than that of rural households. (For burglary and household larceny, however, the opposite was true) For example, suburban households are victimized by personal larceny without contact about as often as urban households but much more frequently than rural households.

• A third (33%) of all urban households were touched by a crime of violence or theft in 1983.

• There was little difference in the percentages of urban and suburban households victimized by the theft of objects away from the home, but urban households were more likely than their suburban counterparts to be victims of theft from around the home.

• The percentage of urban households touched by violent crime by strangers was more than double that for rural households (4.8% vs. 1.9%).

• The biggest relative difference between urban and suburban households was for robbery; the urban estimate is more than twice the suburban estimate, despite the small absolute difference between them (2.1% vs. 0.9%).

• The biggest relative difference between suburban and rural households was for motor vehicle theft; the percentage of rural households victimized by this crime was only half that of suburban households (0.7% vs. 1.4%).

Size of Household

The size of a household is an important factor in assessing its vulnerability to crime. Overall, the more people in a household, the greater its vulnerability, although this tendency is more pronounced for personal crimes than for household crimes. (Larger households have more members at risk for personal crimes; but each household, regardless of size, is the unit at risk for household crimes.)

• 1 in 5 single-person households was touched by crime in 1983 (Table 13-3).

• 2 in 5 households with six or more members were touched by crime.

• The percentage touched by crime varied most by size of household for personal larceny, and varied least by size of household for burglary.

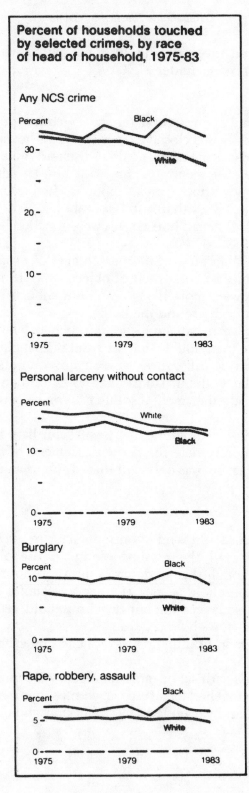

Figure 13-3.

Table 13-2. Percent of households touched by crime by selected characteristics, 1983

| | Race of head | | Annual family income | | | | Place of residence | | |
| | | | Low | Medium | | High | | | |
	White	Black	Under $7,500	$7,500– $14,999	$15,000– $24,999	$25,000 or more	Urban	Suburban	Rural
Any NCS crime	**26.9%**	**31.8%**	**24.7%**	**25.9%**	**27.9%**	**32.4%**	**32.5%**	**28.4%**	**21.6%**
Violent crime	4.9	6.5	5.9	4.9	4.9	5.3	6.5	5.2	3.7
Rape	0.1	0.2	0.3	0.1	0.1	0.1	0.2	0.1	0.2
Robbery	1.0	2.3	1.6	1.2	1.1	0.9	2.1	0.9	0.5
Assault	4.1	4.7	4.5	4.0	4.0	4.6	4.8	4.5	3.3
Aggravated	1.4	2.5	1.8	1.6	1.4	1.4	2.0	1.5	1.1
Simple	3.0	2.5	3.1	2.7	2.9	3.5	3.2	3.3	2.4
Property crime									
Personal larceny	13.0	13.1	9.1	10.9	13.7	18.3	14.8	14.3	9.9
Burglary	5.8	8.5	8.2	6.0	5.4	5.6	8.0	5.8	4.7
Household larceny	8.8	10.1	8.7	9.4	9.2	9.3	10.9	8.8	7.4
Motor vehicle theft	1.3	2.1	1.1	1.3	1.6	1.6	2.1	1.4	0.7
Serious violent crime[1]	2.4	4.6	3.4	2.7	2.5	2.3	4.0	2.4	1.7
Crimes of high concern[2]	8.6	11.7	10.7	8.6	8.2	8.9	11.9	8.8	6.3
Total larceny[3]	19.6	20.4	15.7	18.3	20.6	24.9	22.3	20.9	16.0

NOTE: Detail does not add to total because of overlap in households touched by various crimes.
[1]Rape, robbery, aggravated assault.
[2]Rape, robbery, assault by stranger, or burglary.
[3]Personal larceny, household larceny

Deriving Estimates of Households Touched by Crime

The households-touched-by-crime indicator was introduced by the Bureau of Justice Statistics in 1981. Its aim is to improve our understanding of the impact of crime on our society.[2] The household was chosen as the unit of analysis because the effects of a crime are not limited to the victim alone, but also are felt by other members of the victim's household.

Households-touched-by-crime statistics are derived from National Crime Survey (NCS) data on rape, personal robbery, assault, household burglary, larceny, and motor vehicle theft.[3] Because the NCS counts only crimes for which the victim can be interviewed, homicide is not counted in this analysis; but its exclusion does not noticeably affect the estimates presented here. If each of the homicides during the year had touched a different household and if these households had been touched by no other crime (the largest possible effect), then the inclusion of homicides in these

---

[2]*The Prevalence of Crime*, Bureau of Justice Statistics Bulletin, NCJ-75905, March 1981.

[3]These crimes are defined in *Measuring Crime*, BJS Bulletin, NCJ-75710, February 1981.

findings would not have raised the overall percentage of households touched by crime (27.4%).[4]

Other crimes against persons or their households—such as fraud, confidence games, kidnaping, and arson—were not included because no reliable measures are available for the number of such crimes that occur or the number of households victimized by these crimes.

Traditional measures of crime are in the form of volume or rates. Data on the volume of crime have limited usefulness unless the size of the population base is taken into account. Rates—expressed in the National Crime Survey as crimes per 1,000 households or per 1,000 persons— automatically correct for different population sizes, but they do not show whether a given amount of crime within a population is widely spread or highly concentrated.

Table 13-3. Percent of households touched by selected crimes by size of household, 1983

	Size of household			
	1	2-3	4-5	6+
Any NCS crime	**20.0%**	**26.2%**	**35.7%**	**40.9%**
Violent crime	3.3	4.6	7.1	11.0
Personal larceny	7.8	12.4	18.7	20.7
Burglary	5.8	5.9	6.7	8.0
Household larceny	6.2	8.7	11.5	13.9
Motor vehicle theft	1.1	1.3	1.8	1.8

For each type of crime examined, a household is counted only once regardless of how many times that household was victimized. For example, if a household were burglarized twice and one of its members robbed once during the year, it would be counted once for households touched by burglary even though it was victimized twice by burglary. It also would be counted once for households touched by robbery. Finally, it would be counted once in the overall measure, households touched by crime.

For instance, the households-touched-by-crime estimate for 1983 (27.4%) is less than the sum of the estimates for households touched by personal crimes (16.6%) and those touched by household crimes (15.0%) because 4 percent of U.S. households were victims of *both* personal and household crimes. Similarly, because about 1.5 percent of the U.S. households were touched by both personal theft and violence, the sum of households touched by personal theft (13.0%) and those touched by violence (5.1%) exceeds the estimate of those touched by personal crime (16.6%).

---

[4]1983 homicide estimates are not yet available. There were 21,000 homicides in the United States in 1982 (*Uniform Crime Reports,* Federal Bureau of Investigation, 1982).

Methodology

All data in this bulletin are from the National Crime Survey. The NCS is an ongoing survey conducted for the Bureau of Justice Statistics. Interviews are conducted at 6-month intervals with all occupants age 12 and over of about 60,000 housing units (128,000 persons). Because the NCS does not obtain information about crimes against persons under age 12, households experiencing only these crimes are not included in the estimate of households touched by crime.

"Household" as used throughout this bulletin refers to a dwelling unit and the people who occupy it. No attempt was made to locate people who moved during an interview period. Instead, the people who moved into the vacated dwelling unit were interviewed for the rest of the year. Biases produced by people moving during the year affect the estimates to a minor degree because only about 20 percent of all households move during a typical year. "Family" has been used synonymously with "household." Actually, 73 percent of all households are families, 23 percent are persons living alone, and 4 percent are groups of unrelated persons.

Because the estimates in this bulletin are derived from sample survey data, they are subject to sampling variation.[5] Because the procedure used to produce estimates of households touched by crime differs from that which produces victimization rates, the households touched data have standard errors about 8 percent higher than those for victimization rates with the same population bases even though they are derived from the same sample survey. The estimates are also subject to response errors, including crimes that are forgotten or withheld from the interviewer. Response errors tend to cause understated counts of households touched by crime.[6]

The 1983 data for this report were prepared using a newly introduced NCS data processing system. In order to determine its effect on the data, 1982 data were processed under the new system and compared with 1982 data produced under the old system. This comparison revealed that the effect of the new processing system on the households-touched-by-crime measure is minimal; at most, the percentages touched by any category of crime differed by less than 0.5 percentage points. The 1982 data presented

---

[5]Details of the NCS sample design, the standard error computation, and the customary estimation procedure for victimization rates and counts may be found in appendix III of the BJS report *Criminal Victimization in the United States, 1981*, NCJ-90208, November 1983.

[6]A more detailed description of the procedures used to estimate households touched by crime appears in an unpublished memorandum prepared by the U.S. Bureau of the Census. The memorandum is available on request from the author at BJS.

in this report were prepared under the new procedure, and, therefore, may differ slightly from those presented in *Households Touched by Crime, 1982.* These changes do not affect the year-to-year comparisons discussed in this report.

This bulletin, like its predecessors, *Households Touched by Crime, 1981 and 1982,* examines aspects of the measure, households touched by crime, not covered in the original bulletin, *The Prevalence of Crime.* That first bulletin covered only the characteristics of households touched by crime. The two subsequent bulletins explored other areas such as comparison of victimization risk to other life events, the percentage of households touched by crime during a multiyear period, and multiple victimization of households. This bulletin examines the victimization experience of households of different size. In future years, additional characteristics of the households-touched-by-crime indicator will be examined.

CHAPTER 14

THE PSYCHIATRIC EFFECTS OF POLITICAL PERSECUTION AND TORTURE IN CHILDREN AND FAMILIES OF VICTIMS*

FÉDÉRICO ALLODI

From early 1974 to 1979 about 7,000 political refugees from Latin America arrived in Canada. Many complained of having been tortured by the military forces of their own governments. In Toronto alone there are 150 medically-documented victims of torture, most of them from Chile. They suffered from the Torture Syndrome, as described in Canada by Cathcart, Berger et al., 1979 (1), Allodi, 1979 (2) and in Denmark by Rasmussen et al., 1977 (3,4). They have been subjected to psychological and physical torture including threats, mock executions, prolonged beatings, all forms of psychological and bodily abuse and idiosyncratically in Chile, to electrical torture in more than three-fourths of the cases. The sequelae were both physical and psychiatric, but the most frequent and handicapping were the latter.

The victims were generally young married educated males with skilled occupations. They were arrested at home in the middle of the night and in a violent manner. The rest of the family witnessed and generally was also subject to the violence of the scene. Armed military personnel knocked at or pulled down the doors, pushed into the bedrooms, destroyed furnishings, ripped walls and floors. On occasions they killed family dogs, killed or injured members of the family, raped females, and pulled and pushed children in a violent manner (Allodi, 1979).

In the case of the refugees who later came to Canada, the prisoner eventually returned home after a few weeks or even years of unspeakable experiences. In other cases, however, the prisoner never returned home. Many were reported dead by the authorities and their bodies returned to the families or simply found somewhere. The fate of many has never been determined and the authorities refuse to acknowledge whether they are dead or alive. They have become the "Detained and Disappeared"

---

*Presented in Montreal, May 3, 1980, at a colloquium on "The medical and legal aspects of torture", sponsored by Amnesty International Canada, Francophone section.

people of Chile and Latin America. Their numbers are in the thousands. Recently Amnesty International published a computer list for Argentina alone amounting to 2,665 names, but less conservative estimates bring the estimate to 10,000 and even 30,000. On this scale, the phenomenon has no precedent in the western world. At the same time these acts are used as a technique to maintain a situation of state terrorism, whereby people are crushed into submission, hoping against hope that continued subjugation will move the authorities to spare their imprisoned spouse, son, or brother.

Three Studies

The effects of this type of political repression on families and children have been described in various reports dealing with Chilean and Argentinean populations. In "The Children of Detained and Disappeared People: A Diagnostic Study," 203 cases of children under 12 years seen in a mental health agency in Santiago, Chile, are reported. They were seen between late 1973 and early 1977, physically examined, interviewed and tested, (drawing persons (Goodenough test) and families). Most children (65%) were under six years, and two-thirds were given real explanations of the situation of their fathers (In prison, fate unknown), but some did not accept it. Their traumatic experiences consisted of a family crisis of more than four years duration. A cycle of hope and despair was repeated endlessly, draining and exhausting the emotional reserves of everyone in the family. The normal psychological process of mourning was arrested and the reparation for the loss they had suffered was not possible. The family was in a state of social anomie and disorganization, "Nothing can be planned, we have no legal status, no recourse, we live in limbo, between life and death."

The symptoms reported and observed were those of withdrawal (78%), depression (70%), intense generalized fear and fear triggered by specific environmental stimuli (sirens, uniformed people, car engines at night time) (78%), and loss of appetite and weight, sleep disturbances, regression in behaviour and school performance, dependency and clinging behavior towards their mothers in about half of the cases. The factors associated with the severity of symptoms were younger age, length of exposure to trauma, family and social isolation (due to fear of relatives, of friends and stigma), and to inadequate or untrue explanations for the parental absence.

In a study by another agency in Santiago, nine children of Chilean families subjected to political persecution were investigated. They represented only a small sample of hundreds of cases serviced by that agency. Their experiences were similar to the other group, having witnessed the violent arrest and ill-treatment of their father, mother or both, and the destruction of the furniture, the threats and the personal manhandling. One or both parents died or disappeared and the home life collapsed, after which the children moved to live somewhere else, with relatives or friends. The result was the sudden interruption of psychological development. Fear was the predominant emotion involving all relationships. Profound sentiments of impotence, vulnerability, and paralysis pervaded their lives as they witnessed the collapse of parental protection and security. The mother, oppressed by the disappearance of the husband, grieving her own loss and coping with her own fear and anxiety, could hardly fill the role of mother, let alone compensate for the loss of the father.

Similar experiences and symptoms are reported in another paper dealing with 20 Argentinean families and their 28 children exiled in Mexico. Their ages ranged from zero to four years at the time of the traumatic events in 1976, and from three to seven years at the time of the study in 1979. Twenty-three children were born in Argentina, and five in Mexico. More than half of the parents were professors and teachers. Half of the children had been separated temporarily from their parents, as a result of political persecution and imprisonment, though currently they were together. In a quarter of the cases one parent was still missing (prisoner, dead or disappeared). All families had been subjected to violence that was either direct (prison and torture), social (ostracism and stigma), economic (robbery at time of searching, unemployment), or ideological (book burnings, control of libraries, schools, universities and media, government urging to spy and report on people). The families also had migrated, which is viewed by the authors as a conflictive situation, since it entails a loss of affective bonds with family friends and community, and the new demands placed by the new environment interrupt the process of mourning. The method of investigation included interviews, drawing tests, play therapy, intelligence and psychomotor tests. Questionnaires were filled by the nursery school teachers. In more than half of the cases, the children had experienced the breaking and entering of the home, with destruction and looting of contents and the beating and even torture of one or both parents. About a quarter of the children had one parent still in prison, dead or disappeared at the time of the study. One-third of the children had been separated from the parents before joining them in exile. Others had been in jail with their parents or were born in jail under most unhygienic and crowded conditions.

The symptoms at the time of the experience were most commonly insomnia, feeding disorder, behavioral regression or arrest of development, aggressivity, and somatic complaints. At the time of the study the major problems were overdependency on parents (in most cases and always more frequent in cases exposed directly to violence) and somatic symptoms, depression and aggressivity, which were present in about half of the cases. The drawings showed a blurring or depatterning of family images. Of the children born in exile, more than half were excessively dependent on their parents and frequently showed behavioral immaturity, underdevelopment and somatization reactions under stress. The symptoms that tended to improve with time were sleep and feeding disorders, somatization and regression; aggressivity tended to get worse and dependency, blurring of family images in drawings and loss of sphincter control appeared as new symptoms. The most persistent symptoms were dependency and aggressivity. The authors conclude that the symptoms are those expected for this age group under conditions of severe stress and privations, and that the disturbance is in direct proportion to the severity and frequency of the stress to which the family is exposed. With regards to therapy, it is considered that social conscience is essential in the process of recovery from the loss and re-integration into society.

The Children of Chilean Refugees in Canada

The case records of over 40 victims of political persecution and torture were examined. The general characteristics of this sample have been described already. For the majority of the cases the information about the children was gathered from the mother by the author; the children were not examined in about half of the cases. In the families of 11 victims the children were present during the violent scenes of entering, searching and arrest of their parents or had been pushed around or hit themselves. In 14 families the children had been separated from at least one parent for a period ranging from a few days to years, for most cases ranging from one to twelve months. Some were also exposed to the threats and often violent visits of military to the homes for years after the victim's release from prison. Each family had from one to five children, ranging from zero to fourteen years of age at the time of the first traumatic experience. The symptoms reported were severe behavioral or affective changes in children of six families. Social withdrawal, depression, fear, anxiety and irritability were the most common symptoms. Clearly this is a preliminary report on this group and further collection of data and follow up is intended.

Discussion of Findings

A comparison of the three studies of Chilean and Argentinean children reveals that most children were under six years of age and were subjected to traumatic experiences, including family separation. Their experiences were roughly similar in that they altered profoundly the protective quality of the family atmosphere and the physical integrity of the same. The children reacted with a narrow repertoire of symptoms and most commonly with reactions of social withdrawal, chronic fear, depressive mood, clinging and overdependent behavior, sleep disorders, somatic complaints and an arrest or regression of social habits and school performance. Irritability and aggressiveness were considered a problem and reported only in older children or as a late onset symptom. In the Canadian group the observations are similar.

Comparing the Latin American children with the children whose parents survived the concentration camps during the Nazi regime in Germany, or were subjected to political persecution and imprisonment in Northern Ireland during 1969 and early 1970's, or simply imprisoned for criminal and civil offenses, or separated because of exile and war, it is evident that the symptoms are very similar for the same age groups. They are related to the loss of the parental bond or protective home atmosphere due to the parental preoccupations, psychological disorganization or parent's absence.

Treatment and Rehabilitation

The following discussion borrows heavily from the work of the Chilean and Argentinean groups in the above mentioned studies. They contain clear principles and guidelines for the treatment of victims of torture and political persecution and their families. It is implicit in their approach that the rehabilitation of the children must take place largely within the realm of the family and will therefore be dependent on its remaining structure and protective and nurturing qualities. Thus, children and adults are part of the same process of reparation and therapy and, though the languages used and the levels of personality integration are different, their basic needs are the same.

Explicitly they state that the possibility of recovering from the pain of the loss comes out of two premises:

1. Experiencing it and understanding its meaning to its fullest.
2. Sharing it with other people.

Catharsis, the telling of the story with its emotional load, is the beginning of overcoming the loss and the suffering, but to recover from it, this pain must be actively transformed into the construction of a shared social space. If this should not happen, the pain remains locked as an individual experience in profoundly destructive ways—depression, anguish, despair, and the inability to go on living. The Chilean and Argentinean therapists place great emphasis on group solidarity as the method of treatment. The modalities of therapy are brief in duration and the therapeutic situation is dynamic, changeable and adaptable. Psychiatric treatment is always integrated with other programs, i.e., legal aid, craft workshops, schools, recreation, etc. The process of grieving the loss and sharing the pain is the same under any modality of treatment. "I give you my pain and you give me your sympathy and your affection." This common bond permits that alternatively the grieving person returns affection and the other expresses his pain. In this encounter the harm begins to be repaired. What was unbearable and destructive, supported by the bond with the other person, becomes something constructive. The pain and the suffering permit the first contact, and the closeness of the relationship may result in an extraordinary transformation. Out of the most brutal experience, the quality of this encounter will facilitate the therapeutic relationship. It modifies, of course, the expectations of the Latin American culture, in which masculine strength is incompatible with the open acknowledgement of pain and painful emotions. Even more directly repressed is the experience of a warm affect as a response to the expression of affection by the other person as an act of compassion or love. Immigration and exile also make this task of recovery very difficult because of the scarcity of personal bonds and of opportunities of creating this type of relationship. At the same time that the adults are helped to recuperate their own strength and bearings, the children begin to experience a human environment which is warm, protective and predictable and in which affective bonding can take place again.

Factual information is helpful to adults and especially to young children, whose imaginations are usually worse than reality. A restructuring of personality takes place as families begin to live together as families again, helping the children and leading productive lives. For exiles it requires a direct participation in the community life of the new country in which they live, and an indirect one in their country or origin both through cooperation and solidarity with other exiles and through an understanding of what did happen and is happening presently in their own homeland.

Traditional psychoanalysis has made a significant contribution to the understanding of the psychological reactions to loss, mourning and melancholia. The themes traditionally explored have been anger, guilt, narcissistic withdrawal and the loss of the ability to experience pleasure. In none of the cases of torture victims examined were reactions of anger against the torturers observed. Most commonly the victims were bewildered by the cruelty of their oppressors and deeply ashamed and humiliated, which suggests that the main aim of torture, the humiliation and dehumanization of the victim, had been achieved. No cases of severe melancholia or marked guilt were reported among the families and children of victims, of dead people or of detained and disappeared people. Guilt, as an initial reaction, was only mentioned by the mothers who played games with their children. Games were found to be a most valuable approach to relieve the sadness and social isolation of children and they were most effective when mothers played along with the children. According to psychoanalytic theory a number of healthy mechanisms were encouraged by playing games. The weight of the personal conscience or superego was reduced, a positive or loving aspect of the superego rarely mentioned was encouraged, the ego was supported in its .refusal to submit to self criticism, punishment or death wishes, and consequently the self was maintained in a pleasurable state. The strong emphasis on group support and social activities helped to prevent the key development of melancholia, a regression from object (social) cathexis to narcissistic cathexis.

Bleichmar, with other Argentinean and Uruguayan analysts, who are exiles in Mexico and experienced in the treatment of victims and their children, advocate a more integrated conception of psychoanalysis. They represent a step further from ego psychology, which in its time was a development of European psychoanalysts exiled to the U.S.A. after the Nazi regime came to power in the 1930s.

They argue that psychoanalysis or any other form of understanding the dynamics of loss and suffering must not simply be a contemplative exercise, narcissistic, sterile, and despairing finally, but must aim at a transformation of the social relationships of the individual patient and consequently of the social environment itself. Birth and death, the primal scene, the oedipal situation, and the fear of castration are formal or organizing structures in the unconscious or the fantasy life of people. However, as personal events, they affect each individual at a particular moment in his development and they appear always within a particular historical and social scenario. Psychoanalysis must not be limited to a concern with a narrow structuralism of instinctual life, but must attempt no less than the full understanding of the problem at the encounter point between the personal history of the patient and the social forces that surround him. Less than this is to condemn both patient and analyst to navel gazing or a prison of narcissistic contemplation. Only this kind of understanding and the sharing of it with other people will prevent total psychological collapse, melancholia and despair in families and children of victims of political persecution and torture.

REFERENCES

Allodi, F. (1979, September 26–28). *Psychiatric effects of torture: A Canadian study.* Paper presented at the annual meeting of the Canadian Psychiatric Association, Vancouver, B.C.

Bleichmar, S. (1979, June). Los hijos de la violencia. Psicoanalizar: Contemplar o transformar? *Dialectica,* 4(6). Autonomous University of Puebla, Mexico.

Bowlby, J. (1952). *Maternal care and mental health* (pp. 43–45). World Health Organization, Geneva.

Cathart, L., Berger, P., & Knazan, B. (1979, July). Medical examination of torture victims applying for refugee status. *Canadian Medical Association Journal, 121,* 179–184.

Epstein, H. (1979). *Children of the Holocaust.* Putnam, NY.

Fields, R. M. (1977). *Society under siege* (pp. 67, 156–162). Philadelphia: Temple University Press.

Fraser, M. (1973). *Children in conflict* (pp. 60–87). New York: Basic Books.

Freud, A., & Burlingham, D. (1943). *War and children.* New York: War Books.

Graham-Yool, A. (1978). *Sequalae of political repression. The psychological harm to children.* Santiago, Chile, mimeo, 6 pages.

Graham-Yool, A. (1979). *The children of the detained and disappeared people. A diagnostic study.* Santiago, Chile, mimeo, 10 pages.

Graham-Yool, A. (1979, July 1). Argentina hampers inquiries. *The Manchester Guardian Weekly, 121*(1), 9.

Kjaersgaard, A. R., & Genefke, I. K. (1977). Victims of torture in Uraguay and Argentina: Case studies. In *Evidence of torture: Studies of the amnesty international Danish medical group* (pp. 20–23). London, England: Amnesty International Publications.

Marzolla, M. E. et al. (1979). The child and political repression. Preliminary report. Mexico City, mimeo, 85 pages.

McGowan, B. C., & Blumenthal, K. L. (1978). *Why punish children: A study of children of women in prison.* National Council on Crime and Delinquency. Hackensack, NJ, 124 pages.

Periata, T. M. (1979, March). Psychological damage of political repression and torture on Chilean political prisoners. Santiago, Chile, mimeo, 35 pages.

Rasmussen, O. V., Dam, A. M., & Neilsen, I. L. (1977). Torture: A study of Chilean and Greek victims. In *Evidence of torture: Studies of the amnesty international Danish medical group* (pp. 9–19). London, England: Amnesty International Publications.

Sigal, J. J., Silver, D., Rakoff, V., & Ellin, B. (1977, April). Some second-generation effects of survival of the Nazi persecution. *American Journal of Orthopsychiatry, 43*(3), 320–327.

Sotack, W., Siedler, J., & Thomas, S. (1976). The children of imprisoned parents: A psychosocial exploration. *American Journal of Orthopsychiatry, 46*(4), 618–628.

CHAPTER 15

REACTIONS OF VICTIMS

IRVIN WALLER AND NORMAN OKIHIRO

W e have now examined in some detail what appears to happen in a residential burglary and how frequently burglaries occur. However, we have not yet described how the victim experiences the event, what he does about it, or how the event affects his way of life by increasing his fears, changing his attitudes to punishment, or encouraging him to take additional precautions. In this chapter we examine these questions for the 116 cases in our sample who were victimized. As in Chapter 3 we are again using unweighted data so that relatively more victims come from areas with higher police-recorded burglary rates, but we feel that our data show patterns which are typical of burglary victims across Toronto.

What is it like to have your home broken into? Surprisingly there has been little systematic research to provide an answer to this question. The results of surveys of public attitudes in the United States (USA President's Commission, 1967a; Rosenthal, 1969) suggest that concern for crime including residential burglary is widespread and acute. Furstenberg (1971: 608) has also shown that people have a relatively accurate notion of the amount of crime in their neighborhoods. Apparently this knowledge is attained through accounts given by friends and neighbors, and it may be hypothesized that, if these accounts also communicate the negative feelings of fear or anger felt by victims, concern for crime would grow throughout a neighborhood into a very serious social problem.[1]

Alternatively, particular ways of reporting crime in newspapers (Quinney, 1970) can influence public perception of crime levels even though the crime level itself has not varied. A similar mechanism may apply to concern for crime. There are sensational accounts of burglary victimization that make "news." For example, in *Today's Health*, Arthur Henley relates several dramatic accounts of psychological scars left after burglary.

One evening last summer, a Boston widow returned home from visiting friends and discovered she had been burglarized. Startled, but not dismayed, she telephoned the police. When they arrived, she told them calmly what had

231

happened. An hour later, the widow experienced a delayed reaction to the frightening incident and suffered a heart attack (Henley, 1971: 39).

... The burglar can leave his unseen victims equally demoralized by fear. And it is a contagious fear, with the victim's neighbors likely to worry that they may be next. Poetess Marianne Moore resided for many years in a once-fashionable area in downtown Brooklyn but became so terrified of intruders that she moved.... 'The neighbourhood changed. It just wasn't safe any more,' she explains. 'One of my neighbors, a lovely girl, was robbed three times ... It's a terrible thing to be beset by fear. It wears on you a great deal' (Henley, 1971: 40).

Upon advice from police, the family changed the lock, but were terrified for months to enter their home 'The anxiety is terrible,' confesses the mother. 'I had to take my daughter to a psychiatrist because she became so nervous ... And I've become an awfully protective mother, always warning my daughter to be careful of this and careful of that' (Henley, 1971: 71).

How often do these psychological traumas take place? Are they caused by the event itself or by perceptions of burglary, which distort the significance of a relatively harmless event? Is it just the weak or maladjusted that experience these traumas? As reactions to confrontation appear to be the root of fears, we examine these first.

Reaction of Those Confronted

Neighbors or relatives entering a home without consent were excluded from our definition of burglary. Yet it is important to realize that many of the events involving confrontation were only marginally different. In one extreme case the respondent was "mad that people don't bother to ring our doorbell and just walk in." In contrast, if the offender was known to the respondent (rather than a stranger) the victim was more likely to remember having been afraid.

Forty-four percent of the victims were at home when the event took place, although only half of these actually confronted the offender. The feeling most frequently ($N = 10$) recalled during confrontation was described as "generally upset." However, fear ($N = 8$) and anger ($N = 6$) were mentioned almost as often. Two persons mentioned being surprised and three characterized their feelings during confrontation as calm.

Almost half of the 17 female respondents who were victims of confrontation reported fear, in contrast to none of the 8 males. Not surprisingly, in all four cases where the offender-victim interaction was more "serious" than a verbal interchange, as for example when the victim was threatened or actually harmed, fear was reported, whereas only in one-fifth of the confrontations where nothing more than a few sentences were exchanged (without threats) was fear mentioned as a feeling during confrontation. Feelings of anger and upset were reported about equally by persons of both sexes (though there were only eight men confronted). There was a tendency for feelings of anger to be more prevalent when the offender(s) was known to the victim than when he was a stranger.

Emotional Reactions

The majority of victims were not confronted during the offense. We asked all of the victims to recall their reactions immediately after discovery if they were not confronted, or after the event was over for those confronted.

The most often mentioned emotion was limited to surprise, which one in three of the victims mentioned. Fear and anger directed at the offender were each mentioned by about one in five of the victims and a more general upset feeling by one in four. Only a few persons mentioned feeling relaxed or calm.

It was found that males were less likely to report fear as an immediate reaction to burglary,[2] although there was no difference for surprise or anger.

If the territory that is invaded is more private, then some writers such as Ardrey (1966) or Lorenz (1966), would suggest that the reaction of the householder would be stronger.[3] It was therefore hypothesized that there would be a stronger retributive reaction from victims who placed a higher emotional value on their homes. We used two variables to provide indirect measures of the value of the home to the respondent. One was how long the respondent planned to live there. While many other factors affect this response, it seemed reasonable to suppose that people who plan to live in a house for a long time are more likely to be attached to it than those planning only a short stay. Similarly, we felt that those who had made major alterations to the residence would value their home more than those who had not. However, neither of these variables showed a significant association with fear.

The desire to see the offender imprisoned was a common reaction and was systematically associated with the educational level of the victim and of the damage done to the dwelling. Table 15-1 shows that only 22 percent of the victims with some university education felt that the offenders should be imprisoned, compared to 45 percent of those with less than secondary education and 50 percent of those who completed high school but did not attend a university. Thus, having a university education was associated with less likelihood of immediate retributive reactions reported by victims. Income level of household, however, was not associated with the percentage reporting a desire to see imprisonment for the offender at the time of the incident. This suggests that the relationship between educational attainment and retributive reaction amongst our small number of victims is not so much associated with general socioeconomic status as attendance at a university in particular. This in turn suggests that lack of retributive reactions towards offenders is an element of the liberalization of attitudes associated with university attendance.

Table 15-1 also shows that the degree to which possessions were disarranged or otherwise disturbed during the incident was significantly related to desire for imprisonment. Most respondents reporting extensive disarrangement felt a desire for offender imprisonment, compared to few reporting little or no damage. It was found, however, that other measures of the seriousness of the incident, in particular the value of goods stolen and damage to the dwelling or its contents were not related to desire for imprisonment. This indicates that retributive reactions are affected not so much by how much was taken as by the way the offender treated the possessions of the victims once inside. 'Trashing' behavior within the dwelling, with its connotations of irrational and potentially violent motivations on the part of the offender, usually resulted in retributive reactions.

It was surprising to note that reported feelings of anger, fear, upset, or surprise were not associated with the desire to see imprisonment of the offender. Similarly, retributive reactions were not significantly related to whether confrontation occurred.

Up to now, most household surveys of victims have concentrated on fixing a dollar value or a measure of the seriousness of the crime. These often include medical expenses or treatment in hospitals as well as the value of goods taken and damage done. The effect of a crime on a victim, however, cannot always be measured by dollar costs or scales that attempt to measure the seriousness of the offence from limited data collected shortly after its occurrence. In this subsection we attempt to delve more deeply into aspects of the emotional effect of burglary on victims—aspects which may last long after the incident occurs.

We have seen that residential burglary, even involving confrontation, is generally nonviolent, and at the time of the incident generates feelings of general upset or anger more often than fear. However, victims also reported some long-term consequences of victimization. In over half the cases, the respondents mentioned that the event had generally increased their suspicion or distrust. As shown in Table 15-2, women were more likely than men to report as an aftermath of burglary fear of being alone, and fear of entering the residence or rooms within the residence.

In summary, official punishment is desired by about a quarter of the

Table 15-1. Percentage desiring imprisonment of offender at the time of the offense, by education, disarrangement of dwelling, and mention of fear

	Desiring imprisonment	N	χ^2
Educational level			
Did not complete secondary school	44.8	29	
Secondary school, but not university	50.0	24	
Some university or more	21.6	37	
		90*	p<.05
Disarrangement of contents of dwelling during incident			
Extensive	69.2	13	
A little	12.5	16	
None	37.3	59	
		88*	p<.01

*Does not include cases where respondent was unable to recall his reaction at the time of of the incident.

Table 15-2. Percentage of victims suffering long-term effects from the incident by sex (multiple response)

	Male	Female	χ^2
Fear of being alone (self)	1.9	41.9	p<.01
Fear of entering your residence or rooms within your residence (self)	7.7	30.6	p<.01
N =	52	62	

victims.[4] "Trashing" behavior by the offender results in retributive feelings by the victim, but the magnitude of loss or damage done during the crime does not. Persons with university education tend to be less retributive than others, but there is no relationship between the degree to which a person values his home and feelings of retribution. The emotional reactions experienced by a person immediately after victimization are not related to immediate retributive feelings.

Table 15-3. For burglary victims who reported to police, rank order of reasons*

	Number of times item ranked in top three	Percentage of times reason given
1. It was the right thing to do, it was my duty	39	52.8
2. To prevent the offender from committing similar acts in the future	34	32.1
3. To get the goods back	23	28.8
4. It was just instinct, never thought about it	22	13.2
5. It was necessary to claim insurance	12	9.6
6. Nobody else to call	7	1.9
Other reasons mentioned		28.3

*Question 40d and e

Citizen Discretion in Reporting to the Police

The most important decision taken consciously or implicitly in criminal justice is that of a victim or a witness calling the police and thereby initiating and making possible the official investigations and sanctions of police, lawyers, and the courts. It is also believed that the delay between the occurrence of the offence and calling of the police (especially during the first few minutes after the crimes) is closely related to the probability of the offender being arrested.[5] And so, both the attitude to reporting to the police and the speed with which action is taken are central to the effective operations of criminal justice.

As a phone call to the police is the normal way in which prosecution, judicial hearings, and correctional services are activated,[6] the attitude of a member of the public to the police may also influence attitudes to these other components in criminal justice. In this section we will examine the reasons for reporting to the police of those victims who did so. In Table 15-3 the reasons are set out in rank order of frequency of mention.[7] Apparently, the main reason a Toronto citizen calls the police is because it is his duty. However, victims are also concerned to see the offender prevented from committing the offense again and as many as one in four persons called the police to get their goods back.

In contrast to the 51 victims who called the police, there were 65 who did not. In Table 15-4, the principal reasons for not reporting have been ranked. Lack of confidence in police effectiveness is the principal reason. It is not clear whether this can be related to the fact that the offender would not be caught, that goods would not be returned, or for some other reason. A second important reason for not reporting was that it was not a police matter.

Table 15-5 compares the *most important* reasons given by the respon-

Table 15-4. For burglary victims, who did not report to police, rank order of reasons*

	Number of times item ranked in top three	Percentage of times reason given
1. Police couldn't do anything about it	30	31
2. Thought it was a private, not a criminal matter	23	25
3. Police would not want to be bothered about such things	19	19
4. Did not want harm or punishment to come to the offender	13	17
5. Not sure real offenders would be caught	10	12
6. Did not want to take the time. Might mean time spent in court or loss of work	8	5
7. Afraid of reprisal	7	3
8. Fear of trouble from police	4	5

*Question 50a and b

dents in several American surveys for not notifying the police with the reasons mentioned in our residential burglary-specific survey in Toronto. In these studies, victims not reporting to the police were given a similar (but not identical) list of reasons for not notifying the police. The Toronto study has a slightly more extensive list and some of the alternatives were spelled out in more detail than, for example, in Ennis' NORC study (1967). Hence, only broad categories are considered.

In these studies, the similarities are striking. The reasons for not reporting are related to police ineffectiveness and belief that the offence was not a police matter. We also asked those who reported to the police whether they were hesitant to do so. Only 5 of the 58 respondents replied affirmatively. The main reasons were once again a feeling that this was not a police matter, or the police would not be able to do anything.

Tolerance of Residential Burglary

Because this study focuses on a range of criminal behavior which is relatively homogeneous compared to the broad range of behavior which can be subsumed under the rubric of "crime," it is possible to specify the variation in aspects of residential burglary which are tolerated without calling the police. Other studies have shown that aspects of offenses are related to reporting. For instance, in shoplifting, the decisions of victims to report to the police have been shown to be related among other things to the value of items stolen, what was stolen, and how it was stolen (Hindelang, 1974a).

As with the desire to see the offender imprisoned, the damage and disarrangement done are shown in Table 15-6 to have significant positive associations with rates of reporting to the police. This supports our

Table 15-5. A comparison of most important reasons for notifying police
in several studies (in percentages)

Category	Toronto 1974	USA[*] 1967	Dayton[**] 1974	San Jose[**] 1974
1. Police would not be effective	39	55	32	33
2. Not a police matter	36	34	41	49
3. Personal refusal	9	9	12	9
4. Fear of punishment	4	2	1	1
5. Other	13	-	13	8
	101	100	99	100

[*] Ennis, 1967:44,45
[**] National Crime Panel, 1974a:24

earlier hypothesis that the greater the perceived violation of one's personal territory, the stronger the reaction by the victim. Unlike the desire for imprisonment, however, the value of the property stolen is also closely related to calling the police. This may reflect the fact that higher property losses tended to be in residences insured, where recovery and prevention were crucial.

Apparently, the victim's own assessment of the household's precipitation of the crime by carelessness is not related to a propensity to involve the police. As fear of confrontation appears to be a major element in the public's fear of burglary, it is surprising that there was no significant difference among those households where confrontation occurred, those that were occupied but where no confrontation occurred, and those that were vacant at the time of the incident. However, there were very few where confrontation occurred and the offender got away with any goods. Also, as shown in Chapter 3, over four-fifths of the cases of confrontation involved a nonthreatening verbal exchange as the most serious interaction. Regrettably, there were too few victims in our sample to examine the effect of violence or the threat of violence on reporting to the police. We simply observe that both cases involving actual violence were reported to the police, while the one case of attempted rape was not reported. In one of the two cases involving threat of violence, we know the police were not called. There were no significant relationships between the fear, anger, or surprise felt at the time of the incident and reporting to the police.

Selected victim-related (as opposed to offence-related) variables were related to reporting to the police.[8] In Table 15-7, the significant associations are displayed. Victims who own their residence and who live in attached houses are more likely to call the police. However, no significant differences were found between victims who reported to police and those who did not in household income, in burglary-insurance coverage, or in the burglary rate of the area as known from police records.

Table 15-6. Percentage of victims reporting to the police
by selected characteristics of incident (N = 116)

		Reporting to police	x^2
Value of stolen property	greater than $100.00	87.5	
	less than $100.00	58.1	
	no property stolen	31.1	p<.01
Property damaged	yes	68.3	
	no	40.0	p<.01
Disarrangement	much	80.0	
	a little	76.2	
	none	38.5	p<.01

Table 15-7. Victim related variables in police reporting

	Percentage reporting to the police	N	x^2
Rent/Own			
Rent	42.4		
Own	70.0	115	p<.05
Type of Dwelling			
Single house	55.6		
Attached house	70.4		
Apartment	34.5	109	p<.01
Insurance called (if something taken or damage done)			
Yes	100.0		
No	54.5	51	p<.01

However, it was found that all of those who had something stolen or property damage to their residence *and* who had called their insurance company had also called the police. In contrast, of those who had not called an insurance company, only half called the police. Thus, it appears that a situation which warrants calling the insurance company also warrants a police call, though the reverse is not true.

Our data suggest that the insurance companies usually advise the victim to report the incident to the police. This can also be a stipulation in the insurance policy depending on how burglary is defined. However, two-thirds of the respondents who called the insurance agent had already called the police.

We have seen, then, that the victim has a variety of reasons for calling the police but that aspects of the offence are also correlated with calling. The question remains as to what are the most important factors—especially since some of the variables (e.g., home ownership, type of house, property damage, and property disarrangement) which affect calling the police, are themselves interrelated. We used a multiple-regression technique on our nominal data in order to try to isolate the independent effects of these variables on reporting to the police. Following objective rules, the variable most closely associated with reporting to the police is selected; the computer then follows preestablished rules to find that variable which, combined in our equation, gives the most effective 'prediction' of police reporting. This goes on until the improvement in predictive power is not significant, or the increase in predictive power is very small. Table 15-8 shows the variables which added significantly to explaining police-reporting.

Value of property stolen was the most important variable related to calling the police, while disarrangement added some additional predictive power; both are independent factors related to the decision to report to the police. Table 15-8 suggests that knowledge of aspects of the victim such as home ownership or type of house, whether insured or not, does not add independently to our knowledge of police-reporting behavior.

It is interesting to compare the conclusions on how characteristics of the offence related to victims' desire for imprisonment (Table 15-1) and their behavior in reporting an event to the police (Table 15-6). In both cases, disarrangement is related to the more severe reaction, while value of property was important only in reporting the event to the police. This suggests that the action perceived by the victim as being without any immediate economic motive raises an additional emotional vindictive response in the victim. The victim seems threatened personally more by disarrangement of his personal territory than by the evident economic loss. The lack of simple motive implies also the possibility of personal harm.

The value of property stolen is, however, related to the 'instrumental' response of calling the police. We saw previously in Table 15-7 that all of the victims who had called the insurance company had also called the police. To test whether calling the insurance company was an independent factor not associated with the variables shown in Table 15-8 in predicting police reporting, we performed another stepwise multiple-regression analysis "forcing" into the equation the value of property stolen, property damage, and disarrangement, and then adding insurance agent called to see if significant additional prediction resulted. Calling the insurance company was a factor that added only a small, though statistically significant, increment to our understanding of why people report to the police.[9]

Table 15-8. Summary table of stepwise multiple regression of police reporting by victims (Dependent variable: reporting to police)

Variable entered	R^2	Beta	F	p associated with F
1. Value of property stolen	0.205	−0.307	22.1	<0.01
2. Disarrangement of contents of household	0.273	0.211	8.0	<0.01

In summary, then, the value of property stolen and property disarrangement are the most important factors in predicting whether the victim will report to the police. Calling the insurance company is also, however, an important factor.

Satisfaction with the Police and Their Actions

Police actions in burglary are *reactive* in that they are initiated usually by the victim after the commission of a crime.[10] In addition, police effectiveness in burglary is limited because confrontation is not frequent in events reported to them and so direct evidence is often lacking. However, police actions are also important because they influence the victim's image of and satisfaction with the police, and eventually public support for the police.[11] In spite of this, little has been written on the victim's perceptions of police actions related to an incident. What is it that the police actually do when called to investigate? This is a crucial question in the case of residential burglary in Toronto, since it is clear that the over-all "satisfaction with the police" found by Courtis (1970) is high, yet we found from our analysis of police records that in only 10 percent of burglaries does the action of the police result in a charge or charges being laid. In our sample, only 3 of the 116 cases resulted in an arrest which was known to the victim.

Table 15-9 shows the number of cases in which different actions were taken by police as a percentage of those cases where it was recalled that the police successfully arrived at the victimized household. In most cases, the police asked questions and inspected the premises. Only in a small proportion, however, were fingerprints taken or other evidence collected or action taken. The case was followed up with the resident by another policeman in 43 percent of the reported cases, most often by telephone as opposed to in person. There was no letter follow-up.

Table 15-9. Police actions in victim households reporting to police (multiple response)

Action by police	Number	Percentage
Asked questions	48	94
Inspected residence	38	75
Fingerprinting	5	10
Took samples and other evidence	4	8
Other	4	8
N = 51		

*This is the percentage of respondents who knew what action had been taken and who answered 'yes.' In a few cases, the respondent did not know or the the question did not apply.

We do not know which of the 51 cases where the respondent called the police became part of an official police record. However, findings in the United States suggest that for crime generally an incident is more likely to be officially recorded if the legal category of the incident is more serious, if the complainant is observed to prefer police action, if the complainant and offender are strangers, if the complainant is white collar rather than blue collar, and if the complainant defers to the police (Black, 1970: 733).

In over half the cases where the police arrived, the respondents agreed that the police had filled out an occurrence report, when the interviewer showed them a blank one. Seventy percent mentioned that the officer took notes in a notebook (with or without completing an occurrence form) which might form the basis of an occurrence report filled out later. About 20 percent of the victims did report, however, that the police questioned whether a crime had occurred.

In 30 percent of the cases, the victim reported that either he or someone else in the household emphasized to the police that every effort should be made to have the offender arrested. However, the victims knew of only three persons arrested, one of whom had been convicted and fined; the outcome of the other two cases were either not known to the respondent or had not been settled at the time of the interview.

Two-thirds of the respondents said that, in the end, they were satisfied with the police action. For those not satisfied, the most often mentioned reason was that the police did not follow up the case after the initial contact. In one victim's words, "there was no evidence that the police had done anything." The other, rather less frequently mentioned reason given, was the slow, inefficient service given by the police.

Instrumental Reactions—Others Turned To

Besides the police, people sometimes turn to others for assistance when they find they have been burglarized. Who do they turn to and why? It appears that, as in the case of the police, one of the major reasons for turning to other persons or agencies is to recoup the losses experienced in burglary. Eighteen persons reported the incident to the insurance company. Of these, half received full compensation for their loss, and another quarter received partial compensation. Three were expecting compensation, and only one did not receive anything. Only two persons had or expected to have their insurance premium rise because of the incident, so that the economic impact of burglary on individuals from increased premiums was felt to be minimal.

Of the 57 victims who had something stolen from the residence, recovery of some or all of the items occurred in only four cases. In one case, the value of goods recovered was a substantial $3500. Five persons mentioned they received some form of financial compensation or restitution from the incident, but not surprisingly in view of the rarity of violence in residential burglary no one cited the Criminal Injuries Compensation Board.[12]

When we combine those who had their goods covered by insurance, received compensation, or had some or all of the goods recovered, they added up to fewer than half of the cases where something was taken. Those who had something taken or damage done to their residence, but who did not have insurance coverage or did not receive compensation or whose goods were not recovered, formed a group suffering financial loss, and we asked them whether they would be prepared to settle the case out of court if the offender returned the goods or whatever was taken and repaired any damages that might have been done. Of the 35 victims to whom the question applied, about two-thirds said they would be prepared to accept an out-of-court settlement. This suggests that after the initial feelings of upset, anger, or fear that most victims have, they put the event in perspective and are prepared to settle with simple restitution of the goods stolen. Possibly what happens is that retributive feelings fade and the major remaining concern in burglary is just getting the goods back.

Many victims mentioned turning to persons other than the police and insurance agents for assistance immediately after the incident. The most frequently mentioned persons were the landlord or superintendent, followed by a neighbor or friend. The landlord tended to be called in for

more technical assistance, such as to repair damages, secure the residence to make sure the offender had left, etc., while the friend or
neighbour was usually called to help calm the victim down or to offer
advice.

Table 15-10. First mentioned precautions taken as a result of victimization

Category	N	Percentage
None	27	23
Lock door or window	30	26
More careful (hide valuables, check ID, neighbors check)	11	9
Hardware improvement (more locks, stronger locks, barricade, stronger doors, dog)	25	2
Disguise vacancy	10	9
Move	3	3
Other	7	6
Missing	2	3
Totals	116	101

Prevention Strategies Taken by Victims as a Result of Victimization

Changes in routine behavior or physical structure brought about by
the fact of victimization can be considered another cost of burglary to the
public. This must be distinguished from routine precautions taken if a
social cost is to be attributed to a particular victimization. Table 15.10
shows the first mentioned responses to the question 'What precautions
do you now take as a direct result of this incident?'

Twenty-three percent of the victims said that they took no additional
precautions as a result of victimization. Another 26 percent specifically
mentioned making sure that existing doors and windows were locked,
and an additional 9 per cent cited other minor precautions.

In view of the relatively low rate of victimization found in Toronto
(less than 3 percent of the dwellings per year) and the relatively petty
and peaceful profile of burglary, doing nothing except perhaps being
more careful by locking doors and windows seems like a sensible course
of action.

Failure to take more extreme precautions is tied in with the feeling
expressed by over 35 percent of the respondents that the incident was
partly or fully a result of their own carelessness and with the finding that
one-quarter of the victims felt that just locking existing doors or win-

dows could have prevented the last occurrence. In addition, the one-quarter who felt that nothing could have prevented the incident would probably not have taken more precautions.

In conclusion, the victim of residential burglary is likely to be upset by the experience more than angry. If the victim is a woman, fear is likely to be felt. Even so, as time passes concern for return of goods or compensation seems to be more important. At the time of the offence, official punishment was desired by only a quarter of the victims. Those who called the police did so out of a sense of duty more than to prevent the offender from repeating his offence (or indeed punish him) or to get goods back. Those who did not call the police felt either that the police could not be useful or that the matter was private. If the value of the property stolen was high and the victim's belongings had been disarranged, it was likely that the police had been called. If the police came, the victim was dissatisfied with police action as frequently as one time in three. Over half the victims took no additional precautions as a result of the incident. Only one in five made hardware improvements.

NOTES

1 The way fear of burglary is communicated throughout a neighbourhood is not examined here.

2 Contingency Table $N = 116$ $X^2 = 7.89$ $p < .01$.

3 At a different level, Robert Ardrey in *The Territorial Imperative* (1966) has put forth an argument, based on observation of animals, that the urge to protect property or space which one has come to recognize as one's own is part of a non-rational, biological drive inherent in man and animals.

4 These findings are slightly different from those of Reynolds et al. in Minnesota, who reported that in 36 per cent of the property incidents in their household survey, victims felt that the incident should be handled by the police or some other public agency, while 31 per cent suggested it was a private matter. Reynolds' data were based on ratings on a nine-point private-public handling scale (Reynolds, 1973: vi–5).

5 Conklin notes that the most common means of clearing a robbery in 1968 was an arrest at or near the scene of the crime (1972: 138).

6 Hawkins (1973) found 82 per cent of most 'serious' crimes recorded by the police were reported by citizens, 76 per cent by telephone.

7 Our pre-test experience showed that many persons are surprised at being asked why they called the police. Many felt that no justification was needed for reporting to the police. Calling the police was just a natural response to a crime. Therefore, we phrased our question on reporting reasons: 'Was there any *special* reason you had in mind when you reported the incident to the police?'

8 Because we were concerned primarily with comparing *households* reporting victimization with those not reporting, we did not include a comparison of age and sex of respondents, since the respondent is not always the one who decides whether to call the police, and may have delegated that task to someone else even if he did make that decision. We found that

the respondents placed the call in 62 per cent of the cases, another member of the household in 22 per cent, and someone else in the remainder.

9 Stepwise multiple regression data for the variable 'insurance called' entering into the equation was: $F = 5.002$ with 4,109 *d.f.*, sig. at .01. The change in R^2 was .032.

10 A main duty of the break-and-enter squad of the Metropolitan Toronto Police in fact seems to be the monitoring of pawn shops in hopes of locating an offender after he tries to exchange identifiable goods for cash.

11 Block has shown a negative relationship between victimization, resulting in experience with the police and support for the police (1971: 96).

12 The Criminal Injuries Compensation Board is a provincially funded and federally subsidized agency which compensates victims of crime. Injured people apply showing evidence of injury, loss of pay, expenses, etc.

NAME INDEX

A

Abrahamsen, D., 51, 61
Adams, P., 18, 22
Adler, F., 80, 85
Agoplan, Michael, xi, 68, 111, 120
Alexander, J. F., 66, 69
Allodi, Frederico, xii, 210, 223, 230
Amir, M., 114, 120
Anderson, Gretchen, xi, 68, 111
Andry, R. G., 69
Archer, D., 153, 163
Ardrey, Robert, 233, 245
Avison, N. H., 195, 206

B

Bahn, C., 63
Bakan, D., 88, 108
Bandura, A., 53, 61
Bannon, J., 136, 141, 147
Bard, M., 12, 22, 139, 147
Barnes, B., 152
Baron, M. L., 55, 61
Bart, P., 129, 132
Bartholomew, D., 113, 120
Beezley, P., 165, 184
Benders, 149
Berger, P., 223, 230
Berk, R. A., 18, 23, 131, 132, 139, 147
Black, D., 136, 147, 242
Bleichmar, S., 229, 230
Block, 246
Blood, R. D., 161, 163
Blumberg, A. S., 61
Blumenthal, K. L., 230
Blumer, Herbert, 58
Bohannan, P., 88, 108
Bolton, R. G., 165, 184

Bose, C., 131, 132
Bowlby, J., 230
Brogger, S., 123, 132
Bromberg, W., 51, 61
Brown, R. M., 149, 150, 152
Brownmiller, S., 56, 62
Bruno, Giordano, 66
Bryant, C. D., 110
Burgess, A., 128, 132
Burlingham, D., 230
Burr, W. R., 85, 108
Buzawa, Carl G., xi, 68, 71, 134, 137, 141, 147
Buzawa, Eva S., xi, 68, 71, 134, 137, 140, 141, 147

C

Calissoni, Giorgio, 210
Calvert, R., 17, 22
Cantrell, R. W., 184
Catheart, L., 223, 230
Celarier, M., 121, 132
Chambliss, W. J., 56, 62
Chapman, J. R., 110
Chilton, Roland, 67, 69
Chiricos, T. G., 41, 45
Chretien, James, 121
Christiansen, K. D., 49, 62
Clark, J. P., 41, 45
Clendinen, D., 16, 23
Cline, D., 111, 120
Cloward, R. A., 54, 62
Cohen, A. K., 55, 62
Conklin, J. E., 28, 29, 45, 245
Cooley, Charles Horton, 58
Courtis, 241
Cressey, Paul Frederick, xii, 52, 63, 151, 186
Croft, G., 121, 132
Cumberlege, N. R., 187, 191
Cumming, John, 186, 191

247

Steinmetz, S. K., 7, 22, 23, 43, 45, 73, 88, 90, 92, 93, 98, 99, 101, 104, 107, 108, 109, 110, 111, 120, 121, 133, 166, 167, 172, 184, 185
Straus, Murray, A., xi, xii, 5, 7, 18, 22, 23, 43, 45, 57, 63, 68, 71, 73, 79, 85, 88, 89, 90, 91, 92, 93, 98, 99, 101, 102, 104, 105, 106, 107, 108, 109, 110, 111, 120, 121, 133, 151, 153, 163, 164, 166, 167, 168, 172, 178, 183, 184, 185
Sutherland, Edwin H., 52, 53, 63
Szinovacz, M., 163

T

Taft, D. R., 55, 63
Tannenbaum, F., 59, 63
Tappan, P., 24, 45
Taylor, Meadows, 191, 192
Thio, A., 56, 63
Thomas, S., 230
Thomas, W. I., 51, 58, 83
Thurber, E., 67, 69
Tifft, C. L., 41, 45
Tittle, 85

V

Van Tassel, D., 152
Viano, E. C., 109
Vold, G. B., 55, 63

W

Waite, E., 131, 132

Walder, L. O., 91, 98, 101, 108, 109
Waldo, G. P., 41, 45
Waller, Irvin, xii, 210, 231
Wallerstein, J. S., 41, 45
Weinberg, M. S., 59, 63
Weis, J. G., 154, 163
Wells, J. G., 110
West, D. J., xii, 193, 196, 200, 203, 204, 206
Westman, J., 111, 120
Wilmot, P., 161, 163
Wilt, M., 136, 147
Wise, J. H., 184
Wolfe, D. M., 161, 163
Wolfe, L., 133
Wolfgang, M. E., 53, 63, 98, 110, 114, 120
Wootton, B., 193, 206
Wrench, D. F., 104, 109
Wrench, D. F., 104, 109
Wright, F., 63
Wyle, C. J., 41, 45

Y

Yablonski, L., 66, 67, 69
Yllo, Kersti, xi, 14, 23, 68, 121
Yochelson, 51, 63
Young, L. R., 102, 104, 110
Young, M., 161, 163

Z

Zigler, Edward, 105, 108

SUBJECT INDEX